RESEARCH IN
THE SOCIAL SCIENTIFIC
STUDY OF RELIGION

Volume 1 • 1989

RESEARCH IN THE SOCIAL SCIENTIFIC STUDY OF RELIGION

A Research Annual

Editors: MONTY L. LYNN
Department of Management Sciences
Abilene Christian University

DAVID O. MOBERG
Department of Social and Cultural Sciences
Marquette University

VOLUME 1 • 1989

 JAI PRESS INC.

Greenwich, Connecticut   *London, England*

CONTENTS

INTRODUCTION
Monty L. Lynn and David O. Moberg   vii

A PSYCHOMETRIC ANALYSIS OF THE
ALLPORT-ROSS AND FEAGIN MEASURES
OF INTRINSIC-EXTRINSIC RELIGIOUS
ORIENTATION
Lee A. Kirkpatrick   1

ALTERNATIVE RELIGIONS AND
ECONOMIC INDIVIDUALISM
James T. Richardson, Brock Kilbourne,
and Barry van Driel   33

NEW RELIGIONS, MENTAL HEALTH,
AND SOCIAL CONTROL
E. Burke Rochford, Jr., Sheryl Purvis,
and NeMar Eastman   57

TOWARD COMPLEXITY: THE RIGHT-
TO-LIFE MOVEMENT
James R. Kelly   83

THE FALWELL ISSUE AGENDA:
SOURCES OF SUPPORT AMONG
WHITE PROTESTANT EVANGELICALS
Lyman A. Kellstedt   109

SANCTIONING AND CAUSAL ATTRIBUTIONS
TO GOD: A FUNCTION OF THEOLOGICAL
POSITION AND ACTORS' CHARACTERISTICS
Craig S. Smith and Richard L. Gorsuch   133

ADOLESCENCE AND RELIGION:
A REVIEW OF THE LITERATURE
FROM 1970 TO 1986
  *Peter L. Benson, Michael J. Donahue,
  and Joseph A. Erickson*   153

THE HEBREW SCHOOL EXPERIENCE:
A PHENOMENOLOGICAL ANALYSIS OF
STUDENTS' PERCEPTIONS
  Judith A. Press   183

THE SECULARIZATION OF CANADA
  Hans J. Mol   197

POPULAR RELIGIOSITY AND
THE CHURCH IN ITALY
  Roberto Cipriani   217

THE CONTRIBUTORS   239

AUTHOR INDEX   243

SUBJECT INDEX   253

INTRODUCTION

Religious phenomena provide a significant, fascinating, and open area for social research. Valuable contributions to understanding religion are being made by scholars from numerous countries in several disciplines. International and interdisciplinary communication is usually difficult, yet as the globe shrinks in time-travel and communication distances, it serves an increasingly important function as more and more societies become pluralistic, bringing together diverse religious traditions, organizations, values, and personnel across cultural and political bariers. This new annual aims to provide a multidisciplinary and multinational sharing ground for exploring and summarizing information about religion and religious organizations which will be of use to practitioners, researchers, and educators.

Religion captured the attention of pioneers in the early history of the various social sciences. Early figures in sociology, anthropology, psychology, and economics discoursed about the role of religion in individual life and human society. Yet for a generation or two in the mid-twentieth century, many social scientists lost interest in religious research. Other specialties in their disciplines were more likely to be rewarded with both academic acclaim and funding for study. Some believed religion was a primitive characteristic of society which would pale and ultimately all but disappear in a modern scientific world. When included in research, religion was usually treated as a dependent variable, an epiphenomenon or consequence of something else, rather than an independent variable that produced effects in other areas of human concern.

Beginning with the so-called "mid-century revival of religion" in the United States after World War II, there was first a gradual, then a major, increase in the attention given to religion by writers and educators. Belief in the inevitable advance of secularization and the twilight of religion have been the subject of major revisions for many writers. Their assumption that traditional forms of religion would lose their importance in industrial society has suffered under the impact of major economic and political struggles centered around factions identified at least in part by religion, as conflicts in the Middle East, Ireland, South Africa, and other lands exemplify.

The significant role of religion in the modern world is also seen in the political awakening of religiously grounded groups like the Moral Majority in the United States, the spreading of Eastern religions into Western Europe and North America, the rapid growth of Christianity throughout much of Africa and Asia, the rise of new religious movements in most industrial societies, the growth of theologically conservative Christian groups in America alongside the membership declines of more liberal denominations, the rapid growth of Mormonism and Jehovah's Witnesses despite their unique doctrines, the application of Christian values to freedom movements in Latin America and South Africa as well as among women in all societies, the vigor of Christianity in Communist nations after seven decades of oppression, the resurgence of Islam in much of Asia and Africa, and the appeal of astronomical horoscopes, parapsychology, psychic phenomena, and reincarnation.

One of the results of happenings like these has been the burgeoning of social research in religion. Numerous professional societies have sprung up to support shared interests in specialized areas of study. Reports of religious research are often included in these societies' professional meetings and in the pages of their journals as well as in more general social science meetings and journals. Yet limitations of article length, specialized topical interests of editors and periodicals, disciplinary and methodological restrictions, and other barriers often prevent the dissemination of meaningful scholarship.

Research in the Social Scientific Study of Religion (*RSSSR*) attempts to overcome these barriers. It recognizes the importance of triangulation—the need to examine religious phenomena from many perspectives. While each discipline that analyzes religious belief, behavior, and organization is important, none alone is adequate to provide a holistic understanding of the subject matter. Each methodological approach of the social sciences likewise has much to offer as is true of each sample of respondents or organization studied, each theoretical approach, and each cultural setting.

RSSSR deliberately attempts to be interdisciplinary and international in scope, "ecumenically" encouraging contributions from scholars of diverse religions and ideological orientations, and being theoretically eclectic rather than committed to any particular school of interpretation and explanation. *RSSSR* allows for the publication of contributions of diverse lengths, including some that are longer than the conventional "article length," although shorter than those of most books and monographs.

The current volume is the first of the annual *RSSSR* series. The seventeen authors are from three nations besides the United States, and many of the American writers have had transnational experience as well. Although most are from the disciplines of sociology and psychology, political science, law, and education are also represented. The religions analyzed include new religious movements in addition to Judaism and Christianity. Besides empirical survey research and an innovative methodological study, there is a literature review and several qualitative analyses using a variety of nonquantitative methodologies. Theoretical contributions are evident in many of the papers and some articles contain challenges to conventional wisdom.

Some of the inconsistent and puzzling findings related to intrinsic and extrinsic (I-E) religiosity are explicated by Kirkpatrick's innovative finding that there are three, not just two, factors or dimensions involved in I-E religious orientations. In their analysis of alternative religions, Richardson, Kilbourne, and van Driel review the negative responses to new religious movements which come from mental health, mass media, and public anti-cult sources and then interpret the totalitarianism of economic individualism which the "cults" suggest in American society. In a related vein, Rochford, Purvis, and Eastman counter the popular belief that cult involvement results from a brainwashing of members which makes it impossible to leave the cult. They also make the case that the state has no legitimate basis for legal intervention against cult involvement.

Moving into another controversial subject, Kelly compares the right-to-life movement with Back's "nascent permanence" and discusses ways in which the movement constructively contributes to public policy decisions. Kellstedt's analysis of national survey data on evangelicals identifies several characteristics of supporters of the Christian Right. He uses these to flesh out the sources of support for "the Falwell Platform" of American politics, which proved significant in the 1988 presidential and congressional elections.

The judgments of people with different theological and religious perspectives about God's responsibility for various kinds of events are the focus of attention in the study of sanctioning and causal attributions to God by Smith and Gorsuch. Then the masterful review by Benson, Donahue, and Erickson of the literature on adolescence and religion published from 1970 to 1986 summarizes the findings in terms of such topics as religious development, the influences of parents, conversion, and personality-social variables, thus setting the stage for future investigations. The general lack of sophisticated methodologies and tendency of such research to be merely a by-product of other studies suggest the need for more and higher quality research.

Press summarizes her phenomenological study of Jewish students' attitudes and perceptions regarding their Hebrew schools and the constraints of time and learning which they experience. A critical appraisal of the notion that

Canada is becoming more secularized under the impact of industrialization and increasing rationality is provided by Mol's examination of data from several Canadian religious dominations and social groups. His conclusions will prove disturbing to those scholars of religion who believe that secularization of religion is an inevitable and irreversible trend in modern societies. Finally, Cipriani examines numerous aspects of popular religiosity in Southern Italy and details its relationships to political movements in the Roman Catholic Church.

Each of the contributions in this edition has been refereed carefully by at least three reviewers who provided not only an overall evaluation of their quality but gave the authors and editors many valuable suggestions for improvement. We are grateful to the twenty-two reviewers who evaluated papers for this volume. Inquiries, suggestions about possible contributors or topics, offers to serve as a referee, and manuscripts for consideration for future volumes may be submitted at any time.

Monty L. Lynn
David O. Moberg
Editors

A PSYCHOMETRIC ANALYSIS OF THE ALLPORT-ROSS AND FEAGIN MEASURES OF INTRINSIC-EXTRINSIC RELIGIOUS ORIENTATION

Lee A. Kirkpatrick

ABSTRACT

The most widely used questionnaire measures in the empirical study of religion today are Gordon Allport's scales of Intrinsic-Extrinsic (I-E) religious orientation. Yet despite this popularity, as well as hints in previous research that the scales may suffer important psychometric deficiencies, little attention has been devoted to the question of whether these scales are adequate for measuring what they are intended to measure: namely one intrinsic and one extrinsic dimension that are relatively independent of one another. In the present investigation, data from twelve diverse samples of respondents (total $N = 1070$) who completed the religious orientation scales of Allport and Ross (1967) or Feagin (1964) were subjected to factor analyses and item analyses to explore the psychometric qualities of the scales. The discovery of *three* factors, including two Extrinsic factors concerned respectively with social rewards (Social-Extrinsic, or Es) and gaining personal relief, protection, and comfort (Personal-Extrinsic, or Ep), was replicated consistently across the various samples. Regression analyses indicated

Research in the Social Scientific Study of Religion, Volume 1, pages 1-31.
ISBN: 0-89232-882-7

that these two types of extrinsicness are related differentially to a variety of other variables. Consequently, it is argued, correlations between the traditional Extrinsic scale and other variables may frequently be misleading. Implications of these findings for understanding the relationship between the Intrinsic and Extrinsic dimensions—an issue that has troubled I-E researchers for two decades—are also discussed. Finally, recommendations for improving conceptual and measurement models of religious motivation are proposed.

The most fundamental problem faced by social scientists interested in studying religion empirically has been that of operationally defining and measuring what is meant by "religion." Consequently, investigators in this field have devoted a great deal of time and effort to the development of instruments for measuring various aspects of religiousness. Although these psychometric efforts have been largely successful, researchers' preoccupation with scale development has to some extent been at the expense of more substantive and theoretical applications of the fruits of these labors, leading Gorsuch (1984) to characterize measurement as "the boon and bane of investigating religion."

Of all the conceptual frameworks and corresponding instruments proposed over the last two decades, probably none has been more influential or generated more research than Gordon Allport's intrinsic (I) and extrinsic (E) dimensions. Donahue (1985b) noted that nearly 70 published studies have employed Allport's Religious Orientation Scale. According to Hood (1985), "it is not an exaggeration to state that insofar as the empirical psychology of religion has any consistent theoretical integration, it is from Allport's typology."

In a word, Allport's distinction between *extrinsic* and *intrinsic* religious orientations contrasts a utilitarian, self-serving motivation for being involved in religion, on the one hand, with a genuine faith which represents the central value or commitment in one's life, on the other. Thus, an extrinsically religious person uses religion as a means to other ends, such as personal security and social gain, whereas the intrinsically religious person approaches religion as an ultimate end in itself. In research applications, the Intrinsic scale tends to correlate positively with other "religious" variables, whereas the Extrinsic scale is correlated with measures of dogmatism, prejudice, and the like (Donahue 1985b).

But despite the popularity of the scales proposed by Allport and Ross (1967) for measuring intrinsic and extrinsic orientations toward religion, surprisingly little is known about the psychometric properties of these instruments. There seems to be universal agreement that these items are better described by two separate dimensions rather than a single bipolar one (e.g., Allport and Ross 1967; Dittes 1971; Feagin 1964; Hood 1971; Hunt and King 1971). It is also known that the two dimensions, when scored separately, generally display a slight or moderate negative intercorrelation, depending on the theological orientation of the sample (Donahue 1985b). However, little effort has been made to assess the crucial issue of how well the items actually measure what they are intended to measure, namely one intrinsic and one extrinsic dimension that are largely independent of one another.

Although such psychometric issues are clearly important for any research instrument, they demand particular attention in the case of the I-E scales in light of their somewhat unusual history. The first attempt to measure these constructs was reported by Wilson (1960), who developed a 12-item unidimensional Extrinsic Religious Values Scale based on the theorizing of Adorno, Frenkel-Brunswik, Levinson, and Sanford (1950) and Allport (1954). Although high scores were taken to reflect an extrinsic orientation toward religion, the opposite pole of the continuum was not explicitly defined.

A new set of 21 items, developed in a Harvard seminar to measure an intrinsic-extrinsic dimension of religious orientation based on Allport's prior writings, was given to several hundred churchgoers by Feagin (1964). Although Allport had originally conceived of intrinsic and extrinsic orientations as endpoints of a *bipolar* continuum, Feagin unexpectedly discovered *two* dimensions in a factor analysis of his data, with intrinsically-stated items loading on one factor and extrinsically-worded items on the other. He then proposed two 6-item scales, composed of the highest loading items on the respective factors, for measuring the two orientations independently.

As part of a subsequent investigation of the relationship between religious orientation and prejudice, Allport and Ross (1967) attempted to extend Feagin's work using an "improved" Intrinsic-Extrinsic scale. Although Feagin's work was cursorily acknowledged, the "improvement" to his scale consisted merely of restoring all but one of the original 21 items, including those that Feagin had discarded on the basis of his factor analytic results (and excluding one that Feagin had retained). Eleven of the items were assigned to the Extrinsic scale and nine to the Intrinsic scale, apparently on the basis of face validity.

PSYCHOMETRIC SHORTCOMINGS OF THE I-E SCALES

Thus, although the I and E dimensions had been conceptualized by Allport from the beginning as a single bipolar continuum, the earliest attempts to operationalize this dimension seemed to point to the existence of two factors rather than one. This discrepancy between theory and data led Hoge (1972) to write:

> The researcher today is faced with the question—is the weakness of the existing scales due to Allport's theoretical imprecision, or is it due to poor scale construction which allowed "uninvited" factors to enter into the measurements? There is evidence supporting both contentions (p. 370).

Hoge cited the work of Hunt and King (1971), who had enumerated and analyzed the multiplicity of definitions assigned to the terms "intrinsic" and "extrinsic" by Allport in his various writings, as evidence of a lack of theoretical clarity. With respect to psychometric shortcomings, Hoge noted the generally poor item-scale correlations reported in prior studies. The present investigation will focus primarily on these latter psychometric problems, although we will have reason to return to more theoretical issues after the results have been presented.

As suggested by Hoge (1972), what psychometric evidence does exist for the I-E scales is not encouraging. The item-total correlations for the two scales, as reported by Robinson and Shaver (1973), range as low as .18 for E and .28 for I items, although the 12 items retained by Feagin (1964) fare somewhat better. And whereas the internal consistency estimates for the I scale generally seem adequate, the alpha coefficients of .6 to .7 typically found for the E scale (Donahue 1985a; Spilka, personal communication) are rather unimpressive for a scale of its length.

Factor Analyses of the I-E Scales

Although several researchers have reported factor analyses of the I-E items in support of the purported two-dimensional structure of the scales, the evidence for these claims is not strong. Feagin's (1964) published report does not contain sufficient detail to permit evaluation of his decision to retain only two factors, but the fact that his two factors accounted for only 29% of the variance suggests that additional factors probably should have been examined. In a study using the Allport-Ross scales, Patrick (1979) reported that a two-factor solution "matched the theoretical scales nearly perfectly"; nevertheless, his results prompted him to drop four items from the scales for subsequent analyses. No additional details were provided. Carey (1974a) reported that a factor analysis of the 12 Feagin items "revealed two orthogonal factors which were cohesive enough to be used for analysis," although some anomalies were evident. Details of these analyses reported in an unpublished manuscript (Carey 1974b) indicated that the two-factor solution was chosen based on the size of the first two eigenvalues, even though a third large factor (with an eigenvalue of 1.09) had also appeared.

Another published factor analysis of the I-E items appeared in a relatively unknown Spanish paper by Amón and Yela (1968), who reported the results of a *three*-factor solution. The first and largest factor was clearly an Intrinsic factor. The second factor was composed of those Extrinsic items primarily concerned with the use of religion for social and economic gain; the third factor was defined by a second set of Extrinsic items involving the use of religion as a source of comfort, protection, and refuge.

Hoge (1972) noted in a footnote that he had performed a factor analysis of 30 I-E items, including 8 Allport-Ross items and 22 new items designed to represent the same theoretical domain, and found three major factors. These included one large Intrinsic factor and two Extrinsic factors which emphasized "religion as personal comfort and relief" and "the relation of church-going to social status in the community," respectively (p. 373). These factors appear nearly identical to those reported by Amón and Yela.

Other investigators have conducted factor analyses on large pools of items including, among other scales, all or some of the I-E items (Elifson 1976; Hilty, Morgan, and Burns 1984; King and Hunt 1972; Vincenzo, Hendrick, and Murray 1976). Although such analyses may serve other purposes, they are not very informative with respect to the content of the Intrinsic-Extrinsic scales per se and therefore will not be discussed here.

Thus, although early work led researchers to conclude that a one-factor solution was inadequate to describe the content of the I-E items, what little evidence we have suggests that the scales may not measure two factors very well either. The purpose of the present study is to provide a fairly comprehensive empirical assessment of this issue, employing a wide range of samples and statistical methods.

THE PRESENT INVESTIGATION

In light of the preceding discussion, one wonders just what exactly *is* being measured by the Allport-Ross and Feagin scales, or, stated somewhat differently, how useful are the scales for measuring dimensions of theoretical interest? A careful investigation of these issues is important for at least two reasons. First, and most obvious, is the fact that the I-E theoretical and empirical paradigm is a dominant one in the psychology of religion today, and such popularity warrants good quality measures of the construct(s). Secondly, acceptance of the two-factor conceptualization and scoring procedure has had widespread implications for research and theory that have yet to be resolved. One result of this shift from a bipolar to a two-factor orientation is that the relationship between the Intrinsic and Extrinsic dimensions has become a central problem in the pscyhology of religion literature, with researchers scrambling to figure out what to do about those "muddleheads who refuse to conform to our neat religious logic" (Allport 1966, p. 6) by endorsing both Intrinsic and Extrinsic statements (see Pargament et al. 1986, for a review of some of these research efforts).

The point I wish to address here, however, is not whether the original bipolar conceptualization should be revived, although a reasonable case for this could probably be made (cf. Hoge 1972). Instead, I wish to emphasize the fact that the I-E scales currently in use were *not* originally designed to measure two distinct dimensions. And because the discovery of a two-factor structure seems to have been entirely inadvertent, it would not be surprising if the resultant scales were psychometrically deficient in important ways. After all, scale development typically requires a series of stages of evaluation, revision, and reevaluation before a satisfactory instrument is produced. From this perspective, a comprehensive examination of the psychometric properties of the I-E scales, particularly with respect to the now popular two-factor theory, seems necessary and long overdue.

METHOD

Samples

The data analyzed in this study consisted of twelve independent data sets, three collected by the author and nine by other researchers, that included either the Feagin or the Allport-Ross scales as part of some larger study. Altogether, data from 1070 respondents were included in the analyses.

Samples 1, 2, 3, and 4 were samples of college students from two small Western universities who indicated that they were Christians and at least moderately religious. Sample sizes were 153, 90, 157, and 68, respectively.

Samples 5, 6, and 7 were composed of adult members of various Christian churches. Sample sizes were 50, 110, and 82, respectively. (Data from Sample 5 are from Finney and Malony 1985.)

Samples 8 and 9 consisted of students at a liberal Methodist seminary. Sample sizes were 49 and 106, respectively.

Subjects in samples 10, 11, and 12 were college students at a moderate-sized state university in Texas and a small liberal arts college in Virginia. Only subjects indicating that they were Christians and at least moderately religious were included. The resultant samples sizes were 55, 60, and 90, respectively.

A brief explanation regarding the elimination of nonreligious respondents from the student samples is probably warranted. This is a standard procedure for many researchers in the field (Batson and Gray 1981; Spilka, Kojetin, and McIntosh 1985), under the assumption that in order to understand different ways of being religious, it is necessary to study people who are at least somewhat religious in the first place. Moreover, many of the I-E items are simply not applicable for nonreligious respondents. Items that include phrases such as "One reason for my being a church member is...", "The prayers I say when I am alone...", or "Although I believe in my religion..." all presuppose that the respondent is a church member, says prayers, and so forth. It is not at all clear what a nonreligious respondent's agreement or disagreement with such statements would mean.

On the other hand, Donahue (1985b) has criticized such selection procedures on the grounds that they tend to truncate the range of the Intrinsic scale, thereby restricting variance and attenuating correlations among items and between scales. Donahue's argument is a valid one: In fact, it will be seen below that range restriction presents a thorny problem for using the I-E scales with highly religious seminary students. However, as noted above, inclusion of respondents who are not at all religious presents other difficulties. For research involving heterogeneous samples of students from secular universities then, a reasonable solution is to eliminate respondents who claim to be nonreligious, provided that the range of the Intrinsic scale is not drastically restricted by doing so.

It is also worth noting, at this point, that for many of the analyses of student samples reported below, parallel analyses were conducted with the nonreligious respondents included. In every case, the results were nearly identical to those reported here. To the extent that results did differ, they tended to be *stronger* than those in the restricted samples, that is, factors were "cleaner" and more distinct, and beta weights were larger and more likely to be statistically significant.

Instruments

Intrinsic-Extrinsic Scales

Subjects in Samples 1, 2, 3, 5, and 6 completed all 21 of the original items analyzed by Feagin (1964), which include the 20 items retained by Allport and Ross (1967) plus one additional item. Because of the completeness of these data sets, these samples will be the primary focus of the present investigation.

Subjects in Samples 4, 7, 8, and 9 completed a version of the Allport-Ross scale that omitted a different item from the original 21 than did Allport and Ross ("One reason for my being a church member is that such membership helps to establish a person in the community"), and included in its place the item dropped by them ("Religion helps to keep my life balanced and steady in exactly the same way as my citizenship, friendships and other memberships do"). As will become evident below, this particular omission is a critical one in the context of the analyses to be reported, and so we will have less to say about these samples than the others.

Subjects in Samples 10, 11, and 12 completed the 6-item I and E scales recommended by Feagin (1964).

The 21 I-E items (as used in the studies discussed here), along with the corresponding item numbers used in the text and tables of this report, are listed below for reference. Item numbers are prefixed with an "I" or "E" to denote Intrinsic and Extrinsic items, respectively.

I1.   I try hard to carry my religion over into all my other dealings in life.

I2.   Quite often I have been keenly aware of the presence of God.

I3.   The prayers I say when I am alone carry as much meaning and personal emotion as those said by me during services.

I4.   It is important to me to spend periods of time in private thought and meditation.

I5.   My religious beliefs are what really lie behind my whole approach to life.

I6.   Religion is especially important to me because it answers many questions about the meaning of life.

I7.   I often read literature about my faith or church.

I8.   If I were to join a church group, I would prefer to join (1) a Bible study group or (2) a social fellowship. (Reverse-scored)

I9.   If not prevented by unavoidable circumstances I attend church (1) never. . . (8) more than once a week.

E1.   The church is most important as a place to formulate good social relationships.

E2.   The purpose of prayer is to secure a happy and peaceful life.

E3.   What religion offers me most is comfort when sorrows and misfortune strike.

E4.   It doesn't matter so much what I believe so long as I lead a moral life.

E5.   Although I am a religious person, I refuse to let religious considerations influence my everyday affairs.

E6.   I pray chiefly because I have been taught to pray.

E7.   A primary reason for my interest in religion is that my church is a congenial social activity.

E8.   Occasionally I find it necessary to compromise my religious beliefs in order to protect my social and economic well-being.

E9.   The primary purpose of prayer is to gain relief and protection.

E10.   Although I believe in my religion, I feel there are many more important things in my life.

E11.   Religion helps to keep my life balanced and steady in exactly the same way as my citizenship, friendships and other memberships do.

E12.   One reason for my being a church member is that such membership helps to establish a person in the community.

In addition, each of these studies included a variety of other personality and religiosity instruments. Among these were four Locus of Control scales measuring perceptions of control over events by Self, Chance, and Powerful Others (Levenson 1973) and God (Kopplin 1976); items developed by Spilka and Schmidt (1983) for measuring attributions to these same four causal agents in a series of vignettes depicting hypothetical events; Budner's (1962) Intolerance of Ambiguity scale; Dean's (1961) Alienation Scale, including Powerlessness, Normlessness, and Social Isolation subscales; Batson's (1976) scales for measuring Internal, External, and Quest orientations and Orthodoxy; scales recently developed by Spilka and McIntosh (personal communication,

1986) for measuring the degree to which religion provides individuals with a sense of meaning and self-esteem; and items developed by Finney and Malony (1985) for measuring frequency of church attendance, frequency of prayer, and subjects' self-ratings with respect to written descriptions of Batson's Means, End, and Quest orientations.

Data Analysis

Within each of the 12 data sets separately, the I-E items (either Feagin or Allport-Ross, depending on the sample) were factor analyzed using an iterative principal axes algorithm, using squared multiple correlations as initial communality estimates. (Use of other extraction methods such as generalized and unweighted least squares typically produced nearly identical results.) A scree plot of eigenvalues was constructed for each data set and was used as the primary basis for determining the number of factors to be extracted (Cattell 1978). The extracted factors were rotated according to a variety of criteria including Varimax, Equamax, and Promax, all of which yielded similar results.

Item analyses were then carried out on the individual samples and on pooled samples, where appropriate, including internal consistency analyses and item-scale correlations for the Intrinsic and Extrinsic scales. In addition, new scales were constructed based on the factor analytic results, and comparable item analyses were conducted with respect to these scales. Finally, the intercorrelations among the traditional I and E scales, as well as the new scales, were calculated within each sample.

The last phase of the data analysis consisted of a series of multiple regressions, in which various external variables (i.e., other than I-E measures) were regressed on the proposed new scales, in order to examine the utility of scoring these scales independently.

RESULTS

Factor Analyses of the Allport-Ross Scales

Sample 1

Three factors were extracted according to the scree rule; the results of an Equamax rotation of these factors are presented in Table 1. This factor pattern clearly shows a single Intrinsic factor and two Extrinsic factors. All nine of the I items have positive loadings on the Intrinsic factor, although two of these coefficients are relatively small (i.e., less than .30). Four E items load negatively and substantially (i.e., absolute value greater than .40) on this factor as well. The three items defining the first Extrinsic factor are (E2) "The purpose of prayer is to secure a happy and peaceful life;" (E3) "What religion offers most

Table 1.   Principal Axes Factor Loadings for Sample 1:
Equamax Rotation

Item	Factor 1	Factor 2	Factor 3
I-1	.75	-.01	.18
I-2	.70	.11	.08
I-3	.29	.21	-.13
I-4	.52	.13	-.04
I-5	.79	.03	.19
I-6	.67	.24	.07
I-7	.41	.00	.11
I-8	.24	-.02	-.14
I-9	.50	-.03	.29
E-1	.24	.11	.45
E-2	.07	.67	.04
E-3	.02	.62	.10
E-4	-.46	.16	.04
E-5	-.73	.15	.09
E-6	-.45	.17	.33
E-7	-.09	.07	.56
E-8	-.18	.19	.04
E-9	-.14	.58	.23
E-10	-.56	.08	.17
E-11	.19	.36	.30
E-12	-.04	.23	.66

is comfort when sorrows and misfortune strike;" and (E9) "The primary purpose of prayer is to gain relief and protection." The second Extrinsic factor is defined by the items (E1) "The church is most important as a place to formulate good social relationships;" (E7) "A primary reason for my interest in religion is that my church is a congenial social activity;" and (E12) "One reason for my being a church member is that such membership helps to establish a person in the community."

These factors, which correspond to a distinction between an extrinsic orientation involving social rewards, on the one hand, and procurement of personal relief, comfort, and protection on the other, closely resemble those described by Hoge (1972), and Amón and Yela (1968). Hereafter, they will be referred to as Social-Extrinsic (Es) and Personal-Extrinsic (Ep), respectively. Because this particular set of results is somewhat prototypical, the other factor analytic results will be described in terms of their correspondence to this pattern.

Sample 2

In this case the scree rule dictated that four factors be extracted, and in fact a three-factor solution seemed uninterpretable. The four-factor solution, which

Table 2.   Principal Axes Factor Loadings for Sample 2:
Equamax Rotation

Item	Factor 1	Factor 2	Factor 3	Factor 4
I-1	.65	.45	.13	-.01
I-2	.30	.62	.13	.06
I-3	.08	.49	-.19	.22
I-4	-.15	.67	-.24	.13
I-5	.59	.43	.13	-.07
I-6	.46	.56	.25	.07
I-7	.21	.28	.11	-.08
I-8	.10	.33	-.09	-.08
I-9	.51	.23	.12	.10
E-1	.33	.11	.61	.18
E-2	.03	.12	.08	.79
E-3	.13	.21	.25	.56
E-4	-.69	-.02	.09	.07
E-5	-.52	.08	.07	-.11
E-6	-.31	-.17	.26	.03
E-7	.08	-.15	.66	.18
E-8	-.13	.03	.42	.01
E-9	-.05	-.26	.11	.54
E-10	-.56	-.23	.01	-.11
E-11	.32	.42	.31	.05
E-12	-.06	-.04	.56	.20

is reproduced in Table 2 (with Equamax rotation), corresponded closely to the Sample 1 results with respect to the two Extrinsic factors. Again, the Es factor (Factor 3) is defined by items E1, E7, and E12, whereas the Ep factor (Factor 4) is defined by items E2, E3, and E9. The first two factors, both consisting primarily of Intrinsic items, are highly confounded with each other both empirically and theoretically. These particular Intrinsic factors were not replicated in any other sample, and are therefore probably not worth considering at length. The Extrinsic factors, on the other hand, seem to replicate the Sample 1 data quite well.

Sample 3

In this sample three factors were extracted that again closely resembled the Sample 1 results with the following exceptions: (1) item E1 loaded substantially on both extrinsic factors rather than only Es; and (2) items E6 and E8 ("I pray chiefly because I have been taught to pray;" "Occasionally I find it necessary to compromise my religious beliefs in order to protect my social and economic well-being") joined items E1, E7, and E12 in defining the Extrinsic-Social factor. Again, the failure of these particular anomalies to appear in analyses of the other samples suggests that we not be overly concerned with them. It is worth noting, however, that the presence of item E8—which concerns "social and economic well-being"—on the Es scale is quite consistent with the interpretation of that factor as a social-extrinsic dimension.

Sample 5

The screen rule suggested either a 3- or a 5-factor solution. When three factors were extracted and rotated, the results once again corresponded closely to the Sample 1 results, except that (1) item E12 loaded on both Extrinsic factors, rather than Es alone, and (2) several other Extrinsic items, including E5, E6, E10, and E11, also loaded on the Ep factor. However, it should be noted that each of these "extra" Ep items *also* loaded substantially and negatively on the Intrinsic factor; the marker items for Ep (items E2, E3, and E9), on the other hand, were independent of I as in the other samples.

In the 5-factor solution, the fourth and fifth factors represented Ep and Es respectively. Item E12, which had loaded on both Extrinsic factors in the three-factor solution, loaded only on Es in this solution, as in the other samples. Item E11 ("Religion helps keep my life balanced and steady in exactly the same way as my citizenship, friendships and other memberships do") also loaded on the Extrinsic-Personal factor. The other three factors represented combinations of Intrinsic and Extrinsic items that were not easily interpretable. Thus the general pattern observed in the prior samples was again replicated in both the 3- and 5-factor solutions.

Sample 6

The data from this sample of adult churchgoers from a wide variety of denominations were somewhat less cooperative, although not wholly inconsistent with the previous results. The 4-factor solution suggested by the scree plot produced one Intrinsic (Factor 1) and *three* Extrinsic factors. Factor 2 was defined by the two Es items E7 and E12, and Factor 4 was defined by the two Ep items E2 and E9. The remaining factor was defined by the Es item E1, the Ep item E12, and item E11. Thus, the Ep and Es factors were generally replicated, although a few items did not conform to the structure observed in the other samples.

Sample 4, 7, and 8

The results from these three samples, in which the item E12 was omitted, were inconsistent with both the previously described findings and with each other. This should not be too surprising, though, since the omission leaves only two items to define the Es scale as a dimension distinct from Ep. The intercorrelations among the items were generally consistent with the previous findings, however, as will become evident in the discussion of the item analyses below.

Sample 9

The factor analysis results for this sample of seminary students seemed entirely uninterpretable for any number of factors. The primary reason for this seemed to be that the Intrinsic items were generally uncorrelated with each other due to the fact that they had almost no variance: Respondents nearly always checked the most extreme response on each of these items. Under these circumstances, then, factor analyzing the matrix of correlations seemed inappropriate.

Summary

Factor analyses performed on a variety of college-student and adult-churchgoing samples consistently demonstrated the existence of at least three factors in the Allport-Ross scales. These factors included one Intrinsic factor and *two* Extrinsic factors, the latter of which closely resembled those reported by Amón and Yela (1968) and Hoge (1972). These Extrinsic factors seem to differentiate between an extrinsic orientation concerned primarily with obtaining social rewards from religion (Es), and one in which religion provides personal relief, comfort, and protection (Ep). Discrepancies among results from the various samples generally seemed minor relative to the similarities. Moreover, the consistencies across samples are particularly impressive considering that the Ep and Es factors are generally defined by only three items each, and as such might easily be disrupted by relatively small fluctuations in item intercorrelations due to sampling error.

Factor Analyses of Feagin Scales

Factor analyses of the 12 Feagin items in Samples 10, 11, and 12 produced nearly identical results within each of the three samples analyzed separately. In each case the scree rule suggested that four factors be extracted, and three of the factors corresponded to I, Ep, and Es. The fourth factor was unstable and varied substantially from one sample to the next.

Because the data from these three samples were collected by the same investigator using the same instrument in similar populations, and because the results from the individual samples were so consistent, it seemed reasonable to pool the data and factor analyze the resulting correlation matrix. With more stable estimates of correlations due to the larger sample size ($N = 205$), the scree rule dictated a three-factor solution. The results of an Equamax rotation

Table 3.   Principal Axes Factor Loadings for Sample 10, 11, and 12 (Pooled):
Equamax Rotation

Item	Factor 1	Factor 2	Factor 3
I-1	.71	-.03	.03
I-3	.27	.12	-.00
I-4	.47	-.00	-.02
I-5	.67	-.08	-.03
I-7	.51	.10	.05
I-9	.41	.10	.06
E-1	.06	.05	.47
E-2	.09	.66	.08
E-3	.07	.59	.10
E-9	-.03	.64	.05
E-11	.35	.08	.12
E-12	-.05	.13	.87

of these factors are presented in Table 3. The factor pattern clearly indicates an Intrinsic factor, an Extrinsic-Personal factor defined by the same three items (E2, E3, and E9) as in the Allport-Ross data, and an Extrinsic-Social factor defined by two of the Es items found in the Allport-Ross data (E1 and E12). (The third Es item identified in the other samples, E7, is not included on the Feagin E scale.)

Item Analyses

The results of the factor analyses reported above point to the existence of three factors rather than two within both the Allport-Ross and Feagin I-E scales. In order to more thoroughly examine the relationship between the items and factors, each item was correlated with the traditional I and E scales, as well as with new scales developed on the basis of the factor-analytic results. An Ep scale was constructed as the sum of items E2, E3, and E9, and the Es scale was constructed as the sum of items E1, E7, and E12 (where available). Finally, the remaining Extrinsic items were summed to create a "residual" Extrinsic scale, which will be designated Er. Although this scale did not correspond to any of the factor-analytic results, it was constructed for purposes of comparison with the Ep and Es scales, and represents the Extrinsic scale with the Social and Personal components removed.

In order to obtain more stable estimates of the item-scale correlations, and for ease of presentation, it seemed reasonable to pool the samples in some cases. Therefore, the three samples of college students who completed the 21-item scales (Samples 1, 2, and 3) were pooled, as were the two samples of adult churchgoers who completed these same items (Samples 5 and 6). Because

Table 4.   Corrected Item-Scale Correlations for Samples 1, 2, and 3 (Pooled)

Item	I	E	Ep	Es	Er
I-1	.701	-.138	.062	.077	-.332
I-2	.649	-.065	.103	.081	-.223
I-3	.345	.021	.167	.008	-.077
I-4	.449	-.106	.016	-.024	-.176
I-5	.701	-.159	.052	.081	-.363
I-6	.635	-.013	.180	.144	-.225
I-7	.524	-.043	.067	.120	-.185
I-8	.201	-.274	-.109	-.217	-.262
I-9	.543	-.060	.072	.154	-.251
E-1	.270	.236	.284	.334	.038
E-2	.091	.357	.484	.249	.176
E-3	.181	.379	.459	.246	.202
E-4	-.422	.296	.143	.110	.361
E-5	-.434	.268	.053	.068	.426
E-6	-.107	.340	.190	.271	.282
E-7	-.054	.418	.198	.465	.321
E-8	-.019	.268	.143	.243	.202
E-9	-.014	.417	.477	.287	.232
E-10	-.503	.271	.058	.101	.411
E-11	.329	.243	.279	.320	.013
E-12	-.039	.494	.265	.438	.386

Note: Combined N (Samples 1, 2, and 3) = 400. Correlations of absolute value greater than .098 are significant at .05 level, two-tailed; correlations of absolute value greater than .128 are significant at .01 level, two-tailed. I = Allport-Ross Intrinsic, E = Allport-Ross Extrinsic, Ep = Personal-Extrinsic, Es = Social-Extrinsic, Er = Residual-Extrinsic.

college-student and adult-churchgoing populations obviously differ in many ways, it seemed inadvisable to further combine these groups; whether these populations would provide similar estimates of the correlations was deemed an empirical question rather than a reasonable a priori assumption. The three samples of students who completed the Feagin scales (Samples 10, 11, and 12) were also pooled.

The procedure used for calculating these pooled correlations was as follows. First, the correlation of each item with each scale was calculated separately within the individual samples. In those cases where the scale contained the item with which it was being correlated, that item was removed from the scale before the correlation was calculated. The correlations from the individual samples were then pooled by multiplying each coefficient by its respective sample size, summing these values, and dividing by the sum of the sample sizes.

Samples 1, 2, and 3

The weighted mean correlation coefficients for these pooled samples (combined $N = 400$) are presented in Table 4.

Several important points are illustrated by these data. First, all of the E items correlate positively with the traditional Extrinsic scale, although some correlate more strongly than others. These correlations range from a low of .236 (E1) to a high of .494 (E12). Examination of the last three columns, however, suggests a somewhat different story. Items E1, E7, and E12 correlate more strongly with the Es scale than with the Ep scale, and the reverse is true for items E2, E3 and E9. The correlation of each item with its own scale is particularly impressive when one considers that these values represent the correlations of a single item with the sum of only two other items, and, therefore, the correlations are probably significantly attenuated by unreliability.

A second important point is that these six Ep and Es items have very low (and nonsignificant) correlations with the I scale, whereas several other E items correlate very strongly in a negative direction with I. In particular, the following three items would appear to be ideal marker variables for the I scale if scored in reverse: (E4) "It doesn't matter what I believe so long as I lead a moral life;" (E5) "Although I am a religious person, I refuse to let religious considerations influence my everyday affairs;" and (E10) "Although I believe in my religion, I feel there are many more important things in my life." The correlations of these items with I are -.422, -.434, and -.503, respectively.

Third, the I items generally correlate well with the Intrinsic scale, although items 13 and 18 correlate somewhat less strongly (r's = .345 and .201) than the others, which are all greater than .50. Moreover, the Intrinsic items are generally uncorrelated with the Ep and Es scales (r's range between -.217 and .180), but they are all negatively correlated with the "residual" Extrinsic items. For each of the nine I items, the item's correlation with Er is more negative than its correlation with either Ep or Es. Again it appears that the negative I-E correlation is due primarily to these residual items rather than those items emphasizing the social and personal-support functions of religion.

Samples 5 and 6

The pooled results from the two adult churchgoing samples, based on a total N of 160, are presented in Table 5.

Results for the Extrinsic items are quite similar to those of the student samples, with the Ep and Es items again correlating more highly with their respective scales than with the other scales. Although some of these items correlate negatively and substantially with I, items E4, E5, and E10 again show the strongest negative correlations with I (r's = -.508, -.468, and -.534).

Also similar to the student-sample results is the finding that the I items show much smaller correlations with the Ep and Es scales than with the Er items. This contrast is even more pronounced in Table 5 than in the student samples (Table 4) because the I items are so strongly negatively correlated with the traditional E scale in total but not with Ep and Es. These strong negative

Table 5.   Corrected Item-Scale Correlations for Samples 5, and 6 (Pooled)

Item	I	E	Ep	Es	Er
I-1	.627	-.332	-.008	-.119	-.480
I-2	.609	-.245	.124	-.097	-.420
I-3	.285	-.200	-.034	-.060	-.247
I-4	.646	-.289	.145	-.241	-.432
I-5	.649	-.360	.000	-.169	-.454
I-6	.476	-.101	.191	-.012	-.281
I-7	.454	-.285	-.047	-.058	-.402
I-8	.429	-.409	-.014	-.363	-.458
I-9	.531	-.413	-.034	-.175	-.553
E-1	.159	.086	.137	.189	-.006
E-2	.033	.327	.429	.177	.204
E-3	.191	.213	.251	.246	.053
E-4	-.508	.424	.121	.322	.452
E-5	-.468	.355	.068	.212	.408
E-6	-.404	.437	.187	.287	.448
E-7	-.359	.566	.248	.445	.485
E-8	-.317	.132	.041	.042	.152
E-9	-.152	.299	.368	.063	.228
E-10	-.534	.395	.010	.274	.491
E-11	-.201	.450	.283	.330	.313
E-12	-.314	.432	.130	.303	.435

Note: Combined N (Samples 5, and 6) = 160. Correlations of absolute value greater than .155 are significant at .05 level, two-tailed; correlations of absolute value greater than .202 are significant at .01 level, two-tailed. I = Allport-Ross Intrinsic, E = Allport-Ross Extrinsic, Ep = Personal-Extrinsic, Es = Social-Extrinsic, Er = Residual-Extrinsic.

correlations between the I items and the total E scale in the adult samples—but not in the student samples—are consistent with Donahue's (1985b) observation that more negative I-E correlations are characteristic of highly religious populations. It is therefore important to note that even in these religious samples, the correlation of each I item with Er (and, for that matter, with the total E scale) is more negative than the correlations with Ep and Es. As in the student samples, it appears that the negative correlation between I and E is primarily due to those Extrinsic items *not* associated with the Social- and Personal-Extrinsic dimensions.

Samples 10, 11, and 12

Similar analyses were also performed on the samples in which subjects completed the Feagin items; again the results were pooled across samples by computing weighted mean correlations. These results, based on a total N of 205, appear in Table 6.

Table 6.   Corrected Item-Scale Correlations
for Samples 10, 11, and 12 (Pooled)

Item	I	E	Ep	Es	Er
I-1	.490	.097	.032	.042	.214
I-3	.218	.128	.111	.004	.168
I-4	.376	.087	.020	-.033	.255
I-5	.474	.006	-.066	-.022	.111
I-7	.444	.158	.098	.054	.209
I-9	.320	.144	.077	.068	.232
E-1	.049	.230	.105	.411	.045
E-2	.113	.410	.491	.154	.061
E-3	.108	.376	.450	.151	.064
E-9	.017	.351	.480	.116	.024
E-11	.336	.098	.068	.089	—
E-12	.008	.340	.211	.411	.106

Note: Combined N (Samples 10, 11, and 12) = 205. Correlations of absolute value greater than .136 are
significant at .05 level, two-tailed; correlations of absolute value greater than .178 are significant at
.01 level, two-tailed. I = Allport-Ross Intrinsic, E = Allport-Ross Extrinsic, Ep = Personal-Extrinsic,
Es = Social-Extrinsic, Er = Residual-Extrinsic.

Comparisons between the correlations of Ep and Es items with their respective scales, on the one hand, and with the opposite scales, on the other, are striking. The sole residual Extrinsic item, E11, is the only Extrinsic item substantially correlated with I ($r = .336$; other r's range between .008 and .113), and it is essentially uncorrelated with Ep ($r = .068$ and Es ($r = .089$). The I items, on the other hand, again display stronger correlations (in this case positive correlations) with the Er scale than with either Ep or Es in every case.

Inter-Scale Correlations

Table 7 presents the correlations among the various scales discussed above for Samples 1 through 9 separately. All correlations are again corrected to eliminate redundant items. Table 8 presents the corresponding results for the three data sets including the Feagin scales.

The results in Tables 7 and 8 further confirm the results of the item analyses; the I scale displays a strong negative correlation with Er and generally negligible and nonsignificant correlation with Ep and Es, suggesting that the negative correlation between I and E is due primarily to the residual Extrinsic items rather than the Personal or Social items. Moreover, the Ep and Es scales correlate only moderately—though significantly—with each other.

Table 7. Corrected Correlations Among Intrinsic and Extrinsic Scales:
Allport-Ross Items

	Sample (N)	E	Ep	Es	Er
Ep	1 (152)	.361 **			
	2 (90)	.199			
	3 (155)	.461 **			
	4 (85)	.583 **			
	5 (50)	.307 **			
	6 (122)	.264 **			
	7 (77)	.219			
	8 (47)	.562 **			
	9 (105)	.385 **			
Es	1 (152)	.288 **	.262 **		
	2 (90)	.346 **	.352 **		
	3 (155)	.579 **	.455 **		
	4 (85)	.247 *	.414 **		
	5 (50)	.161	.103		
	6 (122)	.557 **	.296 **		
	7 (77)	.379 **	.294 **		
	8 (47)	.635 **	.502 **		
	9 (105)	.406 **	.311 **		
Er	1 (152)	—	.296 **	.211 **	
	2 (90)	—	.032	.179	
	3 (155)	—	.375 **	.505 **	
	4 (85)	—	.487 **	.114	
	5 (50)	—	.320 *	.152	
	6 (122)	—	.557 *	.528 **	
	7 (77)	—	.124	.272 *	
	8 (47)	—	.483 **	.561 **	
	9 (105)	—	.326 **	.349 **	
I	1 (152)	-.209 **	.095	.119	-.478 **
	2 (90)	-.074 **	.141	.118	-.282 **
	3 (155)	-.260 **	.062	-.012	-.490 **
	4 (85)	-.091	.092	.438 **	-.329 **
	5 (50)	-.329 *	.062	-.122	-.497 **
	6 (122)	-.518 **	.032	-.279 **	-.722 **
	7 (77)	.237 *	.096	-.116	-.344 **
	8 (47)	-.271	-.217	-.073	-.316 *
	9 (105)	-.214 *	.014	-.147	-.300 **

Note: I = Allport-Ross Intrinsic, E = Allport-Ross Extrinsic, Ep = Personal-Extrinsic, Es = Social-Extrinsic,
Er = Residual-Extrinsic.
  * $p < .05$.
  ** $p < .01$.

Table 8.   Corrected Correlations Among Intrinsic and Extrinsic Scales:
Feagin Items

	Sample (N)	E	Ep	Es	Er
	10 (55)	.068			
Ep	11 (60)	.396 **			
	12 (90)	.126			
	10 (55)	-.022	-.058		
	11 (60)	.469 **	.456 **		
	12 (90)	.174	.169		
	10 (55)	—	.221	.076	
Er	11 (60)	—	.062	.155	
	12 (90)	—	-.025	.067	
	10 (55)	.272 *	.135	.156	.275 *
I	11 (60)	.019	-.055	-.073	.309 *
	12 (90)	.251 *	.189	.040	.406 **

Note: I = Allport-Ross Intrinsic, E = Allport-Ross Extrinsic, Ep = Personal-Extrinsic, Es = Social-Extrinsic,
Er = Residual-Extrinsic.
* $p < .05$.
** $p < .01$.

Relationships between Extrinsic Scales and Other Variables

Although the preceding analyses seem to provide persuasive evidence for
the existence of two extrinsic factors in the Allport-Ross and Feagin scales,
it remains to be seen whether scoring the Social-Extrinsic and Personal-
Extrinsic scales separately has any important substantive implications.
Specifically, do these variables relate differentially to other variables of interest
to researchers? In order to address this question, a series of multiple regression
analyses were performed in which external variables were regressed on the Ep,
Es, and Er scales. Each data set included a variety of such variables. Some
dependent variables appeared in more than one data set, thus making it possible
to generate several independent estimates of the regression coefficients for the
various Extrinsic scales. Because the present focus is on differences among the
regression coefficients for the three Extrinsic scales, and because the dependent
variables varied widely in terms of scaling, standardized beta coefficients are
presented here.

Table 9 presents the results of regression analyses predicting various locus
of control measures from the Ep, Es, and Er scales. The measures were available
in five independent data sets and the results are presented separately for each
sample. In addition, the standardized regression coefficient—which is equal

Table 9. Standardized Regression Coefficients for Prediction Locus
of Control Variables from Extrinsic Scales

		Equation 1[a]			Equation 2[b]
	Sample (N)	Ep	Es	Er	E
Chance	1 (129)	.310 **	.070	.162	.386 **
Locus of	4 (66)	.103	.128	.116	.249 *
Control	7 (72)	.111	.128	.320 **	.383 **
	8 (45)	.134	-.243	.378 **	.247
	9 (91)	.104	.200 *	.343 **	.502 **
Powerful	1 (129)	.322 **	-.021	.056	.257 **
Others	4 (66)	.215	.054	.280 *	.438 **
Locus of	7 (72)	.089	.110	.253 *	.309 **
Control	8 (45)	.300	.074	.167	.433 **
	9 (91)	.229 *	.142	.278 **	.491 **
God	1 (129)	.337 **	.122	-.477 **	-.082
Locus of	4 (66)	.305 *	.150	-.665 **	-.225
Control	7 (72)	.206	.039	-.162	.042
	8 (45)	.225	-.271	.166	.104
	9 (91)	.305 **	.019	-.387 **	-.101
Internal	1 (129)	-.159	.127	.285 **	.191 *
Locus of	4 (66)	-.396 **	.182	.503 **	.192
Control	7 (72)	.020	-.002	.045	.045
	8 (45)	-.272	.059	.185	.006
	9 (91)	-.026	.146	.238 *	.286 **

Note: I = Allport-Ross Intrinsic, E = Allport-Ross Extrinsic, Ep = Personal-Extrinsic, Es = Social-Extrinsic,
Er = Residual-Extrinsic.
[a]Equation 1 represents a multiple regression with Ep, Es, and Er included as independent variables.
[b]Equation 2 represents a regression with E as the only independent variable.
* $p < .05$.
** $p < .01$.

to the simple product-moment correlation in this case—for predicting the
dependent variable from the total E scale alone is also given.

For the first two dependent variables, Chance and Powerful Others, each
of the component E scales (especially Ep and Er) contributes positively to the
prediction of the dependent variable in Eq. (1). When all of the E items are
combined into a single Extrinsic scale, a strong positive relationship between
E and the dependent variables is evident [Eq. (2)]. The results for the other
two dependent variables, however, show a quite different pattern. Although
the correlation between God-control and E is near zero, this result masks the
fact that the Ep scale exhibits a strong positive relationship with God-control,
whereas the residual (Er) items show a strong *negative* relationship with God-

Table 10.   Standardized Regression Coefficients for Prediction Locus
of Control Variables from Extrinsic Scales

	Sample (N)	Equation 1[a]			Equation 2[b]
		Ep	Es	Er	E
Attributions to Powerful	1 (129)	.076	.207 *	0.14	.180 *
Attributions to Chance	1 (129)	.252 **	.018	.331 **	.453 **
Attributions to God	1 (129)	.265 **	.106	-.372 **	-.056
Attributions to Personal Faith	1 (129)	.221 **	.305 **	-.401 **	.002
Intolerance of Ambiguity	2 (70)	.248 *	.124	.038	.257 *
Normlessness	3 (145)	.079	.006	.342 **	.360 **
Social Isolation	3 (145)	.029	.196 *	-.230 *	-.029
External Religious Orientation	5 (50)	.220	.204	-.211	.080
Christian Orthodoxy	5 (50)	.283 *	-.062	-.470 **	-.227
Frequency of Church Attendance	5 (50)	-.042	.272 *	-.291 *	-.127
Frequency of Prayer	5 (50)	.302 *	-.151	-.252 *	-.082
Self-Rated "Means" Orientation	5 (50)	.360 *	.178	-.388 **	.015
Self-Rated "End" Orientation	5 (50)	.259	-.009	-.317 *	-.091

Note: I = Allport-Ross Intrinsic, E = Allport-Ross Extrinsic, Ep = Personal-Extrinsic, Es = Social-Extrinsic,
Er = Residual-Extrinsic.
[a]Equation 1 represents a multiple regression with Ep, Es, and Er included as independent variables.
[b]Equation 2 represents a regression with E as the only independent variable.
* $p < .05$.
** $p < .01$.

control. (Recall that the Er scale behaves, in part, like a reversed Intrinsic scale.)
The net result of combining the items into a global E scale is a mutual
cancellation of these two effects. Precisely the opposite pattern is evident with
respect to Internal Locus of Control: Ep displays a negative relationship, and
Er a positive relationship, with the dependent variable, whereas the overall E
scale (as well as the component Es scale) evinces an intermediate degree of
relationship with the variable.

The results of similar regression analyses involving other selected dependent
variables are presented in Table 10, in which a variety of interesting patterns
are evident. For example, number of attributions made by respondents to God
(in a laboratory task involving a series of vignettes) displays a near-zero
relationship with the traditional E scale, but this result masks the fact that the

Ep orientation strongly predicts God-attributions—an effect that is cancelled by the strong negative relationship between the Er items and the dependent variable. A similar pattern occurs in predicting attributions made to personal faith in the same vignettes, in which positive relationships of both Ep and Es with the dependent variable are offset by the negative effect of the residual items. The equations for predicting Batson's External religious orientation follow this same pattern. The correlation between E and Normlessness seems to be due solely to the Er items, with both Ep and Es showing negligible relationships with this variable. In predicting Christian orthodoxy, on the other hand, the negative correlation with the traditional E scale would lead one to overlook the fact that the Ep items are actually *positively* related to orthodoxy.

It should also be noted that some of the relationships depicted in this table provide validating evidence for the interpretation of the Ep and Es scales as Personal and Social extrinsicness, respectively. For example, the Es scale is more strongly related than Ep to feelings of Social Isolation and an independent measure of Church Attendance: That is, persons who turn to religion for social gain tend to be those who feel socially isolated, and they are more frequent church attenders. Conversely, Ep is more strongly related than Es to Frequency of Prayer, suggesting that those who seek comfort and relief in religion are likely to turn to prayer—though not necessarily in church—as a means of attaining this.

Summary

The results of the various regression analyses reported above illustrate that the Ep, Es, and Er components of Extrinsic religious orientation, as measured by the Allport-Ross scales, relate differentially to a variety of external variables. In many examples it was apparent that the correlation betweeen the traditional Extrinsic scale and another variable was due solely to one or two of these components. In other cases a near-zero correlation between E and another variable masked the fact that two components bore strong relationships with the variable, but in opposite directions. Examination of these results should make clear that many interesting and potentially important relationships may be overlooked, and misleading conclusions drawn, when the Extrinsic items are combined into a single global measure.

DISCUSSION

The results of this investigation strongly suggest that the Allport-Ross and Feagin scales are best described as measuring three factors rather than one or two. These factors include one Intrinsic and two Extrinsic factors, the latter concerning religion as a source of comfort, relief, and protection, on the one hand, and as a vehicle for social gain on the other. Although the two Extrinsic factors are moderately intercorrelated, regression analyses revealed that the two dimensions relate differentially to other variables in interesting and theoretically meaningful ways. These analyses also suggest that combining all of the Extrinsic items into a single scale can, in many cases, lead to correlational results that may be quite misleading. For example, a near-zero correlation between E and an external variable may hide the fact that two components of E are both related strongly, but in opposite directions, to that variable.

Although Amón and Yela (1968) and Hoge (1972) have previously reported factor analytic results nearly identical to those described here, these earlier findings seem not to have attracted the attention of other I-E researchers. (There are good reasons for this, however; the Amón and Yela paper appeared in an obscure—at least to Americans—Spanish journal. Hoge relegated his results to a footnote, and then further downplayed their significance by noting the small sample size on which they were based.) In any case, we might add these two studies to the list of replications cited in the results above. Taken in combination, this body of results would seem to provide compelling evidence concerning the factorial structure of the Allport-Ross scales.

These factor analytic findings are also in line with the *theoretical* attempts of a number of other researchers to extend the I-E framework beyond two dimensions. Such proposed extensions have typically been concerned with distinguishing among distinct extrinsic orientations. This approach certainly seems reasonable in principle. If an extrinsic orientation refers to the use of religion as a means to some other end, then perhaps a variety of such "ends" could be identified.

Three years before the publication of Allport and Ross' classic paper, Brown (1964) had introduced an institutional-individual dimension to distinguish between "self-serving extrinsic" and "conventional acceptance" categories of extrinsic orientation. A similar distinction has been made more recently by Meadow and Kahoe (1984), who incorporated these categories into a general model of religious development.

Fleck (1981), and Fleck, Horner, and Castillo (1979) have also proposed an extension of the intrinsic-extrinsic framework. Fleck's trichotomy includes Intrinsic, Extrinsic, and Consensual dimensions, which he described in the 1981 paper as follows:

> . . . an intrinsic-committed religious orientation similar to Spilka's committed and Allport's intrinsic dimension, a consensual religious orientation in which religion supports personal comfort and relief, and an extrinsic religious orientation in which religious membership and participation are used in a self-serving, utilitarian manner for social purposes such as gaining social standing and acceptance in the community (p. 68).

Fleck further proposed that the personal support function of the consensual dimension is manifested in a desire for ritual, ceremony, and order.

The conceptual resemblance between this theoretical framework and the factor-analytic solutions reported by Hoge (1972), Amón and Yela (1968), and the present author is readily apparent. Unfortunately, however, Fleck's (1981) factor-analytic results appear to have yielded a traditional extrinsic factor that included *both* personal support and social gain, whereas the consensual factor was defined solely by items concerning interest in ritual and ceremony. Fleck, Horner, and Castillo (1979) replicated the intrinsic and consensual factors reported by Fleck (1981), but in addition found two distinct extrinsic factors that closely paralleled the social and personal-support dimensions reported in the studies cited above.

Echemendia and Pargament (1982) factor analyzed responses to 71 religion items and obtained *four* factors reflecting various aspects of extrinsic religious orientation that represent different functions or uses of religion. These factors, which differed somewhat from the authors' proposed theoretical framework, were labeled *Personal/Religious Support, Social/Community Support, Obligation,* and *Social Gain.* Given the content of the factors and the intercorrelations among the resultant scales, I would argue that their results are generally in line with the findings of the studies cited above in distinguishing the personal-support and social dimensions of Extrinsic religiosity.

The Relationship Between I and E

The findings of the present investigation also provide some insights into a problem with which many researchers have been concerned, namely the relationship between the intrinsic and extrinsic dimensions. The results presented here indicate that the commonly found negative correlation between I and E (Donahue 1985a) is due almost entirely to those items *not* related to Personal (Ep) or Social (Es) extrinsic orientation. These residual items demonstrate strong negative correlations with I, whereas Ep and Es are essentially uncorrelated with I; this result was observed both for students at secular universities (Table 4) and adult churchgoers (Table 5). The consistency of this pattern across samples suggests that variation in the I-E correlation associated with the theological orientation of the sample (Donahue 1985b) is primarily a function of the "residual" Extrinsic items. Inspection of Table 7 reveals that the correlation between I and Es also becomes more negative in those samples having the strongest I-E correlations—that is, the adult churchgoing and seminary student samples—but these correlations are quite small relative to the I-Er correlations.

The effects of these "residual" Extrinsic items are also evident when one contrasts the Allport-Ross scales with the shorter Feagin scales. Although the former tend to yield a negative correlation between I and E, the Feagin measures tend to produce a *positive* correlation between these scales. This discrepancy apparently derives from differences in the "residual" Extrinsic items: On the Feagin measure there is only one such item, and it is positively correlated with I. Missing from the Feagin E scale are those residual items that correlate negatively with I.

Item analyses revealed that of these six "residual" (Er) items on the Allport-Ross instrument, three in particular were primarily responsible for this negative correlation with I and appear to be ideal marker variables for I if reflected. These items were E4, E5, and E10. In fact, Hoge (1972) chose these very items to be reverse-scored and included in his "validated intrinsic religious motivation scale."

The content of these three particular items seems to depict an explicit denial of an intrinsic or committed orientation toward religion; in fact, it would be a challenging task to write better items for measuring the *absence* of an intrinsic orientation. Perhaps it was these items that Allport had in mind when he referred to his indiscriminately proreligious subject—those subjects who endorse both I and E items—as "muddleheads." Endorsement of both these items and positive Intrinsic items would indeed seem logically inconsistent. However, correlations between these items and I scale, which are probably about as high as the respective reliabilities will allow, indicate that subjects scoring high on I do *not* endorse these particular items. Instead, the items appear to simply indicate reversals of I items that were erroneously placed on the E scale when the bipolar scoring system was abandoned. There is thus little evidence of logical inconsistency or "muddleheadedness" in these data.

The "purified" Ep and Es scales, on the other hand, are uncorrelated with I, suggesting that respondents who score high on I may also score high on Ep or Es or both. Examination of the content of these items suggests that there is really no logical inconsistency in this at all. As noted by Echemendia and Pargament (1982), "an intrinsic orientation may *also* provide support, comfort and solace" (p. 12, emphasis in original). I would add that an intrinsic orientation does not logically preclude the possibility of one's church being a "congenial social activity" or a "place to formulate good social relationships" either.

This finding may have important implications regarding the practice of splitting respondents into low and high groups on the Intrinsic and Extrinsic diemnsions, and then treating the data in terms of a two-way analysis of variance. Donahue (1985b) has called for more research using this "fourfold typology" approach in order to assess the degree to which I and E may interact in relation to other variables. The results of the present study suggest that there are many ways in which respondents may score "high" on the Extrinsic scale, based on various combinations of Ep, Es, and Er items. Item analyses and scale intercorrelations showed that respondents who score high on I tend to score low on the residual Extrinsic items, indicating that "indiscriminate proreligiousness" (i.e., scoring high on both I and E) is not primarily a matter of "muddleheadedness" or logical inconsistency. Detailed examination of this issue is beyond the scope of the present investigation, but suggests an intriguing avenue for future research.

Recommendations

Given the findings just summarized, it seems appropriate and necessary to reconsider the Allport-Ross framework and the scales used to measure it. Three general options for dealing with the problems outlined in this paper appear possible:

1. Since two separate extrinsic factors are evident in the scales, we could bring our theory into line with these empirical results and expand the I-E conceptual framework to include three dimensions rather than two. Fleck and his associates have provided a thoughtful and persuasive conceptual framework that seems quite compatible with the empirical findings reported here, and we might therefore follow their recommendations for reconceptualizing intrinsicness and extrinsicness. Because the appearence of these particular extrinsic factors in the I-E scale seems to have been rather accidental, however—that is, the scales were not originally intended to distinguish two distinct varieties of extrinsicness—I would recommend this approach only if strong theory dictates that Personal and Social Well-Being represent useful and interesting constructs. I leave this question for the reader to decide.

2. We might infer instead that the separate extrinsic factors are themselves an artifact of poor measurement, and improve the I-E scales so as to preclude the emergence of separate E factors. This goal could be accomplished by (1) removing the "reversed intrinsic" items from the E scale to restore the desired orthogonality to the two factors, and (2) developing a wider variety of extrinsic items in such a way that homogeneous clusters of Extrinsic items are not present (that is, by forcing the unique components of the item variances to be uncorrelated). Alternatively, we might keep the "reversed intrinsic" items from the E scale and drop the Ep and Es items in order to re-establish a single unidimensional scale, following the lead of Hoge (1972). One drawback to these approaches, however, is that the Personal and Social components seem to produce interesting patterns of relationships with other variables, and it might be worth examining some of these relationships more closely rather than trying to make them go away.

3. A third option would be to take a few steps back and re-evaluate the whole conceptual framework. Although the I-E distinction proved to be very useful for examining the relationship between prejudice and religion, it may not be sufficiently rich—at least as currently operationalized—for studying other interesting psychological and sociological questions about religious belief and motivation. For example, a much wider range of extrinsic motives might be worth considering, such as those explored by Echemendia and Pargament.

Ironically, an excellent starting point for such a reconceptualization might be Allport's own writings, since our current operationalization of I-E hardly does justice to the richness and depth of Allport's ideas (Batson & Ventis 1982).

Moreover, there are additional problems with Allport's typology that, considered in combination with the psychometric shortcomings described in this paper, provide more than adequate justification for abandoning the current I-E scales. Hunt and King (1971) and Dittes (1971) pointed to a variety of conceptual difficulties with the framework shortly after the scales appeared in the literature (also see Hood 1985). More recently, Batson (1976; Batson and Ventis 1982) has asserted that the Intrinsic scale tends to reflect a rigid adherence to orthodox beliefs, rather than the "mature" religion conceived by Allport, and that the apparent association between intrinsic religion and tolerance is largely an artifact of a social-desirability response set. Although Batson's assessment has in turn been challenged both theoretically and empirically (Donahue 1985b; Hood 1985; Spilka, Kojetin, and McIntosh 1985; Watson, Morris, Foster, and Hood 1986), it provides additional support for the contention that the existing I-E scales may be of dubious utility.

Assuming that the intrinsic-extrinsic distinction is primarily about *motivation* for being involved in religion (Hoge 1972; Hunt and King 1971) there is an even more ambitious approach that I would advocate. That is, we should embed our study of religious motivation within a larger theoretical framework concerning motivation in general, and then examine the ways in which religion can be used by people in the service of these various motives. For example, in a recent paper by Spilka, Shaver, and Kirkpatrick (1985), attribution theory was used as a framework for examining the motives for maintaining a sense of meaning, control, and self-esteem, and it was then asked how religious attributions might help people to attain these goals. Spilka and McIntosh (personal communication, 1986) are currently working toward operationalizing these constructs as motivational factors for being involved in religion. Alternatively, as I have argued elsewhere (Kirkpatrick 1986), a broad-scale theoretical framework such as that provided by Attachment Theory (Bowlby 1969) might serve as a basis for distinguishing among various motivations and psychological benefits of being religious.

Any of these potential courses of action will of course take time, and I hope researchers will direct some of their future efforts toward each until improved scales and/or theoretical frameworks are developed. In the meantime, it is recommended that researchers employing the I-E scale score the Social and Personal scales separately in addition to scoring E in the traditional way. Many interesting results might also be discovered by re-analyzing data from previous studies in this manner. In any case, this modification of the Allport framework will perhaps serve as a useful stepping-stone to a broader and richer conceptualization of religious orientation and motivation for religious involvement.

ACKNOWLEDGMENTS

Portions of this research were previously presented at the Convention of the Rocky Mountain Psychological Association (April 1986) and the Convention of the American Psychological Association (August 1986). The manuscript was completed while the author was a graduate student at the University of Denver, Department of Psychology.

The author is indebted to Robert Bridges, Brian Kojetin, Danny McIntosh, H. Newton Malony, Jennifer Neeman, Bernard Spilka, Donald Sharpsteen, and Scott Stanley for generously sharing their data, and to Charles S. Reichardt, Bernard Spilka, Dan Tweed, the co-editors of this volume, and an anonymous reviewer for their helpful comments on earlier versions of this paper.

Address correpondence to Lee A. Kirkpatrick, Department of Psychology, University of South Carolina, Columbia, SC 29208.

REFERENCES

Adorno, T. W., E. Frenkel-Brunswick, D. J. Levinson, and R. N. Sanford. 1950. *The Authoritarian Personality*. New York: Harper.

Allport, G. W. 1954. *The Nature of Prejudice*. Cambridge, MA: Addison-Wesley.

Allport, G. W. 1966. "Traits Revisited." *American Psychologist* 21:1-10.

Allport, G. W., and J. M. Ross. 1967. "Personal Religious Orientation and Prejudice." *Journal of Personality and Social Psychology* 5:423-443.

Amón, J., and M. Yela. 1968. "Dimensiones de la religiosidad." *Revista de Psicologia General Y Aplicada* 23:989-993.

Batson, C. D., and R. A. Gray. 1981. "Religious Orientation and Helping Behavior: Responding to One's Own or to the Victim's Needs?" *Journal of Personality and Social Psychology* 40:511-520.

Batson, C. D., and W. L. Ventis. 1982. *The Religious Experience: A Social-Psychological Perspective*. New York: Oxford University Press.

Bowlby, J. 1969. *Attachment and Loss. Vol. 1: Attachment*. New York: Basic Books.

Brown, L. B. 1964. "Classifications of Religious Orientation." *Journal for the Scientific Study of Religion* 4:91-99.

Budner, S. 1962. "Intolerance of Ambiguity as a Personality Variable." *Journal of Personality* 30:29-50.

Carey, R. G. 1974a. "Emotional Adjustment in Terminal Patients: A Quantitative Approach." *Journal of Counseling Psychology* 21:433-439.

————. 1974b. *Living Until Death: A Program of Service and Research on the Correlates of Emotional Adjustment to Terminal Illness*. Unpublished manuscript.

Cattell, R. B. 1978. *The Scientific Use of Factor Analysis in Behavioral and Life Sciences*. New York: Plenum Press.

Dean, D. 1961. "Alienation: Its Meaning and Measurement." *American Sociological Review*. 26:753-758.

Dittes, J. E. 1971. "Typing the Typologies: Some Parallels in the Career of Church-Sect and Extrinsic-Intrinsic." *Journal for the Scientific Study of Religion* 10:375-383.

Donahue, M. J. 1985a. "Intrinsic and Extrinsic Religiousness: The Empirical Research." *Journal for the Scientific Study of Religion* 24: 418-423.

————. 1985b. "Intrinsic and Extrinsic Religiousness: Review and Meta-Analysis." *Journal of Personality and Social Psychology* 48:400-419.

Echemendia, R. J., and K. I. Pargament. 1982. The Psychosocial Functions of Religion: Reconceptualization and Measurement." Paper presented at the Convention of the American Psychological Association, Washington, DC, August.

Elifson, K. W. 1976. "Religious Behavior among Urban Southern Baptists: A Casual Inquiry." *Sociological Analysis* 37:32-44.

Feagin, J. R. 1964. "Prejudice and Religious Types: A Focused Study of Southern Fundamentalists." *Journal for the Scientific Study of Religion* 4:3-13.

Finney, J. R., and H. N. Malony. 1985. "Means, End, and Quest: A Research Note." *Review of Religious Research* 26:408-412.

Fleck, J. R. 1981. "Dimensions of Personal Religion: A Trichotomous View." Pp. 66-80. *Psychology and Christianity*, edited by J. R. Fleck and J. D. Carter.

Fleck, J. R., A. J. Horner, and N. L. Castillo. 1979. "Personal Religion and Psychological Schemata: A Cross Cultural Perspective." Paper presented at the Meeting of the Society for the Scientific Study of Religion, San Antonio, TX, October.

Hilty, D. M., R. L. Morgan, and J. E. Burns. 1984. "King and Hunt Revisited: Dimensions of Religious Involvement." *Journal for the Scientific Study of Religion* 23:252-266.

Hoge, D. R. 1972. "A Validated Intrinsic Religious Motivation Scale." *Journal for the Scientific Study of Religion* 11:369-376.

Hood, R. W., Jr. 1971. "A Comparison of the Allport and Feagin Scoring Procedures for Intrinsic/Extrinsic Religious Orientation." *Journal for the Scientific Study of Religion* 10:370-374.

———. 1985. "The Conceptualization of Religious Purity in Allport's Typology." *Journal for the Scientific Study of Religion* 24:413-417.

Hunt, R. A., and M. B. King 1971. "The Intrinsic-Extrinsic Concept: A Review and Evaluation." *Journal for the Scientific Study of Religion* 10:339-356.

King, M., and R. Hunt. 1972. "Measuring the Religious Variable: Replication." *Journal for the Scientific Study of Religion* 11:240-251.

Kirkpatrick, L. A. 1986. "Developmental Psychology and Religion: Potential Applications of Attachment Theory for the Psychology of Religion." Paper presented at the Meeting of the Society for the Scientific Study of Religion, Washington, DC, November.

Kopplin, D. 1976. "Religious Orientations of College Students and Related Personality Characteristics." Paper presented at the Convention of the American Psychological Association, Washington, DC, August.

Levenson, H. 1973. "Multidimensional Locus of Control in Psychiatric Patients." *Journal of Consulting and Clinical Psychology* 41:397-404.

Meadow, M. J., and R. D. Kahoe. 1984. *Psychology of Religion: Religion in Individual Lives.* New York: Harper & Row.

Pargament, K. I., H. Adamakos, M. L. Kelemen, K. Falgout, J. Myers, M. T. Brannic, D. S. Ensing, R. K. Warren, and P. Cook. 1986. "The Direct Measurement of Indiscriminate Proreligiousness: Initial Validation Studies of a New Approach." Paper presented at the Meeting of the Society for the Scientific Study of Religion, Washington, DC, August.

Patrick, J. W. 1979. "Personal Faith and the Fear of Death among Divergent Religious Populations." *Journal for the Scientific Study of Religion* 18:298-305.

Robinson, J. P., and P. Shaver. 1973. *Measures of Social Psychological Attitudes* (rev. ed.). Ann Arbor, MI: Institute for Social Research.

Spilka, B., B. Kojetin, and D. McIntosh. 1985. "Forms and Measures of Personal Faith: Questions, Correlates and Distinctions. *Journal for the Scientific Study of Religion* 24:437-442.

Spilka, B., and G. Schmidt. 1983. "General Attribution Theory for the Psychology of Religion: The Influence of Event-Character on Attributions to God." *Journal for the Scientific Study of Religion* 22:326-339.

Spilka, B., P. Shaver and L. A. Kirkpatrick. 1985. "A General Attribution Theory for the Psychology of Religion." *Journal for the Scientific Study of Religion* 24:1-23.

Vincenzo, J., C. Hendrick, and E. J. Murray. 1976. "The Relationship between Religious Beliefs and Attending the Fear-Provoking Religiously Oriented Movie—'The Exorcist'." *Omega* 7:137-143.

Watson, P. J., R. J. Morris, J. E. Foster, and R. W. Hood Jr., 1986. "Religiosity and Social Desirability." *Journal for the Scientific Study of Religion* 25:215-232.

Wilson, W. W. 1960. "Extrinsic Religious Values and Prejudice." *Journal of Abnormal and Social Psychology* 2:286-288.

ALTERNATIVE RELIGIONS AND ECONOMIC INDIVIDUALISM

James T. Richardson, Brock Kilbourne, and Barry van Driel

ABSTRACT

This paper examines the related negative response of three insitutional sectors of American society—the mass media, certain elements of the mental health professions, and the Anti-Cult Movement—to the growth of new religious movements. That related response reveals a totalitarian ideology of economic individualism in American society and some of the vested economic interests served by it. It also indicates the pervasiveness of mass conformity pressures directed toward individual members of society. In conclusion, religion has taken on a dual role in contemporary American society by allowing individuals to pursue either conventional or nonconventional (i.e., noneconomic) forms of individual self-expression.

INTRODUCTION

A tremendous amount of discussion has been expended in the last decade concerning the value of new religions and their effect on society (Beckford 1981, 1985). The related response of diverse institutions to the growth of new religions, at least in the United States, suggests that the direct investigation

Research in the Social Scientific Study of Religion, Volume 1, pages 33-56.

of new religions may be less important than what that societal reaction reveals about contemporary American society in general, and individual self-concept formation in particular. Ironically, the effort to control or even stamp out new religions suggests the inherent limitations of our cultural conception of individualism by posing the question, "Why is it that, in a society which prides itself on the value it places on individualism, certain forms or expressions of religiosity and social experimentation should be so adamantly opposed?"

The answer to this question requires that we first place new religions within the larger historical context of American society of the last thirty to thirty-five years. The last three or four decades have witnessed Americans individuating themselves and collectively conforming in sometimes contradictory ways. Indeed, several generations of Americans reveal continuing tensions between individuation and conformity needs. More specifically, in the context of this paper we can assert that Americans generally attempt to idealize the idea of the independent, autonomous individual: the unrestrained, free-thinking individual who stands on his own two feet and sinks or swims accordingly (Herberg 1960; Bellah 1976). On the other hand, much social psychological research shows the tendency for Americans to be other-directed (Riesman, 1950) and conforming (Sherif 1935; Asch 1956; Moscovici and Personnaz 1980; Moscovici 1985).

The apparent contradictions between the cultural ideal of individual autonomy and social scientific theorizing and empirical findings on actual conforming behavior makes sense, however, when we consider the larger societal trends of the last four decades in the United States. These trends suggest both how most Americans *define* individualism and the *tensions* between individualism and conformity within American culture. For example, at the risk of sacrificing precision for generality, the 1950s indicated a generation of individuals who generally conformed to the status quo. Most were other-directed and oriented toward getting ahead financially, building their families, worshiping in their communities, and serving their nation under a policy of conscription.

The 1960s and early 1970s, however, witnessed an ostensibly new breed of Americans with different values and beliefs; that is, many young Americans were setting their sights on cultivating self-awareness, meaningful experiences, equality and sharing, love, identity, relationships, and community (Yankelovich 1981). Millions of Americans challenged the terminal values— "an end-state of existence (which) is personally and socially worth striving for" (Rokeach 1968)—and conventional wisdom of prior generations by experimenting with drugs, new forms of sexuality, radical politics, communal life, new sex roles, racial equality, and mysticism. Many individuals literally dropped out of the mainstream and embraced a less materialistic counterculture existence. Some deserted their biological families, substituting instead psychological and/or spiritual surrogates. Others fled the church with the slogan "God is dead," and millions of Americans—old, young, black, white, male, female, worker, nonworker, student, nonstudent, traditional, or nontraditional—took to the streets to *protest* against the war in Vietnam, racism, sexism, poverty, and other social injustices. America's leaders and institutions were under attack, and their legitimacy was deteriorating (Eister 1974; Bellah 1976). Some called it alienation, some called it a "new age," and some called it anarchy. Whatever it was called, it was clearly something new and different: an ad hoc community that emerged which incorporated the confrontation and dissent of the times.

The mid-1970s, a time when American society was winding down after the Vietnam war, brought forth a more stability-conscious generation of Americans, most of whom saw little reason to continue the confrontation politics of the 1960s. Self-growth advancement and an optimistic outlook were the currency of the day—clearly as the new decade's experiential translation of a culturally ingrained ideology of individualism. The "Me" generation (Lasch 1979) thus emerged and ideologically sustained Americans during a time of several major national economic crises. Many of the new ideas and social experiments of the 1960s crystallized into "taken-for-granted" new roles, relationships, identities, lifestyles, and communities (Kilbourne and Richardson 1985). Not too surprisingly, however, given a wave of international crises (e.g., the oil crisis, stagflation, and the Iranian hostage crises), the economic fears and national insecurities of the late 1970s pushed these earlier social changes back, and subsequently established the agenda for the 1980s. Most Americans hurriedly embraced the traditional and safer values of the 1950's and previous generations. A renewed focus on the "old" goals of work, careerism, "get aheadism," family, religion, and national commitment arose again, even among the youth in the society.

What does all this flip-flopping around for several generations of Americans reveal? What does it have to do with the negative reaction to new religions? One thing is clear: different generations of Americans have collectively pursued different *core* ideals/values, and these core ideals/values have at times been in conflict with one another. Cross-generationally we see evidence of conflict and tension between different generations of Americans who adhere to either conventional or nonconventional values (Feuer 1969; Davis 1940; Braungart 1984), which has become the basis for what many refer to as the Generation Gap. We also see as a consequence of these different visions of reality the tendency for different generations of Americans to define their individuality in remarkably different ways.

Individuals with traditional or conventional American values tend to define their individuality in primarily economic terms: how much one earns, the amount of money one has, one's job or career, and/or what one owns. Individuals with counterculture values, on the other hand, are less likely to use or solely emphasize economic criteria in their self-definitions. Such indviduals are more likely to define themselves on the basis of self-growth, experiences, and relationships. They are more likely to emphasize, alternatively, "who one is" rather than "what one has," whether in a psychological, social, or spiritual sense. Starting in the late 1970s and then peaking in the early 1980s, however, we see a definite return by many Americans to conventional values of strict economic individualism. (One could even argue a large-scale *counter* counterculture social movement.)

The potency and pervasiveness of economic individualism as an all-embracing ideology in American society is exemplified particularly well when we examine the related negative response of diverse American institutions to the proliferation of new religions. A normative economic conception of individualism is revealed that culturally dictates the boundaries of acceptable individualism. People should express themselves in terms of their consumption patterns and what they own. This materialistic conception can even be viewed as a *totalitarian ideology* in the sense that it is considered all inclusive and one-dimensional. Expressions of individualism at variance with this economic conception are consistently rejected by powerful segments of society. Nevertheless, periodic alternating dissident expressions of individualism are evident in American society, but to a far lesser degree and with sometimes considerable cost to the individual.

It is the purpose of this paper, then, to examine the generally negative response of three institutionalized sectors of American society—the mass media, certain elements of the mental health professions, and the Anti-Cult Movement—to the growth and proliferation of new religions as a way to facilitate an understanding of the dominant economic conception of individualism in American society. That economic conception and the particular vested interest served by it can account in large part for the adamant opposition by powerful sectors of American society to new forms of religiosity and social experimentation over the last several decades.

THE RESPONSE OF THE MASS MEDIA

The mass media is probably the most influential agent which has molded and transformed public opinion in relation to new religious movements, a point previously made by several authors (Shupe and Bromley 1980; Wilson 1983; Beckford 1983, 1985; van Driel and Richardson 1988a, 1988b). This has probably occurred because only a relatively small percentage of Americans have had anything more than a brief, superficial encounter with any new religious movement or its members. Consequently, most Americans have been dependent on the mass media for information pertaining to new religions or more popularly, cults. In its dealings with subjects of investigation like new religious movements located at the fringe or margin of normal society, the media therefore becomes an all-important source of information.

The "information power" (French and Raven 1959) of the mass media is evidenced by its ability to reach and influence a very broad cross-section of American society, something virtually unattainable by professional social scientific journals. For example, three major weekly news magazines—*Time, Newsweek,* and *U.S. News and World Report*—publish over eleven million copies a week, and television, of course, is an even more ubiquitous medium. That awareness helps us appreciate the extensive reach and penetrating force of the mass media as an instrument of public opinion formation, especially in instances where mediating factors and conditions are absent (Klapper 1960). It is furthermore evident that the mass media generally has its greatest impact by reinforcing existent attitudes or by establishing attitudes toward new social objects (Kraus 1962; Sears and Whitney 1973; Patterson 1980) which, of course, makes new religions subject to prior definitions and labels.

Despite the important role played by the mass media in shaping public opinion in general, surprisingly little research has attempted to systematically investigate trends in the mass media's coverage of new religions. More often than not, there has been a taken-for-granted assumption that the media is generally negative (i.e., suspicious and/or hostile) in its coverage of new religions. The few studies done in this area tend to support this view.

Bromley, Shupe, and Ventimiglia (1979), for example, analyzed newspaper articles on the Unification Church between 1974 and 1977. Although limited in its generalizability (the articles for this analysis came from a clippings file maintained by the U.C. in New York City and only dealt with coverage of ex-members), it is nevertheless a valuable study for the insights provided on some press coverage of one controversial, communal new religious group. Several patterns of atrocity tales were identified; each entailed some flagrant violation of an important cultural value. The major types of tales discerned by Bromley et al., included psychological, physical, economic, "associative" (concerned with conventional patterns of relationships), political-legal, and cultural atrocities.

The authors showed how the dissemination of atrocity tales in the media served to legitimize, authorize, and mobilize actions against a deviant group. As Kilbourne and Richardson (1982b) have noted in relation to such reported atrocity tales:

Atrocity tales are a good example of an important type of indirect violence against new religions. Such tales may serve as the justification for more direct violence against the groups and their members. . . This has had the effect of altercasting new groups into a defensive position whereby they must defend their beliefs and practices against sometimes violent attacks by the established social order. While it is not always evident who "threw the first stone," status quo groups such as anti-cult groups have sometimes provoked counterattacks from new groups (p. 3).

Thus, the reporting of atrocity tales about new religions in the press can have unforeseen and sometimes dramatically negative consequences for new religions.

A study by Lindt (1979) investigated reporting trends in the media in relation to new religious movements. That study, limited to one time period and including only Washington-based newspapers and three weekly news magazines, content analyzed the press coverage of new religions to ascertain their public image, both during and after the Jonestown tragedy. Perhaps overly influenced by contemporaneous events, this study indicated a general negative media bias.

More recently, van Driel and Richardson (1988a) have investigated coverage of new religions across a twelve-year time period (1972-1984). Using five time periods and relying on the indexes of four major newspapers and three major weekly news magazines, over 500 articles were content analyzed. The study also incorporated four control groups (Jehovah's Witnesses, Salvation Army, Christian Science, Mennonites/Amish) to ascertain whether the coverage could be considered specific for this umbrella category of movements, or if other more accepted marginal religions attracted similar coverage.

The findings indicated that coverage of both categories of religious groups was radically different, and was indicated by the following: (1) The control groups received much less attention than new religions from the mid-1970s onward; (2) new religions were discussed in terms of controversy and conflict far more often, and the coverage was much more negative; (3) topics relating to psychological abuse by new religions (and metaphors relating to these subjects) appeared regularly in the print media, but were virtually nonexistent in reports of the control groups; and, (4) the economic successes of the Mennonites especially were embedded within the context of a human interest approach, while the economic successes of newer religions were placed in a social problems and exploitation context. Members of the new religions were depicted as lacking individuality and economic or political power. Mennonites, on the other hand, were portrayed as embodying the higher valued American traits of devotion to work, commitment, and perserverance.

The results of this extensive study also show that the media has been generally quite suspicious of the new religions, and that coverage has vacillated between media peaks and plateaus of negativism, with a narrow valley of ambivalence. Throughout the 1970s coverage became increasingly hostile, and peaked following the Jonestown tragedies. Fewer articles have appeared in recent years, and these tended to adopt a less accusatory tone.

In general, however the results show that: (1) the Unification Church has been the most media-prone movement; (2) new religious groups are not conceived to be legitimate or authentic religions, and are instead depicted as pseudo-religious aberrations; (3) the majority of print media articles describe new religions and their leaders, members, behavior, etc., in a stereotypic fashion; (4) there is a general tendency to ignore historical contextual, and background information as well as balanced explanations; (5) conflicts, controversies, and accusations dominate coverage; (6) pejorative metaphors relating to manipulative processes and psychological abuse are frequently included in accounts of these groups; (7) distinctions between groups are seldom mentioned (they are lumped together and treated as totally similar—the only distinctions relate to different controversies); (8) there exists an *enormous* hiatus between social-scientific and media conceptualizations of new religions and the issues that are deemed to be relevant (anti-cultists' positions appear to have much more influence); and, (9) the actual reality of life in new religions is obscured or missed altogether.

The results of this study (van Driel and Richardson 1988a, 1988b) lend credence to the view that it is not very fruitful to qualify media coverage in terms of atrocity tales (Beckford 1985), as Bromley, Shupe and Ventimiglia (1979) have done, even though they employ a broad definition of an atrocity tale. Beckford (1985) opts for the term "negative summary events" instead. In our opinion, based on the empirical data generated in the van Driel and Richardson study, the coverage by the mass media can best be labeled a "stream of controversies." The documentation of various controversies is the one constant factor in reporting newer religions. The reading audience is presented with a continual procession of controversies that serve to brand these groups as "deviant," "problematic," and, above all, "controversial." Many of these controversies dealt with the enigma of economic illegalities that have engulfed various new religious movements. Accounts of the Rajneesh movement, for instance, constantly brought to the attention of the reading public that members were forced to work long hours for the Bhagwan's financial advantage, illustrated poignantly by his evergrowing fleet of Rolls-Royces. New financial acquisitions of Rev. Moon were the focus of multiple reports, and it was made clear that this economic prosperity was meant only for Moon himself.

In general, then, available evidence indicates that the mass media has for the most part perpetuated a one-sided, stereotypic, simplistic, and negative view of contemporary new religions and those who join them. Uneven or selective attention to the more conspicuous and radical groups has tended to reinforce certain stereotypical conceptions about new groups. Most negative stereotyping seems directed toward creating the impression that new religions or cults are an inherent danger to the individual and/or society (Kilbourne and Richardson 1984a; Beckford 1983, 1985; van Driel and Richardson 1988a, 1988b). Cults allegedly threaten, for example, the autonomy and/or mental health of the individual, economic independence of members, the family, children, democratic processes, Western civilization, the American way of life, and/or authentic religious beliefs (Kilbourne and Richardson 1982a; Kilbourne and Richardson 1986). In solely economic terms, an image is presented of highly-powered multinationals with unlimited financial resources.

The view that all new religions are dangerously the same and that they exert some kind of deleterious influence over the unsuspecting individual (who is willing to sacrifice all his/her financial assets, future career prospects, and individual freedom), tends to make for sensational and attention-getting press. While audience habituation may occur, this pervasive view continues to sell newspapers, magazines, television programs, and movies. It plays on the idea of an inside common threat to cherished norms, values, and ideas of American society (which makes it more sinister), as well as the now culturally institutionalized rebellion of the younger generation in American society.

Another dimension of media coverage of new religions is the general tendency for the media, especially television and movies, to construct plots around *personalities,* rather than situations. This *psychologizing* describes and explains situations by means of the personalities and the histories that compose them, or by explicit personality characterizations, rather than in terms of situational factors and the roles and norms that make particular social performance possible within a given cultural and social context. The print media, for instance, has usually ignored sociocultural explanations of the existence of new religions (van Driel and Richardson 1988a). This reporting strategy goes beyond personalizing accounts to enhance reader identification and interest. Social psychologists refer to this tendency to focus on personalities as the fundamental attribution error (Ross 1977), and have found that observers, as opposed to actors, generally attribute an actor's behavior to internal personal characteristics (Jones and Nisbet 1972). Individuals, groups, nations, and cultures are all viewed as personalities. Within this personality framework, leaders of social movements become media-certified "celebrities" who may be subsequently subjected to a process of status degradation (Garfinkel 1956) by means of "character assassination" (Cromer 1978).

Most important from our perspective, the media-created personalities of cult leaders tend to revolve around conventional, economic values. The cult and its members are obviously unconventional, and the cult leader is often depicted as exploitative; this is usually stated in frank economic terms. The headlines "Prophet for Profit" (*Washington Post* 1976), "Tax Supported Meditation" (*New York Times* 1974), and "A Look at the 'Moonies,' Money, Politics and Confusion" (*Washington Post* 1976) reveal this concern with economic themes. The cult leader is often portrayed as a conniving businessman who has sold his adherents a defective product. The following reasoning is common: an individual's investment of time, affection, energy, and money in new religions could have been better spent by pursuing one's occupational career, education, or financial investments—the real hallmarks of the successful individual. In sum, mass media reports of cult activities generally arouse the public's ire, directly or indirectly, because of our deeply-held *cultural idealization of economic man.*

ELEMENTS OF THE MENTAL HEALTH MOVEMENT

An articulate and out-spoken minority of the mental health community has responded to the alleged threat of new religions to the social order by attempting to confirm the psychological or psychiatric basis of such claims. They have frequently made use of psychopathological, scientific, or medical-sounding coercive group labels (Clark 1978, 1979; Singer 1979; West and Singer 1980; Anderson and Zimbardo 1984) to describe purported cult influences and activities. By medicalizing (Robbins and Anthony 1982) or psychiatrizing (Kecmanovic 1983) new religious affiliation, they have provided fuel to the mass media and others to continue the *public campaign* against the cults. For instance, van Driel and Richardson (1985) have shown that the American print media has made regular use of medical metaphors and that many media discourses on the subject of new religions or cults use medical terminology. In brief, since some mental health professionals view these new groups as a danger to the public's mental health, a legitimizing function is served and the mass media can feel justified in their negatively slanted coverage of the new religions.

Although only a minority of mental health professionals have publicly expressed serious concern about the mental status of new religious adherents, those who have, have done so quite vigorously. West and Singer (1980) are representative of this negative attitude:

> When the adaptation process has progressed for a number of weeks, the elders may judge the recruit ready to assume the duties of full membership. Those duties may include menial labor, raising money on street corners and at airports, parading and chanting, recruiting new members, even scavenging for edible garbage. The new cultist is asked to abandon friend, family, and career and to donate all his material goods and his earnings to the organization. He is required to make a will in favor of the leadership and to agree to carry out all commands given him by those in charge. . . .
>
> When the desired result is achieved, the new cultist does not necessarily appear mentally ill or bizarre. However, family and friends who previously knew him well may observe distressing changes from his former self. Attention is now constricted. New information is avoided. 'His mind seems closed.' Conversation is monotonous and repetitious, filled with the dogma and catchwords and pharases of the cult. Mental mechanisms of dissociation, denial, supression, and regression are implicated in the victim's maintenance of the cult's formulations of life. Of course, such maintenance is reinforced. The more the person conforms to cult requirements, the more approval and affection are forthcoming from the group (pp. 3248-3250).

The credibility of such overgeneralized, negatively stereotyped statements as the above, at first accepted without question by many mental health professionals, have lost much of their punch in recent years. This is primarily due to a growing awareness among mental health professionals of the conflict of interest and/or values between themselves and nontraditional healers. Psychologists and psychiatrists find themselves competing with new religions and other quasi-psychological groups for the same market of serviceable clientele (Kilbourne and Richardson 1984a). Further, a broad-based empirical data set which generally fails to support many allegations made by the vocal minority of mental health professionals has been developed by other scientists.

Kilbourne and Richardson (1984a), for example, have recently summarized evidence of integrative and therapeutic effects sometimes associated with new religious affiliation. They point out that some new religious conversion experiences are directly analogous in structure and outcome to traditional psychotherapy. New religious affiliation and participation is similar to psychotherapy (Frank 1974) in that it can, in some instances, counteract feelings of despair, worthlessness, and/or meaninglessness with positive feelings of heightened self-esteem, mastery, help, hope, and successful outcomes. New religious affiliation has in fact been found to be specifically related to a host of beneficial effects: termination of drug use, vocational and educational motivation, reduced neurotic distress and anxiety, increased self-esteem, self-actualization, suicide prevention, decreased anomie, decreased psychosomatic symptoms, ego clarification, renewed interest in family and community, communal sharing and cohesiveness, increased concern for others, reduced fear of death, reduced criminal activity, reduced alienation, and a greater appreciation of life (see Robbins and Anthony 1982, for a summary of these effects, and Richardson 1985c, for a summary of personality assessment findings).[1]

Even more important for the majority of new religious adherents who evidence no signs of psychological distress or maladaptive behavior, participation in new religions often provides a tangible vehicle for obtaining meaning, positive identity, relatedness to others, and community (Kilbourne and Richardson 1986b). There is a small body of suggestive evidence that some new religions provide an alternative opportunity structure for some adherents who wish to make their work and their religious beliefs an everyday full-time reality (Kilbourne 1986a). One investigation of Unification Church members (Kilbourne 1986a) found, for example, a bimodal pattern of goal orientation (e.g., career and self-growth goals among members and a fairly strong sense of perceived equity regarding church activities). On a less positive note, some who become leaders in new religions may be compensating for past difficulties functioning in conventional society. However, there is evidence of the "reintegrative function" (of new religions, which often serve a "half-way house" role for some who have been "disconnected" from society (Richardson et al. 1979, pp. 97-98; Richardson 1985c).

We see, then, a growing awareness of the diligent efforts by some individuals to search out new experiences and group involvements that provide social support for a desired self-image and particular kinds of experiences and relationships (Kilboune and Richardson 1985). It is ironic that some psychologists and psychatrists view these self-quests as various forms of psychopathology. Of far greater concern to psychology, however, is the concerted attempt by some psychologists to use psychological techniques and institutions to pressure new religious adherents to change their allegiances back to more conventional societal commitments and economic arrangements.[2]

Richardson and Kilbourne (1983) have identified a common characterization of new religious adherents—one they call the "cult syndrome"—that is frequently employed by mental health professionals or mental health advocates with an anti-cult orientation. This syndrome appears in much of the literature of anti-cult mental health professionals. It tends to emphasize the *personal vulnerabilities* of adherents (e.g., some prior ailment involving alienation, meaninglessness, identity crises, dependency, and psychopathology), the *use of powerful and sophisticated techniques of cult recruitment* (e.g., the systematic manipulation of isolation, control, group pressures, deprivation, repetition, altered states of consciousness, confession, and lack of privacy), and the *negative effects allegedly resulting from new religious affiliation* (e.g., depression, loneliness, indecisiveness, slipping into altered states, passivity, obsessional thinking, and depersonalization). Proponents of this view generally believe that anecdotal accounts and/or suggestive evidence of a "cult-syndrome" justify the need for psychotherapeutic intervention in these matters and confirm notions of "mind control" and "brainwashing." These latter notions indirectly confirm the idea of economic man under attack.

Some of the stereotypical conceptions of new religious affiliation referred to above have found their way into professional literature. The best example of this is evident in certain anti-cult oriented diagnostic disorders in the third edition of the *Diagnostic and Statistical Manual of Mental Disorders* (DSM-III, American Psychiatric Association 1980). As Kilbourne and Richardson (1984b) point out, the anticult disorders in the DSM-III-Atypical Dissociative Disorder and Post-Traumatic Stress Disorder—cannot be justified on empirical grounds. There has been no attempt to build a broad and consistent empirical data for each dimension of each of these two diagnostic disorders in the DSM-III. These anti-cult disorders have arisen from the clinical intuitions and personal impressions of a few psychiatrists and psychologists.

Kilbourne and Richardson (1984b) have criticized the inclusion of the disorders that have been used to psychiatrically label cult members on the following grounds: (1) *Atypical Dissociative Disorder* is inordinately vague and incomplete in diagnostic information, lacking in any kind of scientific validity or reliability, conceptually tied to irrelevant issues of brainwashing and terrorism, and does not specify how cult membership per se persumably allows the adherent to dissociate himself/herself; and, (2) *Post-Traumatic Stress Disorder* was never intended to be used to diagnose cult members because it equates, without an empirical basis, cult membership with victims of major disasters (such as earthquakes, war, etc.), fails to separate the multiple influences affecting cult members, does not specify why cult membership is inherently traumatic or what the specific stressors are, ignores blatant inconsistencies in cult experiences and behavior with central characteristics of the diagnostic disorder, and overlooks evidence questioning a common disaster syndrome among victims.

Notwithstanding, the inclusion of cult-related mental disorders in the DSM-III helps us to appreciate the *vested economic interests* served by anti-cultism within the mental health professions. Simply put, a formal diagnosis is a necessary part of any clinical assessment before insurance claims can be filed (Coleman, Butcher, and Carson 1984). It is no secret that third-party payments to cover mental health services costs have skyrocketed in recent years with the growth of mental health movement, and that competition is sometimes intense for the third-party dollar. It is also no secret that the nation-wide growth of professional schools of psychology have significantly increased the supply or number of clinical/professional psychologists, thus paving the way for heightened competition over patients and services (Kilbourne and Richardson 1984a). Accurately or inaccurately, the identification of new target groups for mental health services (e.g., new religious adherents) has the short-term benefit of increasing serviceable people, thereby reducing market pressures resulting from increased numbers of professional psychologists relative to limited consumer demand. Professional psychologists and psychiatrists can even stimulate consumer demand for their services, and thus professional growth, by increasing their actual numbers (to some as-of-yet undetermined level) and by increasing the types of mental health problems (Conrad and Schneider 1980). However, long-term societal costs of this practice may not be self-evident (e.g., the oversupply of services as well as the possible loss of credibility if services entail arbitrary diagnoses and/or false cures).

Consider, for example, the role of forensic psychiatry in an increasingly common courtoom battle between a former cult member and a new religion or cult to which he once belonged. The typical scenario might unfold something like this. The court appoints a psychiatrist or psychologist to assess the past and present mental status of the former cult members. This costs money, whether the psychiatric evaluation is accepted or rejected. The former cult member and his family members may also seek psychiatric services independent of any litigation. This costs even more money. The new religion or cult may, in turn, hire their own psychiatric services independent of any litigation. This costs even more money. In a very real sense, psychiatry stands to gain regardless of the outcome of the court battle. The professional credibility of psychiatry as a legitimate arbitrator of mental health matters is reinforced in the public's eye, and the financial standing of particular forensic psychiatrists is greatly improved as psychiatry extends its purview to include so-called "cult problems." This movement to incorporate cult-related concerns into the field of mental health seems to illustrate well the expansion model described in Conrad and Schneider (1980). (See note 2 as well.)

In sum, anti-cult elements within the mental health professions take the position that they want to protect the mental health of the general public, a most notable and worthy cause. They claim to have identified an "incapacitation effect" associated with new religious affiliation or cult involvement. From this perspective, the new religious adherent is presumably incapacitated in some way from fully participating in the marketplace, and is subsequently discouraged from defining him or herself in culturally acceptable economic terms (such as how much and what one owns, the job/ career one has, what one earns, or the investments one has made). On the other side of the coin, by psychiatrizing or medicalizing religious deviance or experimentation, psychologists and psychiatrists stand to gain professionally and financially by expanding their market of serviceable people. Professional psychologists and psychiatrists also reinforce their own model of economic personhood in this way. This is the case whether anti-cult diagnoses and/or prognostications have any truth to them or not.

We should not mistakenly defend anti-cult diagnoses by mental health practitioners on the same grounds as diagnoses by medical professionals; that assumption is clearly unwarranted. Properly trained in medical science, all physicians will generally concur about the presence of a malignant cancer or a protracted heart disease, but most psychologists and/or psychiatrists will *not* agree about the validity or reliability of the anti-cult disorders. This is primarily because the anti-cult mental disorders and alleged dangers of cult affiliation have not been firmly established using proper scientific methods and procedures. Given the foregoing analysis, it seems questionable whether insurance companies should honor third-party payments for claims filed on the basis of so-called cult-related disabilities.

THE ANTI-CULT MOVEMENT: POLICIES AND RESEARCH STRATEGY

The negative response to the growth of new religions is no better exemplified than in the explicit policies and strategies of the Anti-Cult Movement (ACM) to hinder, or possibly eliminate, the proliferation of new religions. The ACM, according to Shupe and Bromley (1980), is composed of numerous organizations, diverse in size and resources. Some of their organizational tactics include lobbying, lawsuits, media blitzes, educational programs, professional meetings, counseling, and kidnappings for deprogrammings. In general, however, the ACM functions in three different roles: (1) primarily as a disseminator of information on beliefs and practices of new religions (including current publicly available reports on legal battles, recommended tactics, interagency linkages, and new cult operations); (2) aggressive lobbying at local, state, and federal levels to influence lawmakers and elected officials (see

Richardson 1986, for one example of such activities); and (3) in a referral role to maintain ongoing files on extant groups, counseling services, legal assitance, deprogrammers, journal/media contacts, and any professional or nonprofessional advice by sympathizers. Many of the lobbying efforts have been at least partially successful. Though the media has not been completely favorable toward the Anti-Cult Movement, this movement has been able to influence the issues the media has focused on, and it has contributed to how cults are characterized. Van Driel and Richardson (1988b) found that the large majority of explicit accounts of "cults" reflected anti-cultist definitions. One of the major elements in these definitions was an alleged preoccupation with wealth and the relative luxury enjoyed by cult leaders.

The interdependency of the cult and Anti-Cult Movements has been recognized (Shupe, Bromley, and Oliver 1984) in the sense that the former has given rise to the latter, if only in the counter-response of the ACM to the challenge posed by the competing values and lifestyles of the new groups. At times, the two movements feed on one another and appear to benefit from the mutually-perceived threats (Barker 1983).

Social psychologists, for example, have long recognized the positive relationship between external threats to a group and increased cohesiveness and compliance to group norms (Sherif and Sherif 1953, 1969). External threat can have the effect of reducing internal divisiveness and redirecting a group's energies toward the out-group danger. Kilbourne and Richardson (1982a) have previously commented on how certain conflict-ridden families appear to benefit from the alleged cult threat. Attempts by an individual to leave his or her family and join a cult may create a new family consciousness or "we feeling" that had previously dissipated due to family disagreements and tensions. Some families may rediscover their common identity around the sudden departure of a family member into a strange cult. Similarly, the new religions themselves may, in the long run, benefit from the persistent attempts by the Anti-Cult Movement to disband them. The internal doubts, misgivings, and conflicts of cult adherents may pale in significance beside the external threat to the cult, which is sometimes very dramatic or even violent, as in the case of forced deprogrammings and conservatorships to remove members from the cult or new religion. Ironically, then, the Anti-Cult Movement may in some cases strengthen the very loyalty of a new adherent's attachment to the cult that they had hoped to weaken or destroy (Barker 1983).

There are two other unanticipated consequences of the growth of the ACM and their explicitly negative view of new religious movements, both of which have profound implications for appreciating the dominant ideology of economic individualism in contemporary American society. Shupe and Bromley (1981) have identified two major sources of strain between the new religions and the families of adherents: a challenge to the family's authority structure and a threat to the family's goal of preparing offspring for their role in society's economic order. Here we want to focus on the *American family as an economic unit*. From this perspective, the family is a group of producers, or potential producers, and consumers who benefit economically in some way from their close association with one another. Parents invest in the economic future of their children by providing them with the necessities and comforts of life while their children acquire the requisite skills to support themselves. The family is, thus, a basic opportunity structure, and, of course, that structure is a function of the family's position in society. We have long known that a father's education and occupation predicts his son's occupation (Blau and Duncan 1967). Therefore, in large part, the economic unit one grows up with as a child predicts one's later economic status. (There are certainly dramatic exceptions to this rule, as any "self-made" millionaire will testify.) Parent-child economic agreements generally continue in some form into adulthood, whereby family members help one another economically. At the very least, they provide a shared economic environment which they can all enjoy to a greater or lesser degree. Family members give loans, gifts, investment advice, living space, jobs, and access to one another that might not otherwise be as readily available. Parents may save money for a child's future education, thereby deferring their own gratification or self-improvement.

All things being equal, the continued productivity of each family member insures increasing economic security and affluence for the family in general, and the maintenance of the family as an economic unit ensures the continuity of that unit through inheritance of the wealth of prior generations of family members. Inheritance also insures the continuation of one's self symbolically beyond one's lifetime by insuring the good name or secure living of subsequent generations of family members.

Therefore, when the family is treated as an economic unit, new religions present four clearly identifiable economic threats. One threat concerns the *loss of a productive economic individual*. The integrity and maintenance of the economic family unit depends on the productivity of each individual member. A shared economic environment, whether actually used or symbolically referred to, depends on each member carrying his/her own share. The loss of a family member also *threatens the continuity of the family as an economic unit*, since a family member who becomes a new religious adherent could very easily jeopardize that unit by passing on his/her accumulated wealth and material possessions to the new religion, rather than to present and future family members. The *parent's and family's status is dealt a severe blow*, which can have economic repercussions. A parent's identity and status is often times dependent on the achievements and social position of his or her offspring. Children are viewed as extensions of parents, and what happens to the children automatically reflects on the parents. Lastly, the loss of a family member to a new religion implies a *bad economic investment by parents*, since the wayward family member may never contribute to the family's common wealth, the future security of retired parents, or to the economic environment of future generations of family members. Furthermore, the parents may be confronted with a situation in which all their savings and energies invested in the child appear to be "going to waste." Indeed, the family member who joins a new religion may completely renounce his or her family obligations, and even the family surname.

Interestingly, much of the research on new religions sponsored or endorsed by the Anti-Cult Movement tends to generally support, directly or indirectly, the belief in these alleged threats to the economic autonomy of the individual. Richardson (1985a) believes, however, that voluminous findings at variance with anti-cult conceptions can be attributed to the following: (1) differences in perspective and social location of researchers; (2) the fact that researches often are actually studying different things; (3) tendencies to overgeneralize, coupled with a failure to grasp the considerable variation among new religions; and (4) different methodologies of research.

This last factor—different methodologies in research—is illustrated by the fact that most anti-cult researchers use nonrandom, selected samples, nonstatistical techniques, biased data collection techniques, and reactant biographical reports from former members to make their point. (Also see critiques by Kilbourne 1983, 1986b.) Other anti-cult researchers (Langone and Clark 1985) have presented an elaborate thesis on the harm associated with new religious affiliation without making a serious attempt to deal with the growing body of empirical evidence establishing the usually nonharmful and even therapeutic effects of new religious affiliation (see Kilbourne and Richardson 1984a; Richardson 1985c). Interestingly, historical research shows how well-accepted marginal religious groups were often accused in a similar manner in the past (Shupe 1981; Miller 1983; Lindt 1979). Bromley and Shupe (1979) in their study of the Tnevnoc cult ("convent" spelled backwards) show that criticisms of the new religions are rather similar to those leveled against the Catholic Church in the 1800s.

One-sided studies by Anti-Cult researchers are best identified by considering research questions posed by new religious affiliation. Balch (1985) has recently proposed a suggestive guide for much needed ethnographic research on new religions. His list includes, but is not limited to, the following: (1) demographic characteristics of the membership; (2) historical developments and trends; (3) structure and content of the belief system; (4) leadership; (5) social organization; (6) the relationship between members and outsiders; (7) economic system; (8) material culture; (9) patterns of everyday life; (10) talk; (11) sexual relationships; (12) child rearing; (13) deviance and social control; (14) recruitment strategies; (15) commitments demanded of members; (16) socialization techniques; (17) conversion experiences; and (18) defection processes.

There is another unanticipated consequence of new religious affiliation which indirectly supports our belief in the value placed on the sanctity of economic man. Namely, the Anti-Cult Movement has created an *economic opportunity structure* for some individuals to attain their economic and professional identities.[3] Some of the new economic roles and occupations that have emerged as a consequence of the Anti-Cult Movement are deprogrammers, counselors and psychotherapists, consultants, program directors, newspaper editors, lobbyists, and court experts. These various occupational or career opportunities have allowed certain individuals to expand, if not literally create, their economic and/or professional self-concepts. Hence, those who have advanced themselves to various degrees by joining in the fight against the cults may have a problem if they are too successful. If they succeed in abolishing the cults, they may jeopardize some important aspect of their present economic and/or professional situation. At present, however, they can use their experience in the "Anti-Cult Wars" to advance themselves into new positions or professional responsibilities. Perhaps this also helps explain why certain indviduals cannot be persuaded to alter their views in the face of scientific evidence relativizing the dangers associated with new religions. They have a vested economic interest in perceiving the new religions as harmful. Relativizing the threats posted by these groups would create cognitive dissonance.

CONCLUSION

The present paper has examined the related negative response of the mass media, certain elements of the mental health professions, and the Anti-Cult Movement to new religions in America.[4] That similar negative response is an important area of investigation in and of itself. Even if for the sake of argument we were to overlook all of the inconsistent and contradictory evidence and accept on face value alone the negative view of cults by these institutions, we would still have to acknowledge the production of services and wealth associated with the reporting, monitoring, and opposing of new religions. We would also have to acknowledge common ground among these related institutional responses to new religions in their tendency to subscribe to a similar ideology of economic individualism.

Concerning service production, a symbolic interactionist perspective of deviance is germane to understanding the reaction to new religions or cults. Symbolic interactionists (Hewitt 1984) contend that deviance goes beyond the mere violation of norms and laws. This is primarily because people violate norms and break laws on an everyday basis, get away with it, often feel little or no remorse, and frequently do not think of themselves as deviant. Furthermore, there is differential detection, apprehension, prosecution, and sentencing of people in the criminal justice system, and we do not label all people the same who engage in deviance or objectionable behavior. In some cases, social control agents *actually create deviance* with arbitrary definitions or elicit deviant reactions from others. Correctional institutions often do not eradicate, but instead *breed* crime and violence. *Thus, from a symbolic interactionist perspective, what is deviant is negotiated and definitional.* That understanding can help us appreciate why some people view new religious affiliation as deviant and some do not. It can also help us appreciate why some groups in conflict are more likely to use a particular label as opposed to others to describe their adversaries (Kilbourne and Richardson 1986a; Richardson, van der Lans, and Derks 1986).[5]

There is an important implication of this symbolic interactionist focus on the social construction of deviance. For instance, crime and fighting crime are major industries in the United States that depend on certain shared definitions. They stimulate compensatory consumption, redistribute wealth, create opportunities for criminals (illegitimate) and crime fighters (legitimate), and, hence, contribute to the overall growth of the service sector of society. The analogy of crime and crime fighting is useful to understanding service production in relation to new religions or cults. As market pressures (e.g., high labor costs and the high costs of materials) continue to push the manufacturing sector of the American economy outside of its borders, there are increasing economic pressures to compensate for lost jobs by expanding the service sector of the economy. There are also economic pressures to provide maintenance services to the general population to help citizens maintain their present standard of living and psychological well-being.

Psychological maintenance services come in many different forms. Some believe that the social and cultural milieu in the United States is particularly favorable to the proliferation of psychotherapies of all kinds (Garfield 1981) and to new religious, self-growth, and self-help groups as well (Kilbourne and Richardson 1984a). In relation to the self-growth subculture, Kilbourne and Richardson (1985) have specifically commented on the development of *entrepreneurs of experience* of that subculture who provide social experimenters with the opportunity to experience different identities, relationships, and group affiliations (see Richardson and Davis 1984). Similarly, *moral entrepreneurs* (Becker 1963) have long existed in American society for the purpose of identifying social deviance. Usually a whole nexus of related professional services develop around the designation of social deviance. Such services have the *manifest function* of controlling, protecting, and compensating for the effects of identified deviance; they have the *latent function* of producing wealth around the identification of and controlling efforts directed toward social deviance.

Concerning the second point of a dominant ideology of economic individualism in contemporary American society,[6] it is self-evident that the mass media, certain elements of the mental health professions, and the Anti-Cult Movement have all focused directly or indirectly on the threat of new religions to the economic autonomy of the individual. The economic exploitation theme is common throughout much of the negative press, psychological theorizing, and anti-cult allegations and fears. These negative themes concerning new religions reveal the value placed on economic individualism in American culture. Indeed, there are norms governing how individuals in American society *should* express their individuality. Such norms generally have to do with expectations of financial success, security, and group approval. This applies especially to that strata and society where new religions attract their major following—the upper middle-class. It is in that strata that economically-defined expectations are pervasive.

Totalitarianism is generally thought to incorporate subordination of the individual to some state system, and the stringent control or influence by that system over all aspects of the individual's life, often times by coercive (or the threat of coercive) measures. In American society, there are ubiquitous social pressures exerted on members of society to define themselves in largely economic terms. Those social pressures are related to an ideology of economic individualism that is all-inclusive, one-dimensional, and threatens, directly or indirectly, noncompliers with disapproval and rejection; therefore, it arguably satisfies a general definition of totalitarianism, even though it is not regulated by law. Individuals in American society (including adherents to new religions) who attempted publicly to adhere to alternative values or lifestyles have usually been rejected in some way by society and are sometimes socially ostracized. The fact that most Americans feel they must be economically minded in a broad sense, and that they have no other choice if they want to feel good about themselves or if they want to function effectively, evidences the pervasive, totalitarian nature of economic individualism in American society.

Some individuals, on the other hand, have rejected the dominant economic conception of individualism in American society by socially and spiritually experimenting with new religions and self-growth groups. They often work long hours for their religious group with little or no monetary compensation, perhaps even giving their possessions to the group. Such activities are in conflict with both implicit and explicit norms of economic individualism in contemporary American society. Consequently, these individuals have often found themselves being castigated for their anti-normative ways of expressing their personhood. They have frequently been labeled brainwashed and/or mentally ill, and sometimes they have been incarcerated in mental hospitals, prisons, or kidnapped by unsympathetic strangers. (See note 2 and accompanying discussion.)

We see, then, systematic control efforts by agents of the dominant ideology of society (e.g., the mass media and certain elements of the mental health professions) to limit significantly the self-quests of certain individuals because they refuse in one way or another to conform to the dominant ideology of economic individualism. We see repeated attempts by some to pressure people into a one-dimensional mold of mass conformity, where individuals express their individuality by their consumption patterns, by the things they own, and/

or the career positions they occupy—where individuals are made to feel bad about themselves because they do not want to be or cannot hope to be individuals in the narrow sense of economic consumption and production.

Religion has consequently taken on a very important role for some individuals in contemporary American society. It has become a source of *liberation from* the dictates of economic individualism. Some individuals have self-consciously experimented with the new religions to pursue what they feel constitutes their real selves, and the diversification of modern society has in many ways made this possible (Kilbourne and Richardson 1985; Richardson 1985b). Religion appears to have taken on the important role of defining both majority and minority views in American society, as well as in safeguarding the minority from an overzealous and potentially oppressive majority. Thus, religion is a vehicle of both social stability and social change. Time will tell whether American society can learn to be more tolerant of such noneconomic forms of individual self-expression.

ACKNOWLEDGMENT

First presented at Annual Meeting of Western Social Science Association, Reno, Nevada, 1986.

NOTES

1.   Here again we can point to the crucial role of the media. The beneficial effects related to participation in newer religions are almost totally missed by the media. In their longitudinal study of U.S. print media, van Driel and Richardson (1985) found that 30% of their sample items referred to negative consequences of such participation, while less than 2% contained any reference to positive consequences.

2.   For one of the more revealing such efforts, see the symposium published in the *Journal of the National Association of Private Psychiatric Hospitals* 1978 on the topic "Socio and Religious Cults: Religion or Brainwashing." The presentations by Singer (1979) and by Clark (1978) attempt to support the notion that cult membership is, ipso facto, mental illness and thus justifies deprogramming or incarceration by mental health authorities. The articles by Rosenberg (1978) and Hopkins (1978) point out difficulties with such a simplistic approach, even if they do seem to share the basic perspective of Singer and Clark. Rosenberg (1978, p. 23) says, for instance, the major point of discussion is: "Given the unwillingness, as I see it, of a majority of cult members to seek psychiatric help, even when necessary, what legal means are available to invoke hospitalization?"

3.   As noted earlier, many new religions also offer an economic opportunity structure. This is, however, largely denigrated by anti-cultists. See Richardson (1982, 1988) for discussions of this overlooked aspect of new religions.

4.   To a certain degree, an ideology of economic individualism, in some form or the other, characterizes all Western industrialized nations: it is in this sense a world-wide ideology. Capitalism's greatest achievement may be its success in providing millions of individuals of different racial, ethnic, class, religious, cultural, national background and interests with a common self-definitional system and social reality. Even Third World and developing nations aspire for the economic conditions of Western Europe, the United States, and Japan-further evidence of the

far-reaching hand of economic individualism. The poorer economic conditions of Communist and Third World nations are held up as living proof for true believers of what happens to those who do not embrace the ideology of economic individualism.

5.   The deviance associated with new religions can be socially defined in varying ways. Beckford (1983, 1985), drawing from a broad base of anti-cult campaigns, reports of concerned relatives, a highly-suspicious press, atrocity tales by apostates, and numerous court cases and investigations, has identified two analytically distinct, mostly negative, response patterns to new religions that incorporate distinctive patterns of deviance labeling. The first response pattern he calls the "Anglo-Saxon" response, characteristic of the United States and Great Britain, which emphasizes pscyhological explanations and religious deviance. New religious affiliation is generally frowned upon and explained by various psychological processes occurring before, during, and after affiliation. Psychopathological processes and "brainwashing" or "mind control" allegations are common. A second response pattern, the "organicist" response characteristic of France and West Germany, focuses on the interrelationships between new religious movements and the social institutions of society. The "cult-problem" is defined as a socio-political conflict by emphasizing ideological totalitarianism, subversion, and conspiracy.

6.   The fact that those in the United States excluded for one reason or another from full enjoyment of the economic benefits of the social system (e.g., the poor, certain minorities, the unemployed, the imprisoned, and the mentally ill) still aspire to achieve such benefits tends to confirm their value to those who presently enjoy them. One study designed to measure adherence to individualism, for instance, required respondents to indicate whether there should be a ceiling on the amount that one can earn (*Society* 1982). While more respondents from high-income families rejected such a ceiling, there was still only 33% support for imposing a ceiling among those with annual incomes of $5,000 or less a year. The ideology of economic individualism is, thus, firmly entrenched in the minds of the "haves" and "have-nots" and, therefore, acquires a reified and absolute nature all its own.

REFERENCES

Andersen, S. M., and P. G. Zimbardo. 1979. "On Resisting Social Influence." Washington, D.C. Office of Naval Research. Technical Report Z-79-01.

Ash, S. E. 1956. "Studies in Independence and Conformity: I. A Minority of One Against a Unanimous Majority." *Psychological Monographs* 70, 9 (Whole No. 416).

Balch, R. W. 1985. "What's Wrong With the Study of New Religions and What We Can Do About It." In *Scientific Research and New Religions: Divergent Perspectives,* edited by B. K. Kilbourne. San Francisco: Pacific Division, American Association for the Advancement of Science.

Barker, E. 1983. "With Enemies Like That: Some Functions of Deprogramming as an Aid to Sectarian Membership." Pp. 329-344 in *The Brainwashing/Deprogramming Controversy,* edited by D. Bromley and J. T. Richardson. New York: Edwin Mellen Press.

Becker, H. 1963. *Outsiders.* New York: Free Press.

Beckford, J. A. 1981. "Functionalism and Ethics in Sociology: The Relationship Between 'Ought and Function.' " *Annual Review of the Social Sciences of Religion* 5:101-131.

————. 1983. "The Public Response to New Religions in Britain." *Social Compass* 30:49-62.

————. 1985. *Cult Controversies.* London: Travistock Publications, Ltd.

Bellah, R. N. 1976. "New Religious Consciousness and the Crisis in Modernity." In *The New Religious Consciousness,* edited by C. Y. Glock and R. N. Bellah. Berkeley: University of California Press.

Blau, P.M., and O. D. Duncan. 1967. *The American Occupational Structure.* New York: Wiley.

Braungart, R. G. 1984. "Historical Generations and Youth Movements: A Theoretical Perspective." Pp. 95-142 in *Research in Social Movements, Conflict and Change,* vol. 6, edited by L. Kriesberg. Greenwich, CT: JAI Press.

Bromley, D. G., and A. Shupe. 1979. "The Tnevnoc Cult." *Sociological Analysis* 4:361-366.

Bromley, D. G., A. Shupe, and J.C. Ventimiglia. 1979. "Atrocity Tales, the Unification Church and the Social Construction of Evil." *Journal of Communication* 29(3):42-53.

Clark, J. 1978. "Problems in Referral of Cult Members." *Journal of the National Association of Private Psychiatric Hospitals* 9(4):19-21.

————. 1979. "Cults." *Journal of the American Medical Association* (242):279-281.

Coleman, J. C., J. N. Butcher, and R. C. Carson. 1984. *Abnormal Psychology and Modern Life,* 7th ed. Glenview, IL: Scott.

Conrad, P., and J. Schneider. 1980. *Deviance and Medicalization.* St. Louis: C. V. Mosby.

Cromer, G. 1978. "Character Assassination in the Press." In *Deviance and Mass Media,* edited by C. Winick. Beverley Hills, CA: Sage Publications.

Davis, K. 1940. "The Sociology of Parent-Youth Conflict." *American Sociological Review* 5:523-535.

Eister, A. 1974. "Culture Crises and New Religious Movements: A Paradigmatic Statement of a Theory of Cults." Pp. 612-627 *Religious Movements in Contemporary America,* edited by H. Zaretsky and M. Leone. Princeton, NJ: Princeton University Press.

Feuer, L. 1969. *The Conflict of Generations.* New York: Basic Books.

Frank, J. 1974. *Persuasion and Healing: A Comparative Study of Psychotherapy.* New York: Schocken Books.

French, J. R. R., Jr., and B. H. Raven. 1959. "The Bases of Social Power." In *Studies in Social Power,* edited by D. Cartwright. Ann Arbor: Institute for Social Research, University of Michigan.

Garfield, S. L. 1981. "Psychotherapy: A 40-year Appraisal." *American Psychologist* 36:174-183.

Garfinkel, H. 1956. "Conditions of Successful Degradation Ceremonies." *American Journal of Sociology* 61:420-424.

Gitlin, T. 1980. *The Whole World is Watching.* Berkeley: University of California Press.

Herberg, W. 1960. *Protestant-Catholic-Jew.* Garden City, NY: Anchor.

Hewitt, J. P. 1984. *Self and Society: A Symbolic Interactionist Social Psychology,* 3rd ed. Boston: Allyn and Bacon.

Hopkins, R.P. 1978. "The Hospital Viewpoint: Mental Illness on Social Maladjustment?" *Journal of the National Association of Private Psychiatric Hospitals* 9(4):19-21.

Jones, E. E., and R. Nisbet. 1971. "The Actor and Observer: Divergent Perspectives of the Causes of Behavior." *Attribution: Perceiving the Causes of Behavior* edited by E. Jones and R. Nisbet. Morristown, NJ: General Learning Press.

Kecmanovic, D. 1983. "Psychiatrization: A General View." *The International Journal of Social Psychiatry* 29:308-310.

Kilbourne, B. K. 1983. "The Conway and Siegelman Claims Against Religious Cults: An Assessment of Their Data." *Journal for the Scientific Study of Religion* 22:380-385.

————. 1986a. "Equity or Exploitation: The Case of the Unification Church." *Review of Religious Research* 28:143-150.

————. 1986b. "A Reply to Maher and Langone's Statistical Critique of Kilbourne." *Journal or the Scientific Study of Religion* 25:116-123.

Kilbourne, B. K., and J. T. Richardson. 1982a. "Cults Versus Families: A Case of Misattribution of Cause." *Marriage and Family Review* 4(3-4):81-100.

————. 1982b. "Violence and the New Religions: An Interactional Perspective." Paper presented at the annual meeting of the Society for the Scientific Study of Religion, Baltimore, Maryland, October.

————. 1984a. "Psychotherapy and New Religions in a Pluralistic Society." *American Psychologist* 39(3):237-251.

————. 1984b. "The DSM-III and its Relation to Psychotherapy for Cult Converts." Paper presented at the annual meeting of the Society for the Scientific Study of Religion, Chicago.

————. 1985. "Social Experimentation: Self-process or Social Role." *The International Journal of Social Psychiatry* 31(1):13-22.

————. 1986a. "Cultphobia." *Thought* 61:258-266.

————. 1986b. "The Communalization of Religious Experience in Contemporary Religious Groups." *Journal of Community Psychology* 14:206-213.

Klapper, J. T. 1960. *The Effects of Mass Communication.* New York: Free Press.

Kraus, S. 1962. *The Great Debates.* Bloomington: Indiana University Press.

Langone, M. D., and J. Clark. 1985. "New Religions and Public Policy: Research Implications for Social and Behavioral Scientists." In *Scientific Research and New Religions: Divergent Perspectives,* edited by B. K. Kilbourne. San Francisco: Pacific Division, American Association for the Advancement of Science.

Lasch, C. 1979. *The Culture of Narcicism.* New York: Norton.

Lindt, G. 1979. "Religious Cults in America: Public Opinion and the Media." Paper presented at the annual meeting of the American Association for Public Opinion Research.

Miller, D. E. 1983. "Deprogramming in Historical Perspective." In *The Brainwashing/ Deprogramming Controversy,* edited by D. C. Bromley and J. T. Richardson. Toronto: Edwin Mellen Press.

Moscovici, S. 1985. "Social Influence and Conformity." In *The Handbook of Social Psychology,* vol. 2, 3rd ed., edited by E.Aronson and G. Lindzey. New York: Random House.

Moscovici, S., and B. Personnaz. 1980. "Studies in Social Influence, Minority Influence and Conversion Behavior in a Perceptual Task." *Journal of Experimental Social Psychology* 16:270-282.

New York Times. 1974. "Tax Supported Meditation." Feb. 14.

Patterson, T. E. 1980. *The Mass Media Election: How Americans Choose Their President.* New York: Praeger.

Richardson, J. T. 1982. "Financing the New Religions: Comparative and Theoretical Perspectives." *Journal for the Scientific Study of Religion* 21:255-267.

————. 1985a. "Methodological Considerations in the Study of New Religions." *Scientific Research and New Religions: Divergent Perspectives,* edited by B. K. Kilbourne. San Francisco: Pacific Division, American Association for the Advancement of Science.

————. 1985b. "The Active vs. Passive Convert. Paradigm of Conflict in Conversion/ Recruitment Research." *Journal for the Scientific Study of Religion* 24:163-174.

————. 1985c. "Psychological and Psychiatric Studies of New Religions." In *Advances in Psychology of Religion,* edited by L. Brown. New York: Pergamon Press.

————. 1988. *Money and Power in the New Religions.* New York: Edwin Mellen Press.

Richardson, J. T., and R. Davis. 1984. "Experiential Fundamentalism: Revisions of Orthodoxy in the Jesus Movement." *Journal of the American Academy of Religion* 54:397-425.

Richardson, J. T., and B. K. Kilbourne, 1983. "Classical and Contemporary Brainwashing Models: A Comparison and Critique." In *The Brainwashing/Deprogramming Controversy,* edited by D. Bromley and J. T. Richardson. Toronto: Edwin Mellen Press.

Richardson, J. T., M. W. Stewart, and R. B. Simmonds. 1979. *Organized Miracles.* New Brunswick, NJ: Transaction Books.

Richardson, J. T., J. van der Lans, and F. Derks. 1986. "Leaving and Labeling: Voluntary and Coerced Disaffiliation from Religious Social Movements." In *Research in Social Movements, Conflict and Change,* vol. 9, edited by G. Lang and K. Lang. Greenwich, CT: JAI Press.

Riesman, D. 1950. *The Lonely Crowd.* New Haven, CT: Yale University Press.

Robbins, T., and D. Anthony. 1982. "Deprogramming, Brainwashing and the Medicalization of Deviant Religious Groups." *Social Problems* 29:283-297.

Rokeach, M. 1968. *Beliefs, Attitudes and Values.* San Francisco: Jossey-Bass.

Rosenberg, A.H. 1978. "Legal Issues in the Treatment of Cult Members." *Journal of the National Association of Private Psychiatric Hospitals* 9(4):22-25.

Ross, L. 1977. "The Intutitive Psychologist and His Shortcomings: Distortions in the Attribution Process." In *Advances in Experimental Social Psychology*, vol. 10, edited by L. Berkowitz. New York: Academic Press.

Sears, D. D., and R. E. Whitney. 1973. "Political Persuasion." In *Handbook of Communication*, edited by I. D. Pool. Chicago: Rand McNally.

Sherif, M. 1935. "A Study of Some Social Factors in Perception." *Archives of Psychology*, 187.

Sherif, M., and C. W. Sherif. 1953. *Groups in Harmony and Tension.* New York: Harper and Row.

————. 1969. *Social Psychology.* New York: Harper and Row.

Shupe, A. 1981. *Six Perspectives on New Religions: A Case Study Approach.* New York: Edwin Mellen Press.

Shupe, A., and D. Bromley. 1980. *The New Vigilantes.* Beverly Hills, CA: Sage.

————. 1981. "Apostates and Atrocity Stories: Some Parameters in the Dynamics of Deprogramming." In *The Social Impact of New Religious Movements*, edited by B. Wilson. New York: Rose of Sharon Press.

Shupe, A., D. Bromley, and D. Oliver. 1984. *The Anti-Cult Movement in America.* New York: Garland Publishing.

Singer, M. 1979. "Coming Out of the Cults." *Psychology Today* 12(8):72-82.

"Social Science and the Citizen." *Society* 19(5):2.

van Driel, B., and J. T. Richardson. 1988a. "The Print Media and New Religious Movements: A Longitudinal Study." *Journal of Communication* 38(3):37-61.

————. 1988b. "Research Note on Categorization of New Religious Movements in the American Print Media." *Sociological Analysis* 49:171-183.

Washington Post. 1976. "Sun Myung Moon: Prophet for Profit." May 30.

————. 1976. "A Look at 'Moonies' Money, Politics, and Confusion." September 2.

West, L. J., and M. T. Singer. 1980. "Cults, Quacks and Nonprofessional Psychotherapies." In *Comprehensive Textbook of Psychiatry*, edited by H. Y. Kaplan, A. M. Freedman, and B. J. Sadock, 3rd ed. Baltimore: Williams and Wilkins.

Wilson, B. 1983. "Time, Generations and Sectarianism." In *The Social Impact of New Religions*, edited by B. Wilson. New York: Rose of Sharon Press.

Yankelovich, D. 1981. *New Rules.* New York: Random House.

NEW RELIGIONS, MENTAL HEALTH, AND SOCIAL CONTROL

E. Burke Rochford, Jr., Sheryl Purvis, and NeMar Eastman

ABSTRACT

Critics of cults claim that the brainwashing techniques used by these groups have pathological consequences resulting in members being unable to freely leave the cult. These claims and the supporting testimony of some psychiatrists have been instrumental in legal cases involving the cults. We analyze the findings on the mental health effects of cult involvement and present data on defection from one of the more controversial new religions. We conclude that there is no legitimate basis for state intervention in the cult phenomena.

Since the 1970s deviant religious groups—popularly known as cults—have gained widespread notoriety in the United States and worldwide. While reliable statistics are hard to come by, it is estimated that anywhere from several hundred thousand to as many as several million young people have joined deviant religious groups in America alone (Lucksted and Martell 1982; Melton 1983; *U.S. News and World Report,* 1976). Regardless of the exact figure, it is clear that America over the past two decades has witnessed what some have called "an epidemic of sudden personality change" (Conway and Siegelman 1978, p. 11) and an "age of conversion" (Richardson and Stewart 1978, p. 24).

Research in the Social Scientific Study of Religion, Volume 1, pages 57-82.

The growth and expansion of deviant religious groups such as the Unification Church, Hare Krishna, and the Church of Scientology have resulted in a vociferous public outcry. A major issue fueling the conflict has involved the recruitment strategies and indoctrination practices of the cults.[1] Charges of cult brainwashing and mind control and attempts by anti-cultists to deprogram members of deviant religious groups reflects the intensity of the conflict. This controversy has increasingly involved society's medical and legal institutions as the expertise of these professions have been called upon by the state to help clarify and perhaps draw the line with respect to First Amendment protections to be afforded the new religions (Coleman 1984; Richardson 1980; Robbins 1981). Although the U.S. Constitution protects the freedom of religious belief for all citizens, legal protections are more ambiguous with respect to the *actions* of religious groups and organizations. As Delgado explains in an article widely cited by anti-cultists:

> It is when religious belief spills over into action that the degree of protection afforded (by the First Amendment) to an individual or group is no longer absolute. Instead, religious practices are subject to a balancing test, in which the courts weight the state's interest in forbidding or regulating conduct against the interest of the religious organization in carrying out its activities. In determining the state's interest in intervening in religious activities, the court must ascertain both the individual and societal harms presented by these practices (1980, p. 25).

Because the controversy surrounding the new religions largely involves their recruitment and conversion practices, the state has called upon the clinical skills of psychiatrists and other mental health professionals to help determine the influence of cults on the psychological well-being of their adherents (Galanter et al. 1979; LeMoult 1978; Richardson 1980; Robbins and Anthony 1982).

While the legal issues surrounding the cults have been complex, and clearly differ in content on a case-by-case basis, psychiatrists have been asked by the courts to judge whether cult members join largely out of voluntary choice, or because they have been subject to coercive persuasion or brainwashing. In conservatorship hearings, litigation involving deprogramming, and lawsuits by ex-members against their former religious groups, psychiatrists have been asked to testify with regard to whether participation in cults is primarily an expression of individual free will or the result of cult manipulation and indoctrination practices which renders members psychologically impaired and unable to leave the group on their own. In numerous legal cases, the supposed negative influences of the cults on the safety and well-being of members has been influential, if not crucial, to judicial decisions involving new religions.

Given the overall importance of mental health issues and the role of some psychiatrists in helping to define First Amendment protections to be afforded the cults, the question arises as to what the clinical findings in this area conclude. Relatedly, are members of deviant religions able to freely choose to leave the groups or are interventive measures by families of cult members and the state required to safeguard the personal freedom and safety of participants? If the case can be made that competent adults freely join and leave new religious groups and that these groups do not inflict emotional or psychological harm on their members, then the case for intervention by the state would lack legitimacy on constitutional grounds. Intervention by the state would then suggest efforts to socially control unconventional religious beliefs—forbidden under the Constitution—rather than a legitimate concern for protecting the rights of believers against harms inflicted by deviant groups acting in the name of religion.

Our purpose in this paper is (1) to systematically review and analyze the psychological and psychiatric findings relating to the mental health impact of new religions on their members, and (2) to report the findings of our research on defection rates from the International Society for Krishna Consciousness (ISKCON), more widely known as the Hare Krishna movement.[2] While other researchers have suggested that attrition from most new religions is quite high (Beckford 1978, 1985; Bromley and Shupe 1979; Galanter 1980; Solomon 1981; Wright 1983), no systematic quantitative studies have thus far been conducted on defection from any of the new religions.[3]

METHOD AND DATA

The present study relies upon three sources of data:

(1) We reviewed and critically analyzed the findings of psychiatric and psychological studies addressing the mental health effects of cult participation. We located 17 empirical studies reporting on the mental health status of over 2100 members and ex-members of a wide variety of new religious groups and movements including: The Unification Church, Hare Krishna, The Children of God, Zen Buddhism, Scientology, and the Divine Light Mission. We excluded from consideration commentaries and review articles focusing on mental health issues and the new religions which lacked primary sources of data on members' psychological well-being (see, for example, Ash 1983; Clark 1979; Clark, Langone, Schecter, and Daly 1981; Coleman 1984; Galanter 1982; Levine 1979, 1981; Richardson 1985; Shapiro 1977; Singer 1978). The studies included ranged in methodology from clinical interpretations and conclusions of psychiatrists based upon therapy sessions with deprogrammed ex-cult members, to investigations of current members and prospective recruits using standardized psychological tests and measures.

(2) The senior author conducted a nonrandom survey of six ISKCON communities in the United States in 1980. Data were collected from 214 ISKCON members residing in Los Angeles, Denver, Chicago, New York, Boston, and a

farm community near Port Royal, Pennsylvania. This sample represents approximately 10% of the total ISKCON membership in the United States. Findings relating to ISKCON members' psychological state at the time they joined are reported. This includes previous involvements in therapy, and psychologically oriented groups and movements, pre-involvement feelings of anxiety and discouragement about life, and past experience with drugs and alcohol.

(3) We present data from an ongoing study of defection from ISKCON between the years 1973 and 1977. These data were compiled from membership lists which were part of a yearly tribute paid by ISKCON's members to their founding spiritual master, A. C. Bhaktivedanta Swami Prabhupada on his birthday. Since 1969, devotees from each of ISKCON's communities worldwide have included their names in the *Sri Vyasa-Puja* which continues to be published each year by the movement's publishing company, the Bhaktivedanta Book Trust. Our ability to calculate rates of defection from ISKCON is made possible because Prabhupada gave unique Sanskrit names to each of his disciples at the time of their initiation into Krishna Consciousness. After Prabhupada's death in November of 1977, eleven of his disciples were appointed as ISKCON gurus (see Rochford 1985). These new gurus gave the same Sanskrit names to their disciples as those given by Prabhupada to his followers. As a result, it was impossible to reliably differentiate between individual devotees after 1977 on the basis of names recorded in the *Sri Vyasa-Puja*. Prior to 1973, ISKCON members' names were handwritten in the *Sri Vyasa-Puja* making it difficult to accurately decipher the spelling of their names. Because of the practical problems this posed, we chose to exclude these early years from this research.

For the years 1973 to 1976, we drew a random sample of 312 initiated ISKCON members' names from the membership list contained in the yearly *Sri Vyasa-Puja*. We placed each devotee's name, sex, and community of residence on the computer to allow for tracking membership patterns through 1977. If an ISKCON member's name failed to appear in the years following its initial appearance in the *Sri Vyasa-Puja*, he/she was counted as a defector from the movement. This method of compiling defection figures means that only those members who left ISKCON *permanently* during this period were treated as defectors.[4] This procedure has allowed for calculating total defections from ISKCON between 1974 and 1977.

We should note one problem with the data which influences the reliability of the defection figures reported. One ISKCON community—the movement's farm community in West Virginia with a devotee population of approximately 175 adults—failed to report individual devotee's names each year in the *Sri Vyasa-Puja*. As a result we are left unable to compute defection figures for one of ISKCON's largest communities. In addition, it is possible that some ISKCON members who previously resided in another movement community and whose name appeared previously in the *Sri Vyasa-Puja* may have relocated to ISKCON's West Virginia community, thus inadvertently showing up as a defector in our study. Since ISKCON members often move from community to community during their tenure with the movement, however, it is likely that some of these latter devotees would at some point reappear in the *Sri Vyasa-Puja* as residents of another ISKCON community. This, in part, is why we have chosen to count only permanent defectors from the movement, excluding members who appear to have defected for a period of a year or more. Although the defection rates reported should not be treated as exact, we believe that they are a close approximation and clearly represent the most comprehensive findings on the membership patterns of any one of the new religious movements.

FINDINGS AND DISCUSSION

At the center of the controversy surrounding the new religions have been charges that some cults have employed mind control tactics meant to seduce young persons into the group to allow for intensive indoctrination which, in turn, renders them psychologically disabled and virtually unable to freely leave the group (Clark et al. 1981; Robbins 1981; West and Singer 1980). Conversion, from this view, "is simply a case of induced mental illness" (Hargrove 1980, p. 22). Cult members have been diagnosed as suffering from "dissociative states" (Ash 1983; Clark et al. 1981; Singer 1979), "information disease" (Conway and Siegelman 1978, 1982), and "cult indoctrinee syndrome" (Delgado 1980; West and Singer 1980).

The findings from previous research on the relationship between cult participation and the mental health of members are summarized in Table 1. Of the seventeen studies, ten report some degree of psychological impairment among members sampled from a variety of new religious groups. Psychological symptoms identified include: depression, anxiety, hallucinations, suicidal tendencies, neurotic distress, an incapacity to make decisions, and feelings of powerlessness and self-estrangement.

Our findings regarding the mental health status of Hare Krishna members are largely consistent with those just presented. As indicated in Table 2, approximately half of the ISKCON members in our survey admitted to feeling "discouraged and/or anxious about life" prior to becoming a Krishna devotee. More than a third reported taking part in therapy, or participating in psychological groups and movements such as "T" groups, Erhard Seminars Training (est), the Esalen Institute, encounter groups and a variety of lesser known self-help groups. We should note that only 3% of the devotees were actually undergoing therapy at the time they joined ISKCON and only 15% had ever been in therapy. This degree of involvement in therapy is less than that found for converts to other contemporary religious cults such as the

Table 1. Summary of Previous Studies of the Relationship Between
Cult Participation and the Mental Health of Members

Author/Year	Name of New Religions Studied	Sample Size	Sample Comprised Of:	Methods and Measures	Psychological or Psychiatric Impairment Found	Type of Symptoms or Disorders Identified
Conway and Siegelman (1982)	Total of 48 Cults Represented in Sample, Including: 1. Unification Church 2. Hare Krishna 3. Scientology 4. Divine Light Mission 5. Children of God 6. Bhagwan Shree Rajneesh 7. Erhard Seminars (est)[a]	N = 262	Former members: 71% were deprogrammed	Questionnaire Survey	Yes	Long Term: • floating in and out of altered states • nightmares • amnesia • hallucinations and delusions • inability to break mental rhythms or chanting • violent outbursts • suicidal or self-destructive tendencies
Deutsch (1975)	Baba Family (Hindu Group)	N = 14	Current Members	• Clinical Interviews • Semi-structured interviews of 1-5 hours duration	Yes	• Depression • Anxiety
Galanter and Buckley (1978)	Divine Light Mission	N = 119	Current Members	• Inteviews • 170 Item Multiple Choice Questionnaire Dealing with: Group Functions, Psychiatric Symptoms, Drug Use, Meditation Practices • Cochran Q Text • Multiple Regression Analysis	Yes	• Hearing voices • Anxiety • Depression • Suicide ideation • Referential thinking • Anomie • Behavioral problems

Author (Year)	Group	N	Sample	Instruments	Control	Findings
Galanter, et al. (1979)	Unification Church	N = 237	Current Members	• 216 Item Computer Codeable Questionnaire • Neurotic Stress Scale • Religiosity Scale • General Well-Being	Yes	• Neurotic distress
Galanter (1980)	Unification Church	N = 104	Potential Members • Attending a 21-day Unification Workshop	• Clinical Interviews/ Interpretations • Group Therapy • General Well Being Schedule • Cohesion Scale • Creed Scale • Sense of Purpose Scale	Yes	• Low emotional states • Neurotic stress
Kuner (1983)	German Members of: 1. Unification Church 2. Children of God 3. Ananda Marga	(303) (42) (47) N = 392	Current Members	MMPI	No	
Levine and Salter (1976)	1. Hare Krishna 2. Divine Light Mission 3. 3 HO 4. Unification Church 5. Foundation 6. Process 7. Jesus People 8. Scientology 9. Children of God	(15) (14) (12) (11) (14) (10) (9) (14) (7) N = 106	Current Members	Interviews	Yes	• Feeling of normlessness • Powerlessness • Isolation • Self estrangement • Demoralized
MacPhillamy (1986)	Zen Buddhist	N=31	Current Members	MMPI	No	

(continued)

Table 1. (continued)

Author/Year	Name of New Religions Studied	Sample Size	Sample Comprised Of:	Methods and Measures	Psychological or Psychiatric Impairment Found	Type of Symptoms or Disorders Identified
Rosen and Nordquist (1980)	Ananda	N=28	Current Members	• The Sentence Completion Test • Rokeach's Value Survey (Form D) • Counter-Cultural Attitudes Scale	No	
Ross[b] (1983)	Hare Krishna	N = 42	Current Members	• Clinical Interview & Interpretations • Individual Therapy • MMPI • Eysenck Personality • General Health • Present State Examination (Interview)	No	
Ross (1985b)	Scientology	N = 48	Current Members	• Adjective Checklist • Barron Ego-Strength Scale of the MMPI • Purpose in Life Scale	No	
Simmonds (1978)	Fundamentalist Jesus movement group	N = 96	Current Members	• Gough's Adjective Check List • Spielberger's State-Trait Anxiety Inventory	Yes	Scored Low:[c] • Defensiveness • Self-confidence • Self-control • Personal adjustment • Achievement • Dominance • Nurturance Scored High: • Succorance • Counseling-readiness • Trait anxiety

Study	Name of Group(s)	Sample	Methods/Tests		Findings
Singer (1979)	1. Children of God 2. Unification Church 3. Hare Krishna 4. Scientology 5. Divine Light Mission	N = 300 • Current Members • Voluntary Defectors • Deprogrammed/ Involuntary Defectors (Conservatorships) (Sought Psychiatric Treatment)	• Interviews/ Clinical Interpret. • Individual Therapy • Group Therapy	Yes	• Depression & confusion • Feelings of meaninglessness • Guilt • "Slippage into Disassociated States" • Severe incapacity to make decisions • Loneliness • "Floating" • Blurring of mental activity — Cognitive inefficiencies • Uncritical passivity • Fear • "Fishbowl effect"
Spero (1982)	Name of Group(s) Unspecified	N = 65 • Voluntary and deprogrammed defectors	• Clinical Interviews & Interpretations • Wechsler Adult Intelligence Scale • Bender-Gestalt Test • Draw-a-Person Test • Sentence Completion Test • Thematic Apperception Test • Rorschach Test	Yes	• Preference for stereotypy • Manic denial or depressive trends • Ego restriction
Ungerleider and Wellisch (1979a)	Variety of Cults - None Specified	N = 50 22-Concerned Members (feared deprogramming) 11-returnees (deprogrammed/ returned to cult) 9-non-returnees (deprogrammed/had not returned to cult) 8-Voluntary Ex- members *6 of the 9 non- returnees were members of anti-cult movement	• Psychiatric Data: 1. structured interviews 2. traditional mental status examination • Psychological Data: 1. Weschler Adult Intelligence Scale 2. MMPI 3. Draw-A-Person Test 4. Interpersonal Check List (ICL)	No	

(continued)

Table 1. (continued)

Author/Year	Name of New Religions Studied	Sample Size	Sample Comprised Of:	Methods and Measures	Psychological or Psychiatric Impairment Found	Type of Symptoms or Disorders Identified
Ungerleider and Wellisch (1979b)	Unidentified Christian Group	N = 2 Clinical opinions also based on interviews with 8 members of the group who feared deprogramming.	• Current Members • Resisted Attempted Deprogramming	• MMPI • WAIS • Leary Interpersonal Checklist • Interview	Yes (Legally Mentally Competent)	• Difficulties with management of aggressive impulses • Strong dependency needs • Both cases had histories of difficulties in social relations
Weiss (1985)	Hare Krishna	N = 226	• Current Full-time Members (N = 186) • Congregational Members (N = 40)	• Mental Health Inventory • Comrey Personality Scales	No[d]	

[a] There are two additional studies which have focused on the psychological and psychiatric effects of Erhard Seminars Training on participants (Kirsch and Glass 1977; Glass, et al. 1977). Reporting on a total of seven est participants, the latter investigators found evidence of psychotic symptoms including "grandiosity, paranoia, uncontrollable mood swings, and delusions" (1977 p. 245). The researchers do admit that their limited data source on est limits the generalizability of their findings with regard to questions of causality and overall rates of psychopathology. We have not included studies on est within our review because it does not fit neatly within the cult phenomena as such, being more a therapeutic group than a religious movement or organization.

[b] Ross (1985a) retested 25 of his original sample of 42 after a four year period using the MMPI. Those retested were similar in terms of demographic characteristics and initial MMPI scores with those who did not take part in the follow-up study. Results indicated that Hare Krishna members who participated in both studies continued to show good mental health, although there was an increase in anxiety over the four year period but still within the normal range.

[c] Results are based on a comparison with "Scores from normative samples of college students who were similar in age, educational, and socioeconomic characteristics" (Simmonds 1978, p. 119).

[d] The mental health of Hare Krishna members was within the normal range when compared with independent control groups matched by gender and age for both the Mental Health Inventory and the Comrey Personality Scales (Weiss, 1985, pp. 250-251). The only personality characteristic which significantly differentiated between Hare Krishna members and normative comparison groups was a prominent compulsivity trait. This personality trait is characterized by "very meticulous, compulsive people who are highly organized, conscientious, punctual, neat, and tidy. They are driven to complete tasks, feel compelled to correct errors, and often fall prey to obsessive behaviors" (Comrey 1980, quoted in Weiss 1985, p. 238). Weiss notes (1985, pp. 238-242, 260) that this personality trait is adaptive to the Krishna lifestyle and does not reflect evidence of a compulsive personality disorder.

Table 2. Psychological Symptoms, Involvements in Therapy and Psychological Groups, and Patterns of Drug Use for 214 ISKCON Members Prior to Joining

	N	Percentage (%)
Psychological Symptoms		
Feeling Discouraged and/or Anxious about Life	103	48%
Experiencing Family Problems	32	15%
Participation in Therapy and Psychologically Oriented Groups or Movements:		
Seeing a Therapist or Counselor at the Time Joined ISKCON	7	3%
Previously Took Part in Therapy or Counseling	32	15%
Participated in Self-Awareness or Psychologically Oriented Groups or Movements	80	37%
Use of Drugs:		
All Types of Drugs and Intoxicants (i.e., Alcohol, Marijuana, and Hallucinogens)	101	47%
Marijuana and Hallucinogens Only	30	14%
Alcohol and Marijuana Only	18	8%
Hallucinogens (i.e., "LSD," Peyote) Only	2	1%
Marijuana Only	24	11%
Alcohol Only	10	5%
No Drug Use	27	13%

Unification Church and the Divine Light Mission (see Clark et al. 1981; Deutsch 1975; Galanter and Buckley 1978; Galanter et al. 1979; Levine and Salter 1976).

Consistent with the findings of Deutsch (1975), Galanter and Buckley (1978), and Galanter et al. (1979), Hare Krishna members also have a history of drug and alcohol use prior to joining ISKCON. Only 13% of the devotees reported no previous use of drugs or alcohol; 80% had previously used marijuana, and 62% had taken hallucinogens such as "LSD."[5] As others have argued (Daner 1976; Judah 1974; Roszak 1969), the use of drugs by young people joining new religions suggests some degree of alienation from the dominant culture and general willingness to experiment with alternative forms of consciousness, lifestyles, and belief systems. As one early ISKCON member commented in a 1976 interview, "When I first joined in 1969 in San Francisco, everyone [ISKCON members] thought that taking LSD was a prerequisite for Krishna Consciousness. It came as a shock when people started joining who hadn't at least experimented with psychedelic drugs."

Taken at face value, one might logically conclude that the weight of evidence supports the claim that cults do, in fact, pose a serious mental health hazard to their members. But to gain a valid appraisal of the evidence requires that we ask an additional set of questions, questions which move beyond the content of the findings to more methodological and conceptual issues. Two focal questions guide this portion of our discussion: (1) are the findings from previous research based upon reliable methodologies which allow for generalization from subjects studied to clinical conclusions about a particular religious group, or the cults as a whole? and, (2) relatedly, can we validly interpret the presence of psychological impairment among some cult members to be related *causally* to the social environment of the cult, or are the symptoms identified by these studies largely an artifact of other influences which either pre- or post-date involvement?

Methodological and Conceptual Considerations

In the broadest sense, all of the previous studies reported in Table 1 can be questioned on methodological and/or conceptual grounds. Methodologically, none of the studies are based upon samples randomly selected from the new religion(s) investigated. At best, a convenience sample comprised of members from one or more new religious communities provides the data-base for the study (Deutsch 1975; Galanter 1980; Galanter and Buckley 1978; Galanter et al. 1979; Kuner 1983; Levine and Salter 1976; MacPhillamy 1986; Ross 1983, 1985b; Simmonds 1978; Weiss 1985). Moreover, with the exception of the research by Galanter and his associates (1979, 1980) and Weiss (1985) none of the studies have used control groups matching the background characteristics of cult members. These investigators employed age and sex matched comparison groups to investigate the psychological effects of participation in the Unification Church and Hare Krishna, respectively. Unfortunately, these efforts have not gone far enough to assure adequate controls. Without carefully matched control groups it becomes difficult to interpret findings on the mental health status of cult members. Findings from such studies may well confuse the causal relationship between cult involvement and psychological disturbance.

A further methodological issue which makes interpreting several of the studies problematic involves treating the retrospective statements of ex-cultists—many of whom have been deprogrammed and/or have sought psychiatric treatment—as objective data (Conway and Siegelman 1982; Singer 1979; Spero 1982; Ungerleider and Wellisch 1979a). Previous studies by Beckford (1978, 1985), Solomon (1981), and Shupe and Bromley (1980) suggest that former cult members often reinterpret their cult experiences in line with the anti-cult views of parents, friends, and the anti-cult movement. Because brainwashing interpretations ultimately absolve ex-converts of responsibility for past cult involvement (Beckford 1985; Robbins and Anthony 1982; Shupe and Bromley 1980), it is not surprising that many offer such explanations in an effort to preserve their competency in the eyes of others. Such responses are therefore better treated as "accounts" (Scott and Lyman 1968) or "motive talk" (Blum and McHugh 1971; Mills 1940). Because of these problems of distortion, one must interpret studies whose conclusions are based solely or largely on the statements of ex-members with caution.[6]

Beyond problems of methodology which uniformly plague all the studies reviewed, there are also conceptual issues which further cloud the validity of these investigations of cults and mental health. Putting aside questions of methodology, the question still remains as to whether the evidence from these studies is able to establish a causal relationship between the levels of psychological impairment found and the cultic milieu. The underlying assumption of anti-cultists—be they mental health professionals or otherwise— is that the cults' religious practices and lifestyles are ultimately the cause of members' psychological problems (Clark 1978; Conway and Siegelman 1978, 1982; Schwartz and Zemel 1980; Singer 1979). Two leading anti-cult psychiatrists, for example, state the following about the ways in which the cults' indoctrination practices influence the psychological well-being of their members:

> As time passes [during the initial indoctrination phase], the member's psychological condition may deteriorate. He becomes incapable of complex, rational thought; his responses to questions become stereotyped; he finds it difficult to make even simple decisions unaided; his judgment about events in the outside world is impaired. At the same time, there may be such a reduction of insight that he fails to realize how much he has changed (West and Singer 1980, p. 3249).

If we look more critically at the studies finding psychological problems among cult members, it becomes arguable what, if any, role the new religions have played in promoting psychopathology among their members. Table 3 addresses the question of causality by reporting on: (1) whether the psychological impairment found was an outcome of cult involvement or a condition which appears to have predated cult participation; and (2) what, if any, influence did the cult have in either further promoting psychological disorder or relieving symptoms and overall levels of impairment?

Of the ten studies finding evidence of psychological impairment, seven suggest that the symptoms uncovered were attributable to causes which *pre-dated* cult involvement (also see Clark 1979). Our findings on ISKCON members lend support to this conclusion. Singer (1979) and Spero (1982) argue that the presence of symptoms may be the result of both pre-involvement influences and cult indoctrination practices. Only one of the ten studies (Conway and Siegelman 1982) openly argues that cult involvement is the direct cause of psychological disturbance found among respondents. Conway and Seigelman conclude, "Put simply: our findings appear to confirm that *the psychological trauma cults inflict upon their members is directly related to the amount of time spent in indoctrination and mind-control rituals"* (1982, p. 90,

Table 3. Causes of Psychological Impairment Found and the New Religions Role in Increasing/Decreasing Symptoms

Author/Year	Psychological Impairment Caused by Involvement in NRM	Involvement in NRM Increased or Reduces Symptoms
Conway and Siegelman (1982)	Yes	Involvement Causes Psychological Impairment
Deutsch (1975)	No; Pre-existing Resulting From Family Problems and Use of Psychedelic Drugs	Reduced Symptoms
Galanter and Buckley (1978)	No; Pre-existing	Group Cohesiveness and Meditation Reduces Symptoms
Galanter et al. (1979)	No; Pre-existing	Religious Commitment Reduces Symptoms
Galanter (1980)	No; Pre-existing	Reduces Symptoms and Increased Sense of Well-Being
Levine and Salter (1976)	No; Pre-existing	Involvement Reduces Symptoms
Simmonds (1978)	No; Pre-existing	No Personality Changes Over a Two and One-half Month Interval
Singer (1979)	Yes and No; Some Symptoms Caused by Involvement (e.g., Dissociated States, Incapacity to Make Decisions) Other Symptoms Pre-existing (e.g., Depression, Meaninglessness)	Involvement Reduces Pre-existing Symptoms But Causes Other Sources of Disorder
Spero (1982)	Yes and No; Some Symptoms Caused by Involvement, Other Symptoms Pre-existing (e.g., Weakness in Ego Functions)	Involvement May Reduce Symptoms, But More Likely Causes, or Exacerbates Pre-existing Symptoms
Ungerleider and Wellisch (1979)	No; Pre-existing Resulting From Family Conflict and Substance Abuse	Involvement Reduces Symptoms

emphasis in the original). A serious challenge to this conclusion has recently been made by Kilbourne (1983, 1986). After statistically analyzing Conway and Siegelman's data, Kilbourne concluded that ". . . there was no statistical support for the claims of 'information disease.' In fact, the only significant correlations that emerged from their data tended to support a 'therapeutic' view of some cult affiliation" (1983, p. 380). (See Maher and Langone 1985, for a critique of Kilbourne's analysis and interpretation of Conway and Siegelman's data, and Kilbourne 1986, for his response.)[7]

Some investigators and clinicians have noted that the symptoms of disability apparent among some ex-converts of new religions may well result, not from cult involvement, but from "the traumatic manner in which some of these persons have been removed from sects and subjected to confrontational deprogramming, or to the difficult situation of ex-devotees who are stigmatized for their past involvements with a cult" (Robbins and Anthony 1982 p. 291). Levine (1979) reports that failed deprogrammings may well result in devotees feeling estranged from their families and left emotionally disturbed by the experience. These observations suggest that research which attempts to address the question of cults and mental health by studying the psychological status of ex-members (especially those subject to deprogramming) may well confound the whole issue of causality. Do the findings from such studies speak to the psychological consequences of cult involvement, or to problems of adjustment and adaptation faced by ex-cult members?[8]

But Table 3 reveals another finding which further undermines anti-cult notions of causality as they relate to cults and mental health. With the exception of Conway and Siegelman (1982) and Simmonds (1978), the remaining investigators report that cult involvement may prove *therapeutic* rather than a mental health hazard: cult participation may reduce some pre-movement symptoms of impairment and actually increase members' overall sense of psychological well-being (also see Anthony and Robbins 1974; Galanter 1982; Downton 1979; Pattison 1980; Robbins and Anthony 1982). Galanter (1978) has referred to this therapeutic side of cult participation as a "relief effect." By participating in religious and group functions, cult members who previously experienced symptoms of disorder often undergo an amelioration in feelings of distress. Galanter and his associates (1978, 1979) report that for adherents of the Divine Light Mission and the Unification Church that growing religious commitment, feelings of group cohesiveness, and participation in the religious practices and rituals of the movement all had the effect of reducing previous levels of psychological impairment.[9]

Robbins (1981) argues that cults may serve a therapeutic function for young people because they represent mediating structures, institutions which offer the opportunity for close face-to-face relationships with people who share a collective sense of belonging based upon a unifying religious belief. In modern society, traditional mediating structures between the individual and the larger society, such as the family, the neighborhood, personal work settings or conventional churches have been undermined by "social changes involving increased geographical mobility, [and] bureaucratization of instrumental structures" (Robbins 1981, p. 215). New religious groups because of their emphasis upon communal fellowship and the provision of loving familiar roles provide "ideological primary groups" (Marx and Holzner 1975) for their members (see Pattison 1980). Moreover, these groups tend to offer "a *holistic self-concept* whereby the participant can perceive all of their various activities and experiences as integrated under the auspices of a single ideal or symbol system. The goal of these movements may thus be said to be 'therapeutic'" (Robbins 1981, p. 216).

Given the above methodological and conceptual considerations, and in light of the fact that research has demonstrated that many U.S. citizens experience tensions, worries, anxieties, and symptoms of disorder (Gallup 1978; Institute of Social Research 1979; Robbins et al. 1984; Srole et al. 1962), one might logically ask what previous studies on the mental health status of cult members have actually measured—levels of disorder which are unique and attributable to participation in deviant religious groups, or levels of disability no different than that found within the larger society? Previous studies of cults and mental health leave this question largely unanswered. One investigator of this issue concludes, however, that:

> There is no evidence that devotees are any more disturbed, using any nosological classification, than any comparable peers in the general population. . . Any like population—white, young (18 to 30), middle class—has its share of symptoms and psychiatric disorders and cult members fare no better or worse in this regard (Levine 1981, p. 535).

All things considered, it remains arguable as to whether cult members' psychological status differs either in kind or degree from Americans of similar age and background (Kenniston 1965; Masterson 1967; Rutter et al. 1976). Needless to say, methodologically and conceptually informed research is required before we can hope to solve what remains the puzzle of cults and mental health.

Defection From Hare Krishna

Although the past two decades have produced an explosion of research addressing the processes of movement recruitment and religious conversion (Lofland and Skonovd 1981; Marx and Wood 1975; Rambo 1982; Snow and Machalek 1984), only recently have researchers turned to the other side of the membership issue: how and why some previously committed adherents of new religions defect from their respective movements? Studies of defection from the new religions have largely focused on two types of apostates: ex-members who have been removed against their will from a new religion as a consequence of deprogramming and conservatorships and former adherents who have chosen to voluntarily exit their religious group (Beckford 1985; Jacobs 1984; Kim 1979; Shupe and Bromley 1980; Skonovd 1981, 1983; Solomon 1981; Wright 1983, 1984). A limited amount of research has also considered members who have been expelled from one of the cults (Galanter 1980; Rochford 1982b.)

Much of the research on defection has more or less borrowed conceptual frameworks used to explain recruitment and conversion to cults. If young people join new religions largely because of a pre-existing convergence between their beliefs and values and those of a particular movement, or if such a cognitive linkage is imposed because of cult indoctrination, then it seems logical to assume that a breakdown in this linkage is crucial to voluntary and involuntary decisions to leave. Defection, from this perspective, is viewed as a process of "falling from the faith" or perhaps one of "reverse snapping" (Conway and Siegelman 1982), where cult members are brought back to normal awareness through deprogramming and/or therapy.

Other researchers have suggested that defection from new religions is also influenced by organizational factors as well as social psychological processes. Rochford (1985, 1988, forthcoming) argues that the Hare Krishna movement faced growing defections during the 1970s as a result of two factors: economic policies which were deemed controversial among a portion of ISKCON's membership and conflicts arising after the death of the movement's founding charismatic leader. Wright's (1983, 1984) investigation of former members of several new religions suggests the role of both organizational and social psychological factors in voluntary defections. He concludes that members defect from contemporary religious cults largely because of: (1) the breakdown of members' insulation from the outside society; (2) unregulated dyadic relationships within the communal context; (3) perceived lack of success in achieving the movement's religious aims and purposes; and, (4) inconsistencies between the actions of the leaders and the beliefs of the movement. But despite these recent theoretical and substantive treatments of the defection process, no research has yet appeared on patterns of defection from any one of the new religions. (See Levine 1984, on defection from communal groups, and Bird and Reimer 1983, on defection patterns among persons affiliated with new and para-religious movements in Montreal.)

The findings presented in Table 4 report on patterns of defection from ISKCON between 1973 and 1977. As the data demonstrate, there has been considerable defection from the movement during this period. Fifty-six percent of those initiated into ISKCON during these years, or who were initiated disciples of Prabhupada prior to 1973, had defected from the movement by 1977. As the data further indicate, over half (55%) of those ISKCON members who received initiation between 1974 and 1976 defected from the movement within the first year. Since the present findings report only on initiated devotees,

Table 4. Defection by Year of Initiated ISKCON Members (1973-77)
($N = 312$)

Year of Initiation	1974	1975	1976	1977	Total % Defection
1973* ($N = 93$)	17% (16)	16% (15)	4% (4)	15% (14)	53% (49)
1974 ($N = 77$)		40% (31)	9% (7)	13% (10)	62% (48)
1975 ($N = 86$)			31% (27)	26% (22)	57% (49)
1976 ($N = 56$)				52% (29)	52% (29)
Total Defections	9% (16)	26% (46)	22% (38)	43% (75)	56% (175)

*Note: ISKCON members included in our sample for 1973 include devotees who were initiated between 1966 and 1973. Thereafter, ISKCON members were initiated in the year indicated, or at least their initiated name first appeared in the *Sri Vyasa-Puja* in that year.

who are normally required to reside within an ISKCON community for six months prior to receiving initiation, the actual number of defections would be considerably larger if short-term recruits who never reach the stage of initiation were also accounted for. Unfortunately, the membership record contained within the *Sri Vyasa-Puja* does not allow for tracking uninitiated members over time. Finally, the large percentage of defections occurring in 1977, particularly among more recent converts to Hare Krishna, represents the *beginning* of the mass defections which occurred following Prabhupada's death, in November of 1977. After his death, ISKCON endured a series of succession crises resulting in the defection of many of the movement's members (Rochford 1985). Estimates from within ISKCON suggest that only about 1000 of the nearly 5000 devotees initiated by Prabhuapada remained in the movement after 1983.

CONCLUSION

The findings and discussion presented seriously challenge anti-cult views that deviant religious movements pose a threat to the mental health of their members. While some psychiatrists have argued that conversion to cults represents induced mental illness, such claims are not clearly supported by the literature. In those instances where researchers have discovered psychological disturbance among some adherents of new religions, it appears that such conditions existed prior to membership rather than being caused by the cult's indoctrination practices. Moreover, the corollary proposition that cult members are effectively left unable to leave the cult on their own, because of cult precipitated psychopathology, also appears to be misplaced. Findings on membership patterns for the Hare Krishna movement suggest that defection is more the *norm* than the exception. Most ISKCON members ultimately choose to defect at some point during their tenure with the movement. Given the requirements of the devotees' lifestyle, it is not surprising to find that most prove unable or perhaps unwilling to live up to the movement's spiritual practices and leave voluntarily.

In our view, there is no legitimate basis for continued state intervention in the cult phenomena on the grounds that deviant religions represent a threat to the mental health and personal freedom of their members. Clearly, some members of new religions do suffer from psychological disorders which may require professional treatment, but this can be said about virtually any other group or organization within the larger society, yet the state does not see fit to intervene in these latter cases. Intervention by the state (especially with regard to sanctioning legal deprogramming where parents are granted 30 day conservatorships for purposes of "treating" their adult children) can reasonably be interpreted as measures which threaten the freedom of religious belief protected under the First Amendment.

But the whole question of cults and mental health raises two additional concerns regarding church/state issues and the role of psychiatry in the social control of deviant religious movements. The ongoing involvement of psychiatry in the cult phenomena represents the medicalization of new religions (Robbins and Anthony 1982). As Conrad has described, medicalization involves a process of "defining behavior as a medical problem or illness and mandating or licensing the medical profession to provide some form of treatment for it" (1975, p. 12). By bringing the cult phenomena into the realm of psychiatry, anti-cultists have been able to attack these groups under the guise of mental health concerns. Rather than directly challenge the religious status of contemporary cults—a constitutionally risky strategy—opponents have enlisted the aid of prominent psychiatrists (and thereby the power of psychiatry as a profession) to help undermine the cult influence in America and worldwide. As others have noted, psychiatric theories may be used as "rhetorical tools to discredit political opponents and members of disvalued classes or subcultures" (Bainbridge 1984, p. 224). Accusations of brainwashing and mind control directed against new religions by anti-cultists rest not on scientific evidence but are largely matters of *strategy* (Coleman 1984). Charges of cult brainwashing provide little more than the rhetoric of social control. From this view, brainwashing, as Thomas Szasz has argued, is largely a metaphor: a term used to discredit influences of which we disapprove (1976, p. 11).

Controversy surrounding the cults raises a broader issue involving conceptions of the self in Western society and the role of psychiatry in contemporary culture. As Beckford has suggested, the root of much of the conflict involving new religions is tied to Western notions of the need for "a well balanced compromise between egoism and communalism" (1979, p. 179). Challenges to the cults in large part represent claims that they are unnatural and unhealthy precisely because they exceed the balance between the private and public spheres of individual existence. Cult members are thus viewed as having relinquished their "real self" by aligning their present and future with the collective needs and goals of the cult. This is seen as coming at the expense of individual autonomy and independence. From the time of Freud, psychiatry has embodied this stance of individualism by remaining largely antagonistic to collective enterprises, especially those of a religious orientation. As one commentator suggests, "the essentially secular aim of the Freudian spiritual guidance is to wean away the ego from either a heroic or a compliant attitude to the community. . . . What is needed is to free men from their sick communities. To emancipate man's 'I' from the communal 'we'" (Rieff 1961, p. 362).

NOTES

1. For purposes of this paper we will use the concepts "new religions," "deviant religious groups," and "cults" interchangeably. While most of the new religions are neither "new," or "cults" in the strict sense, these terms, for right or wrong, have been widely used by both scholars and members of the general public. The concept cult is popularly applied to groups which are viewed as using forms of "mind control" or "coercive persuasion," which tend to be authoritarian in their leadership, and which proselytize aggressively in an effort to recruit largely among young people. While the term is often applied to a wide range of groups—religious and nonreligious—our discussion in this paper only focuses on deviant religious movements.

2. The Hare Krishna movement originated in India and was brought to this country by A. C. Bhaktivedanta Swami Prabhupada in 1965. ISKCON is dedicated to spreading Krishna Consciousness throughout the world and has communities and preaching centers on every continent. At its height in the early 1970s, ISKCON had approximately 5000 core members throughout the world. The aim of the Krishna devotee is to become self-realized by practicing the *bhakti*-yoga process which involves chanting Hare Krishna and living an austere lifestyle that requires avoiding meat, intoxicants, illicit sex, and gambling. For a discussion of the movement's historical roots in India, see Judah (1974). For a more detailed history of the movement's growth and expansion in America and internationally, see Rochford (1982a, 1985) and Goswami (1983).

3. Rates of disengagement have been investigated for persons who have attended workshops sponsored by the Unification Church in Britain and the United States. Barker (1981) reports that only 12% of her sample of respondents attending a two-day workshop in Britain become full-time Moonies. An additional 9% of the respondents became less committed Home Church members. Barker points out that many of those who agreed to join the Moonies subsequently left the movement (also see Barker 1983). Galanter's (1980) study of induction processes employed by the Unification Church in the United States reported similar rates of disengagement. Of 104 prospective members attending a 21 day workshop, 71% did not continue their involvement past

the second day. After 21 days, only 9 people decided to join but four months later only six remained as full-time members. The present study of defection from the Hare Krishna movement focuses on members who have been in the movement for six months or longer. As such, it is the first study which systematically investigates defection patterns among *members* rather than prospective adherents.

4. A surprising number of ISKCON members have apparently defected from the movement only to rejoin at some later time. Findings from the senior author's 1980 devotee survey revealed that 20% of the 214 ISKCON members surveyed reported defecting from the movement only to return weeks, months, and sometimes years later.

5. Drug use among American adults aged 18-25 years progressively increased throughout the decade of the 1970s (Kelleher et al. 1983). While marijuana use among members of this age group was less than 50% in 1972, the use of this substance increased to nearly 70% by 1979. The use of hallucinogens increased from approximately 15% to 25% during the same period. Likewise the use of alcohol, cocaine, and every other major drug increased among young American adults (Inciardi 1986; Kelleher et al. 1983). Overall, however, past drug use by ISKCON members who joined the movement during the late 1960s and 1970s is greater than the national average for their age group.

6. Problems of respondent distortion work both ways. Ungerleider and Wellisch report that the cult members in their study had an elevated Lie scale indicating "an intentional attempt to make a good impression and to deny faults . . . Thus, it is likely that many of the in-group's subscales [on the MMPI] would have been elevated had they not consciously skewed their responses" (1979, p. 281). Whether from interviews or standardized measures, the responses of members and ex-members should be considered as motivated in light of their present circumstances. For this reason researchers should be cautious about uncritically accepting the reports of members and ex-members as objective data.

7. Maher and Langone (1985) argue that Kilbourne's statistical analyses and interpretation of Conway and Siegelman's data should be rejected as "faulty." Their critique and Kilbourne's (1986) response involve differences over statistical techniques (i.e., whether using both Spearman's rho and and Kendall's tau "increase the chances of finding adventitious significances") and, more critically, whether Kilbourne was mistaken in his definition of the appropriate sample size. Without going into the statistical details here, we think it enough to say that Kilbourne demonstrates rather conclusively that he did *not* err by inadvertently including a sixth group which included "the average of all 48 cults in the calculation of his coefficients" (1985, p. 117), as charged by Maher and Langone. Rather, Kilbourne correctly used data on only the five largest cults, as he reported in his original 1983 paper. Because the issues under dispute are more technical than substantive, and hence difficult to address fully here, we would direct the interested reader to the original Kilbourne (1983) paper and the subsequent comments generated (Kilbourne 1986; Maher and Langone 1985). Our reading of these three papers leads us to conclude that Kilbourne's original findings and interpretation that cults may be therapeutic is both accurate for the data analyzed and largely compatible with previous research, as reported in Table 3.

8. Galanter (1983), in the only study which attempts to systematically consider members' psychological adjustments in the period after *leaving* a deviant religious movement, reports that over one-third of the former Moonies he studied suffered "serious emotional problems" after disaffiliating from the Unification Church. He, unfortunately, does not say whether those in his sample who were deprogrammed were any more or less likely to have suffered psychological distress than members who left voluntarily. He goes on to report that after an average of 3.8 years from the time of defecting, that the 66 ex-Moonies studied apparently improved in their overall psychological well-being. Galanter summarizes his finding from the General Well-Being Schedule as follows: "[ex-Moonie respondents'] mean scores were higher than those of active members [Galanter et al. 1979] and higher still than those of workshop recruits [Galanter 1980]. Their mean scores now were no different from those of the matched sample from the general population"

(1983, p. 985). Because Galanter's study does not employ a panel design, it remains uncertain whether the initial problems encountered by a portion of his ex-Moonie sample reflect residual effects of participation in the Unification Church, or are conditions directly attributable to the problematics of becoming readjusted into the dominant society. Moreover, one cannot assume, as Galanter's analysis implicitly does, that the ex-Moonies he studied are representative of the Unification Church membership as a whole, or even of the respondents in his 1979 study (Galanter et al. 1979).

9.   There have been only three longitudinal studies of cult participation and mental health effects. Ross (1985a) found that members of Hare Krishna actually improved in their psychological well-being over a four year period. MacPhillamy's study of a sample of Zen Buddhists in California revealed "a general improvement in psychological adjustment over the course of 5 years of intensive monastic Zen training" (1986, p. 310). In a less revealing study because of the limited time period involved, Simmond's (1978) found no significant changes in the personality profiles of a sample of Jesus movement members after a two and one-half month period. A more indirect determination of the potentially positive effects of cult involvement is suggested by Ross who reports that long-time members of Scientology (1985b) and Hare Krishna (1983) have less psychological problems than do newer members.

REFERENCES

Anthony, D. and T.Robbins. 1974. "The Meher Baba Movement: Its Effects on Post-Adolescent Youthful Alienation." In *Religious Movements in Contemporary America,* edited by I. Zaretsky and M. Leone. Princeton, NJ: Princeton University Press.

Ash, S. 1983. *Cult Induced Psychopathology: A Critical Review of Presuppositions, Conversion, Clinical Picture, and Treatment.* University Microfilms, Ann Arbor, MI.

Bainbridge, W. 1984. "Religious Insanity in America: The Official Nineteenth-century Theory." *Sociological Analysis* 45:223-240.

Barker, E. 1981. "Who'd Be A Moonie? A Comparative Study of Those Who Join the Unification Church in Britain." In *The Social Impact of New Religious Movements,* edited by Bryan Wilson. New York: The Rose of Sharon Press.

_____. 1983. "The Ones Who Got Away: People who Attend Unification Church Workshops and Do Not Become Members." In *Of Gods and Men: New Religious Movements in the West,* edited by E. Barker. Macon, GA: Mercer University Press.

Beckford, J. 1978. "Through the Looking Glass and Out the Other Side: Withdrawal from Reverend Moon's Unification Church. *Archives de Sciences Sociales des Religions* 45:95-116.

_____. 1979. "Politics and the Anticult Movement." *Annual Review of the Social Sciences of Religion* 3:169-190.

_____. 1985. *Cult Controversies.* New York: Tavistock Publishers.

Bird, F. and B. Reimer. 1983. "Participation Rates in New Religious and Para-Religious Movements." *Journal for the Scientific Study of Religion* 21:1-14.

Blum, A. and P. McHugh. 1971. "The Social Ascription of Motives." *American Sociological Review* 46:98-109.

Bromley, D. and A. Shupe. 1979. *Moonies in America: Cult, Church and Crusade.* Beverly Hills, CA: Sage.

Clark, J. 1978. "Problems in Referral of Cult Members." *Journal of the National Association of Private Psychiatric Hospitals* 9:27.

_____. 1979. "Cults." *Journal of the American Medical Association* 242:279-281.

Clark, J., M. Langone, R. Schecter, and R. Daly. 1981. "Destructive Cult Conversion: Theory, Research, and Treatment." *American Family Foundation,* Weston, MA.

Coleman L. 1984. "New Religions and the Myth of Mind Control." *American Journal of Orthopsychiatry* 54:322-325.

Conrad, P. 1975. "The Discovery of Hyperkinesis: Notes on the Medicalization of Deviant Behavior." *Social Problems* 23:12-21.

Conway, F. and J. Siegelman. 1978. *Snapping: America's Epidemic of Sudden Personality Change.* New York: Lippincott.

_____. 1982. "Information Disease: Have Cults Created a New Mental Illness?" *Science Digest* (Jan):86-92.

Daner, F. 1976. *The American Children of Krsna: A Study of the Hare Krsna Movement.* New York: Holt, Rinehart and Winston.

Delgado, R. 1980. "Limits to Proselytizing." *Society* 17:25-33.

Deutsch, A. 1975. "Observations on a Sidewalk Ashram." *Archives of General Psychiatry* 32:166-175.

Downton, J. 1979. *Sacred Journeys: The Conversion of Young Americans to Divine Light Mission.* New York: Columbia University Press.

Galanter, M. 1978. "The 'Relief Effect': A Sociobiologic Model for Neurotic Distress and Large-Group Therapy. *American Journal of Psychiatry* 135:588-591.

_____. 1980. "Psychological Induction into The Large-Group: Findings from a Modern Religious Sect." *American Journal of Psychiatry* 137:1574-1579.

_____. 1982. "Charismatic Religious Sects and Psychiatry: An Overview." *American Journal of Psychiatry* 139:1539-1548.

_____. 1983. "Unification Church (Moonies") Dropouts: Psychological Readjustment after Leaving a Charismatic Religious Group." *American Journal of Psychiatry* 140:984-989.

Galanter, M. and P. Buckley. 1978. "Evangelical Religion and Meditation: Psychotherapeutic Effects." *Journal of Nervous and Mental Disease* 166:685-691.

Galanter, M., R. Rabkin, J. Rabkin, and A. Deutsch. 1979. "The 'Moonies': A Psychological Study of Conversion and Membership in a Contemporary Religious Sect." *American Journal of Psychiatry* 136:165-170.

Gallup, G. 1978. *The Gallop Poll: Public Opinion 1972-1977.* Wilmington, DE: Scholarly Resources.

Glass, L., M. Kirsch, and F. Parris. 1977. "Psychiatric Disturbances Associated with Erhard Seminars Training: I. A Report of Cases." *American Journal of Psychiatry* 134:245-247.

Goswami, Satsvrupa dasa. 1983. *Prabhupada.* Los Angeles: Bhaktivedanta Book Trust.

Hargrove, B. 1980. "Evil Eyes and Religious Choices." *Society* 17:20-24.

Inciardi, J. 1986. *The War on Drugs.* Palo Alto, CA: Mayfield.

Institute of Social Research. 1979. "Americans Seek Self-Development, Suffer Anxiety from Changing Roles." *IRS Newsletter.* University of Michigan, (Winter):4-5.

Jacobs, J. 1984. "The Economy of Love in Religious Commitment: The Deconversion of Women from Nontraditional Religious Movements." *Journal for the Scientific Study of Religion* 23:155-171.

Judah, S. 1974. *Hare Krishna and the Counterculture:* New York: John Wiley.

Kelleher, M., B. MacMurray, and T. Shapiro. 1983. *Drugs and Society.* Dubuque, IA: Kendall/Hall.

Kenniston, K. 1965. *The Uncommitted: Alienated Youth in American Society.* New York: Dell.

Kilbourne, B. 1983. "The Conway and Siegelman Claims Against Religious Cults: An Assessment of Their Data." *Journal for the Scientific Study of Religion* 22:380-385.

_____. 1986. "A Reply to Maher and Langone's Statistical Critique of Kilbourne." *Journal for the Scientific Study of Religion* 25:116-123.

Kim, B. 1979. "Deprogramming and Subjective Reality." *Sociological Analysis* 40:197-208.

Kirsch, M. and L. Glass. 1977. "Psychiatric Disturbances Associated with Erhard Seminars Training: II. Additional Cases and Theoretical Considerations." *American Journal of Psychiatry* 134: 1254-1258.

Kuner, W. 1983. "New Religious Movements and Mental Health." In *Of Gods and Men: New Religious Movements In The West,* edited by E. Barker. Macon, GA: Mercer University Press.

LeMoult, J. 1978. "Deprogramming Members of Religious Sects." *Fordham Law Review* 46:599-640.

Levine, S. 1979. "The Role of Psychiatry in the Phenomena of Cults." *Canadian Journal of Psychiatry* 24:593-603.

_____. 1981. "Cults and Mental Health: Clinical Conclusions." *Canadian Journal of Psychiatry* 26:534-539.

_____. 1984. "Radical Departures." *Psychology Today* 18:21-27.

Levine S. and N. Salter. 1976. "Youth and Contemporary Religious Movements: Psychosocial Findings." *Canadian Psychiatric Association Journal* 21(6):411-420.

Lofland, J. and N. Skonovd. 1981. "Conversion Motifs." *Journal for the Scientific Study of Religion* 20:373-385.

Lucksted, O. and D. Martell. 1982. "Cults: A Conflict Between Religious Liberty and Involuntary Servitude?" (Part I). *FBI Law Enforcement Bulletin* (April):16-20.

MacPhillamy, D. 1986. "Some Personality Effects of Long-Term Zen Monasticism and Religious Understanding." *Journal for the Scientific Study of Religion* 25(3):304-319.

Maher, B. and M. Langone. 1985. "Kilbourne on Conway and Siegelman: A Statistical Critique." *Journal for the Scientific Study of Religion* 24(3):325-326.

Marx, G. and J. Wood. 1975. "Strands of Theory and Research in Collective Behavior." *Annual Review of Sociology* 1:363-428.

Marx, J. and B. Holzner. 1975. "Ideological Primary Groups in Contemporary Cultural Movements." *Sociological Focus* 8:312-329.

Masterson, J. 1967. *The Psychiatric Dilemma of Adolescence.* New York: Arm-Hill.

Melton, J. 1983. "The Flowering of the 'New Religious Consciousness': Factors in its Sudden Growth." Paper presented at the Fourth International Conference on the New Religious Movements, Berkeley, CA (October).

Mills, C. 1940. "Situated Actions and Vocabularies of Action." *American Sociological Review* 5:904-913.

Pattison, E. 1980. "Religious Youth Cults: Alternative Healing Social Networks." *Journal of Religion and Health* 19:275-286.

Rambo, L. 1982. "Bibliography: Current Research on Religious Conversion." *Religious Studies Review* 8:146-159.

Richardson, H. 1980. "Introduction." In *New Religions and Mental Health.* New York: The Edwin Mellen Press.

Richardson, J. 1985. "Psychological and Psychiatric Studies of New Religions." In *Advances in the Psychology of Religion,* edited by L. B. Brown. New York: Pergamon Press.

Richardson, J. and M. Stewart. 1978. "Conversion Process Models and the Jesus Movement." In *Conversion Careers: In and Out of the New Religions,* edited by J. Richardson. Beverly Hills, CA: Sage.

Rieff, P. 1961. *Freud: The Mind of the Moralist.* Garden City, NY: Anchor Books.

Robbins, L., J. Helzer, M. Weissman, H. Orvaschel, E. Gruenberg, J. Burke, and D. Regier. 1984. "Lifetime Prevalence of Specific Psychiatric Disorders in Three Sites." *Archives of General Psychiatry* 41:949-958.

Robbins, T. 1981. "Church, State and Cult." *Sociological Analysis* 42(3):209-226.

Robbins, T. and D. Anthony. 1982. "Deprogramming, Brainwashing and the Medicalization of Deviant Religious Groups." *Social Problems* 29(3):283-297.

Rochford, E. B., Jr. 1982a. "Recruitment Strategies, Ideology, and Organization in the Hare Krishna Movement." *Social Problems* 29(4):399-410.

————. 1982b. *A Study of Recruitment and Transformation Processess in the Hare Krishna Movement.* University Microfilms, Ann Arbor, MI.

————. 1985. *Hare Krishna in America.* New Brunswick, NJ: Rutgers University Press.

————. 1988. "Movement and Public in Conflict: Values, Finances, and the Decline of Hare Krishna." In *Money and Power in the New Religions,* edited by J. Richardson. New York: Edwin Mellen Press.

————. forthcoming. "Factionalism, Group Defection, and Schism in the Hare Krishna Movement." *Journal for the Scientific Study of Religion.*

Rosen, A. and T. Nordquist, 1980. "Ego Development Level and Values in Yogic Community." *Journal of Personality and Social Psychology* 39(6):1152-1160.

Ross, M. 1983. "Clinical Profiles of Hare Krishna Devotees." *American Journal of Psychiatry* 140(4):416-420.

————. 1985a. "Mental Health in Hare Kirshna Devotees: A Longitudinal Study." *American Journal of Social Psychiatry* 5(4):65-67.

————. 1985b. "Personality Changes in Scientologists: Effects of Membership." Unpublished Manuscript, Department of Psychiatry, Flinders University of South Australia.

Roszak, T. 1969. *The Making of a Counter Culture.* Garden City, NY: Doubleday.

Rutter, M., P. Graham, O. Chadwick, and W. Yule. 1976. "Adolescent Turmoil—Fact or Fiction?" *Journal of Child Psychiatry and Related Disciplines* 17:35-76.

Schwartz, L. and J. Zemel. 1980. "Religious Cults: Family Concerns and the Law." *Journal of Marital and Family Therapy* 6(7):301-308.

Scott, M. and S. Lyman. 1968. "Accounts." *American Sociological Review* 33:46-62.

Shapiro, E. 1977. "Destructive Cults." *American Family Physician* 15:80-83.

Shupe, A. and D. Bromley. 1980. *The New Vigilantes.* Beverly Hills, CA: Sage.

Simmonds, R. 1978. "Conversion or Addiction: Consequences of Joining a Jesus Movement Group." In *Conversion Careers: In and Out of the New Religions,* edited by J. Richardson. Beverly Hills, CA: Sage.

Singer, M. 1978. "Therapy With Ex-Cult Members." *Journal of the National Association of Private Psychiatric Hospitals* 9(4):14-18.

————. 1979. "Coming Out of the Cults." *Psychology Today* 12(8):72-82.

Skonovd, N. 1981. *Apostasy: The Process of Defection from Religious Totalism.* Ph.D. dissertation, University of California, Davis.

————. 1983. "Leaving the Cultic Religious Milieu." In *The Brainwashing Deprogramming Controversy: Sociological, Psychological, Legal and Historical Perspectives,* edited by D. Bromley and J. Richardson. New York: The Edwin Mellen Press.

Snow, D. and R. Machalek. 1984. "The Sociology of Conversion." *Annual Review of Sociology* 10:167-190.

Solomon, T. 1981. "Integrating the "Moonie" Experience: A Survey of Ex-Members of the Unification Church." In *In Gods We Trust,* edited by T. Robbins and D. Anthony. New Brunswick, NJ: Transaction Books.

Spero, M. 1982. "Psychotherapeutic Procedure with Religious Cult Devotees." *The Journal of Nervous and Mental Disease* 170(6):332-344.

Srole, L., T. Langner, S. Michael, M. Opler, and T. Rennie. 1962. *Mental Health in the Metropolis.* New York: McGraw-Hill.

Szasz, T. 1976. "Some Call It Brainwashing." *New Republic* 174(10):10-12.

Ungerleider, J. and D. Wellisch. 1979a. "Coercive Persuasion (Brainwashing), Religious Cults, and Deprogramming." *American Journal of Psychiatry* 136:279-282.

————. 1979b. "Cultism, Thought Control and Deprogramming: Observations on a Phenomena." *Psychiatric Opinion* (January):10-13.

U.S. News and World Report. 1976. "Religious Cults: Newest Magnet for Youth." 80(24):52-54.

Weiss, A. 1985. *Mental Health and Personality Characteristics of Hare Krishna Devotees and Sympathizers as a Function of Acculturation into the Hare Krishna Movement.* Ph.D. dissertation, California School of Professional Psychology, Los Angeles, CA.

West, L. and M. Singer. 1980. "Cults Quacks, and Non-Professional Psychotherapists." In *Comprehensive Textbook of Psychiatry III,* edited by H. Kaplan, A. Freedman, and B. Sadock. Baltimore, MD: Williams and Wilkins.

Wright, S. 1983. "Defection from New Religious Movements: A Test of Some Theoretical Propositions." In *The Brainwashing/Deprogramming Controversy: Sociological, Psychological, Legal and Historical Perspectives,* edited by D. Bromley and J. Richardson. New York: The Edwin Mellen Press.

————. 1984. "Post-Involvement Attitudes of Voluntary Defectors from Controversial New Religious Movements." *Journal for the Scientific Study of Religion* 23:172-182.

TOWARD COMPLEXITY:
THE RIGHT-TO-LIFE MOVEMENT

James R. Kelly

ABSTRACT

Social movements are not always either successes or failures, especially when they find roots in groups that are carriers of religious traditions and moral traditionalism. Back's (1986) seminal notion of "nascent permanence" applies to the right-to-life movement which shows no likelihood of either success or declension. The resources of the right to life movement include the fact that most Americans do not wish it to either succeed or fail, the proliferation of right-to-life organizations that create new constituencies, and the distrust of the elitist connotations of a "quality of life ethic" as operationalized in decisions not to treat handicapped neonates, the terminally ill, and the senile old. These pro-life resources are weaker than the pro-choice resources of elite support, dominant feminism, contemporary liberalism, and the likelihood of the nonenforceability of abortion prohibitions. But the resources of the right-to-life movement make it likely to persist as a marginal, but not tangential, element of modern culture and society. Failure to note the progressive egalitarian basis of right-to-life arguments and the diversity of right-to-life organizations distorts analyses of the abortion controversy and hinders continuing attempts to construe constructive policy suggestions.

Research in the Social Scientific Study of Religion, Volume 1, pages 83-107.
Copyright © 1989 by JAI Press Inc.
All rights of reproduction in any form reserved.
ISBN: 0-89232-882-7

The one certain fact about the opposition to legal abortion that arose in the mid 1960s in American society and continues through the 1980s without any evidence of declension is that it is a social movement. Indeed, it is a spectacular example of a social movement that illustrates most of the themes found in the social movement literature and calls attention to some that are underemphasized. Since abortion and its legalization also involves fundamental questions about the beginning of life, the conditions when life can be taken, and the relationship between law and morality, the right-to-life movement involves dimensions of religion and requires for its understanding many of the resources of the sociology of religion. I will draw upon the literature of social movement analysis and the sociology of religion to better understand the right-to-life movement and the implications that the right-to-life movement, in turn, has for both social movement theory and the sociology of religion. The data used in this essay include over 75 interviews (about half personal and half by telephone) with pro-life activists from around the country,[1] references to the pertinent scholarship on the issue and some attention to the chronology of the abortion debate. My interpretation of the significance of the right-to-life movement will draw on some seminal notions of Kurt Back (1986) who asks the interesting question of whether social movements that remain in a nascent state can assume a kind of permanence.

RIGHT-TO-LIFE AS A SOCIAL MOVEMENT

At various times in the controversy proponents of liberal abortion laws have portrayed their opponents as, first, agents of hierarchical Catholicism and, later, as elements of a politically driven "New Christian Right." A key strategy of pro-choice polemicists has been a moral reductionism whereby pro-life moral claims have been classifed as religious ones, and then polemically reduced to authoritarian psychological categories. Nathanson (1983, p. 177ff), one of the founders of the National Association for the Repeal of Abortion Laws (NARAL), reports that the description of opposition to abortion as financed by the American Bishops was a conscious strategy adopted by NARAL. On occasion the strategy led to the use of gross stereotypes.[2]

By the 1980s evangelical Protestantism, usually simplistically identified as the "Moral Majority" or "Fundamentalists," were included with Roman Catholic Bishops as the primary causes of continuing opposition to legal abortion. Opposition to elective abortion was frequently described as a kind of "moral lag" kept alive only because it was institutionally lodged in the most illiberal and authoritarian sectors of American life, namely Roman Catholicism and biblical fundamentalism. Both traditions were portrayed as uncomfortable with key dimensions of modernity, such as pluralism, the separation of church and state and the primacy of individual conscience in moral matters, and in this way more widespread resistances to legal abortion were ignored and unstudied and any possibly progressive elements in the right-to-life movement were overlooked. Legal abortion, on the other hand, was most commonly represented as a dimension of the growing equality of women, an extension of the respect for conscience and pluralism that characterized American liberal denominationalism and as a technological innovation that further freed human beings from the constraints of both nature and traditional mores.

OPPOSITION TO ABORTION AS SPONTANEOUS AND VOLUNTARY

Scholarly accounts of the right-to-life movement do not sustain the pejorative characterization of antiabortion activists as passive agents of religious authorities. These studies (Leahy 1982, pp. 45ff, 66; Luker 1984, p. 146ff; Kelly 1981, p. 659)[3] found that the first opponents to legal abortion—the right-to-life pioneers—invariably described themselves as spontaneously experiencing a quick and powerful sense of moral repulsion to the notion that the state would make abortion legal. "Abortion kills babies," they frequently said. An acceptance of such behavior and, worse, its legalization, seemed to them an unraveling of the moral universe and a corruption of the basic principle of any humane society. "If abortion can be legal," they said in different ways, "then the state can do anything and call it moral." They claimed that morality and biology and not theology were their animating frames of reference. That abortion was, in a word, a self-evident evil seemed to them not a church teaching, although it was also that, but a rudimentary and nonsectarian moral fact.

Groups promoting abortion rights, on the other hand, generally portray the opposition to abortion as resulting, however unconsciously, from an opposition to contemporary sexual mores that is part of an effort to retain both traditional sexual morality and gender roles. While it is notoriously difficult to resolve the question of "actual" motivation, as opposed to the reasons an actor subjectively feels or publicly gives for a behavior, studies of right-to-life activists support their proclaimed motivation that they are motivated by what they describe as a defense of human life rather than an animus against women or birth control. Secondary analyses of national survey data that inspect, for example, the associations among variables such as religious membership and attitudes toward sex education, ease of divorce laws, acceptance of birth control, and opposition to abortion, have shown no general relationship between opposition to abortion and measures supportive of "sexual constraint" among Catholics and most Protestants, and is pronounced only among some fundamentalists (Jelen 1984, p. 222, 225; Hall 1986.) In this context it is worth noting that the most prominent pro-life organizations themselves say that they have no official position on birth control or, for that matter, on other issues besides abortion (and for reasons discussed later, infanticide and euthanasia.) All major right-to-life organizations, for example, support an equal rights amendment if it includes "abortion neutral language," on the grounds that some states have interpreted their equal rights amendments as implying the right to medicaid funded abortions. Granberg's and Granberg's (1981) study of National Right to Life Committee leaders concluded that, compared to the general public, they were more likely to support an expanded role for women in public life. It is of some significance that within the right-to-life movement there is a group called "Feminists for Life" that disputes dominant feminist organizations, such as the National Organization for Women, only on the point of abortion.

The motivation and personal sacrifices of the opponents of abortion match those of other social movements, a further indication of the internalized and self-propelled character of pro-life activists. All accounts of right-to-life activists note the high levels of commitment they show. Studies have found activity levels as high as 30-40 hours a week (Luker 1984, p. 218; Leahy 1982, p. 68). The great majority of activists finance their activities out of their own pockets (Luker 1984, p. 223; Burtchaell 1982, pp. 124-126). This was especially true in the formative stages of the right-to-life movement when activists report that they used their kitchen tables as their pro-life "offices." The evidence is clear that the first great sociological lesson to be learned about the right-to-life movement is the power of moral conceptions, when they represent the central conceptions of what it means to be human, to mobilize large numbers of people to engage in sustained, difficult, and financially nonremunerative collective behavior. The heart of any social movement of any duration is moral—that is, a concern with questions of ultimacy rather than simply self-interest—and to better understand social movements, sociologists have begun to take this dimension more centrally into their analysis (Wood and Hughes 1984, p. 96; Simpson 1985, p. 160; Kandermans 1984, p. 585; Killian 1984, p. 781). Moral commitments, after all, are central to the self-descriptions provided by movement activists and it is hard to explain the persistance of social movements, especially when they seem unlikely to achieve their goals, without reference to the power of moral commitment.

WHO WERE THE ACTIVISTS? THE ESTABLISHMENT ROOTS OF SPONTANEOUS SOCIAL MOVEMENTS

The first opponents of abortion were like the first proponents of abortion legalization, doctors and lawyers who learned from their professional contacts and professional journals that some relaxation of the states' restrictive abortion laws was beginning to be discussed. What had seemed to be a long settled moral constituent of morality was now questioned,[4] although with great circumspection. As part of its provisions for a model penal code, the American Law Institute included the recommendation of some relaxation of the states' restrictive abortion laws so that, besides those performed to save the mother's life, abortions indicated for risks to mental health or pregnancies from rape and incest, or pregnancies involving grave fetal deformity, should now be permitted.

Social Disorganization and Resource Mobilization Aspects of the Right-To-Life Movement

The social origins of the right-to-life activists illustrate both the "social disorganization" and "resource mobilization" tendencies in social movement analyses, but far more the applicability of the latter. Indeed, even the "social disorganization" elements here refer to the sense among pro-life women activists (Luker 1984) that contemporary life had led to a devalorization of the investments of women who followed traditional gender roles and thus refers more to a purported state of "anomie" or "status insecurity" rather than to the usual elements of social disorganization, such as economic insecurity or political disorientation. Indeed, in interviews pro-life activists display little "anomie," for they are convinced that abortion is morally wrong and, except for those who bombed or burned abortion clinics, none of whom were members of any organized right-to-life groups, pro-life activists use the conventional instruments of American politics, such as lobbying, voter registration and political action committees. They display few symptoms of suffering from social disorganization and most are members of intact families with ties to churches.

While part of the definition of a social movement is that it emerges outside of existing channels of elite influence and brings to public attention a matter ignored or downplayed by political elites, this is always a matter of degree (Freeman 1973). After all, a movement lacking all ties to existing institutions and leadership networks might better be called a revolution than a social movement. The early opposition to legal abortion contained this mixture of populist spontaneity and connection to established institutions. A major element in terms of prior channels of support was the resources of the Roman Catholic Church. The first example I can find of a local anti-abortion group is the Metropolitan Life Committee, founded in 1963 by Robert M. Byrn, a Fordham University Law School professor. This group met in the Madison Avenue offices of the New York Archdiocese. The first public opponents of changes in the abortion laws were mostly doctors and lawyers, and mainly Catholic, who saw in these proposed laws, besides a moral dimension, an issue that would soon confront Catholic hospitals and social welfare agencies. No other denomination had such a vast institutional network of service institutions, and these institutional investments undoubtedly prompted an early

Catholic reaction to the first discussions of change in the abortion laws. But there was no initial expectation among Catholic agencies or the hierarchy that abortion reform would succeed (Francome 1984, p. 90). That abortion represents the ending of a human life, and thus an impermissable means of birth control, seemed to them a settled fact of moral and public life. Indeed, one of the main difficulties confronting abortion law reformers was their realization that most Americans also felt this way (Lader 1973, pp. ix-x). Luker (1984, pp. 101, 107) found that even those who had obtained illegal abortions did not think that the laws would be changed. To become pro-abortion activists requires exposure to one of the ideologies of feminism to counter the internalized conviction that abortion remained a "taboo" topic beyond political change. To make the "morally settled" unsettled and changeable a new ideology redefining abortion was required, for the notion of legal elective abortion had not yet become "thinkable." Before 1930 only one article on abortion was indexed in the Reader's Guide to Periodical Literature. During the time of the epoch-making Second Vatican Council the Harvard "Roman-Catholic/ Protestant Colloquium" was held March 27-30, 1963 and although two of the sessions and one of the seminars dealt with questions of morality, conscience and pluralism, there was no mention of abortion. "Abortion" does not appear in the index of the published proceedings either.

The Complexity and Diffuseness of the Right-To-Life Movement

With the exception of the Roman Catholic Church, before 1973 there was no organized national or even central organizational loci of opposition to legal abortion. The first changes in the abortion laws occurred in the states (before the 1973 Supreme Court decision, the federal government had no jurisdiction regarding abortion law), and in 1965 the first local right-to-life groups formed in states where changes in the abortion laws were publicly discussed. More than half of the membership of these groups were and are women, almost always housewives with small children at home (Leahy 1983; Luker 1984, p. 138; Kelly 1981, p. 655). Very few of these activists, men or women, had prior political experience or were even active in local community organizations (Luker 1984, p. 139) apart from church groups. Most were Catholics, but even at this stage there were conscious efforts to make their groups ecumenical and they had some success in attracting Orthodox and Conservative Jews and some Protestants. Indeed, one of the conclusions of a September 1967 International and Ecumenical Conference sponsored by the Harvard Divinity School and the Kennedy Foundation was that scholars and theologians from all traditions were in broad agreement that unrestricted or elective abortion violated a fundamental and long-standing conviction of Western Judeo-Christian civilization. The early grass roots opponents of legal abortion persistently described their opposition to abortion as moral rather than religious, and used pictures and slides to convey their contention that biology and the human eye were sufficient to understand that abortion stopped innocent human life and thus violated an elementary and foundational moral principle. While these activists complain that they received little help from their local clergy, and financed their groups voluntarily, a major resource in their mobilization was the Catholic teaching that all direct abortions were immoral. Protestant theology took more varied positions, and it seemed in the beginning of the abortion controversy, at least for nonfundamentalist Protestantism, that the limited aims that the abortion reformers first publicly proclaimed did not directly contradict Protestant moral reasoning about abortion. As late as 1967 the President of the Association for the Study of Abortion, Robert Hall, described the association's goal as bringing current law into greater harmony with present medical practice, which included therapeutic abortion but not elective abortion. It was not until 1969, with the formation of the National Association for the Repeal of Abortion Laws, that the goal of elective abortion was first publicly formulated. When the American public heard of abortion reform they were encouraged by abortion law reformers to think of making legal those abortions that preserved maternal health or which ended pregancies caused by rape or incest. The original public presentation of the abortion reformers stressed continuity with themes congruent with moral traditionalism, namely that legal abortion would prevent death from illegal abortion, that maternal health should be a valid reason for abortion, and that abortion would help family stability by allowing family resources to be expended on those already born. Only after the 1973 Supreme Court decision *Roe* v. *Wade* were arguments widely advanced that defined abortion positively, as opposed to "tragically necessary," that is, as right with intrinsic self-justification involving no other morally relevant elements than the choice of woman.

EARLY PRO-LIFE SUCCESS

It can be said that on the whole the right-to-life movement was not unsuccessful on the state level. This wording is circuituous, but the facts themselves are not linear. While abortion reform had succeeded in 18 states (Florida, Alaska, Hawaii, New York, Washington, South Carolina, Virginia, Arkansas, Delaware, Kansas, New Mexico, Oregon, Georgia, Maryland, California, Colorado, North Carolina, and Mississippi), abortion reform had not been successful in the great majority of states. Moreover, the state reforms were for the most part along the restrictive lines suggested in 1959 by the American Law Institute and made legal only abortions for the "hard" or "tragic" cases. Those few states that made elective abortion legal (Alaska, Hawaii, New York, and Washington) permitted abortion only until "viability," calculated then as around the 24th week of gestation. The National Association for the Repeal of Abortion Laws impatiently described (Lader 1973, p. 70) these reforms as inadequate. Finally, in 1972 abortion reform was defeated in two state referenda (Michigan and North Carolina) by wide margins. When the Supreme Court the next year declared abortion to be a constitutionally protected right, and thus struck down all state laws, even abortion reformers were surprised.[5]

Roe v. *Wade* seemed at first to restrict as well as permit abortions, because it said that after viability the state could exercise its interest in human life; but in the companion decision, *Doe* v. *Bolton,* the Court explained that maternal health included psychological and economic well-being and thus in actuality Roe made elective abortion a constitutionally protected right throughout pregnancy. In its June 26, 1986 ruling "*Thornburg* v. *American College of Obstetricians and Gynecologists,*" the Supreme Court (5-4) ruled unconstitutional Pennsylvania's Abortion Control Act that, among other things, required that a woman considering an abortion be given information about the probable age of the fetus and the fact that medical assistance may be available should she continue her pregnancy, thus confirming the judgment that in effect the Court had permitted elective abortion throughout pregnancy.

THE RIGHT-TO-LIFE MOVEMENT GOES NATIONAL

It is of some significance that the first national pro-life groups to form were in the "service" wing, groups that immediately realized that it would be an inadequate response to legal abortion to simply oppose legal abortion without trying to help women who were pregnant and did not want to be. In 1970 Louise Somerhill founded "Birthright," a pro-life service organization that helps women who might consider abortion because they lack money or a place to live. Birthright provides counseling, financial assistance, medical help and even private "birthright" homes where women can stay until delivery. In November, 1971 Lori Maier founded another pro-life service organization called "Alternatives to Abortion International," which provides similar services but grants more local autonomy than Birthright. These local service groups, including later groups such as those started in the 1980s by the Christian Action Council, the Pearson Foundation and others, probably now number close to 3,000.

Steps Toward More Political National Organizations

With the Supreme Court decision invalidating all state restrictions on abortion, the right-to-life movement required a national focus, since now any change in the law would require a constitutional amendment of some sort. This stage in the right-to-life movement illustrates several basic themes found in social movement analysis, such as the persistent disputes among centralizing social movement organizations and grass roots organizations, the difficulty in establishing authoritative claims for movement leadership, the schism and fractionation inherent in movements involving volunteers, and the tension between ideological purity and the exigencies of politics. The formation of a national right-to-life organization was greatly facilitated by the inherent centralizing capacity of the Roman Catholic Church. Later the Catholic Church itself would become an element in the fractionation of the right-to-life movement.

THE ROLE OF THE CATHOLIC FAMILY LIFE BUREAU

By June 1966 the Family Life Bureau (FLB) of the United States Catholic Conference was directed to monitor for State Catholic Conferences all efforts to alter the states' abortion laws. In 1970 the director of the FLB, Rev. James McHugh, called the first national meeting of local right-to-life activists and by this time there were thousands of independent right-to-life groups in many states. New York State, for instance, had between 50 and 70 such groups. The grass roots pro-life organizations were a vital force before any attempt to achieve centralization was made and the initial function of the National Right-to-Life Committee was mainly to serve as a clearing house for those local groups that already existed (Leahy 1982, p. 37). There was (and is) no central authoritative pro-life organization or voice. About 70 people attended this first meeting—paying their own way—in Chicago. In the summer following the January 22, 1973 Roe decision, the National Right-to-Life Committee became a fully autonomous organization with legal incorporation. Its nine person board of directors was ecumenical, including Methodists and Episcopalians as well as Catholics. Although it is now stable, the National Right-to-Life Committee has led a precarious existence. For several years it was close to bankruptcy. Major problems included schisms, internal disputes over the wording and degree of restriction of abortion in a human life amendment and over the appropriateness of direct nonviolent action. One of the interesting aspects of the right-to-life movement is that in time it seemed to become even more fractionated than in its origin. The reasons for this include not merely the perennial social movement difficulty of establishing the legitimacy of any central voice (in lieu of an unquestioned charismatic person), disagreements about strategies, and the inevitable clashes of personality, but also the difficulty of confronting the question of how making abortions illegal would stop abortions and, thus, how right-to-life groups could truly be "pro-life" rather than simply "anti-abortion." For a movement based on moral principles, this issue remains its unresolved basic dilemma. Given the complexity of the abortion issue, the fractionation of the right-to-life movement, although lamented by pro-life activists, is probably more objectively viewed as a movement asset since it allows individuals who would not feel morally and politically comfortable in one group to affiliate with another.

THE DIVERSITY AND COMPLEXITY OF THE RIGHT-TO-LIFE MOVEMENT

The National Right-to-Life Committee, as mentioned above, was formed in 1973 and claims (from membership and subscription rates to its biweekly *National Right-to-Life News*) a membership of several million. It is organized in right-to-life chapters in each state and has a board of directors, a president and a staff now numbering in the mid-twenties. It also has its own political action committee. Its yearly convention attracts about 2,000 activists and NRLC correctly describes itself as the main voice in the right-to-life movement. Even those in disagreement with the NRLC rent space for a booth or a room at its annual convention, and thus tacitly acknowledge its central place in the right-to-life movement. The NRLC is centrist, in that it takes no position on any topic save the "life" issues of abortion, infanticide, and euthanasia.

The group that openly challenges the NRLC for dominance is the American Life League (ALL) started in 1977 by Judy Brown, who had been the executive secretary of NRLC. ALL best fits the stereotype of the antiabortion movement as favoring conservative politics and Christian fundamentalism. The ALL, indeed, received financial help and advice from right-wing strategists and fund-raisers, such as Paul Weyreich. The American Life League asserts its claim to centrality by contending that it alone represents the pure principle of the pro-life movement. It accuses the NRLC as compromising on abortion by not insisting on a human life amendment that prohibits all abortions, including those performed to save the mother's life, and for supporting the so-called Hatch Amendment that would have returned the question of abortion to the state legislatures. ALL criticizes the American Bishops' National Committee for a Human Life Amendment for its compromising tendencies, as well as for linking opposition to abortion to other issues, such as the arms race and poverty, which ALL claims dilutes pro-life voting strength.[6] A main ideological foe of ALL is "secular humanism." The ALL agenda supports prayer in the school and attacks on sex education, issues never mentioned by the NRLC which steadfastly characterizes abortion as a moral issue without explicit religious implications. ALL claims a membership of about 2 million but it has no national convention, no formal state offices and exists largely as the ideological antiabortion center of fundamentalist Protestants and Catholics unsympathetic to both economic and theological liberalism. Their slant is clearly conservative in economic terms as well, with frequent criticisms of economic liberalism and of those who criticize American nuclear policy. In

1978 Paul Brown, Judy Brown's husband, started an independent political action committee called Life Amendment Political Action Committee. By 1985 LAPAC had been transferred to Rick Woodrow and was no longer associated with the American Life League. ALL has not successfully challenged the central position of the NRLC.

If the National Right-to-Life Committee, in terms of the usual sociopolitical labels, represents a centrist position in the right-to-life movement, and the American Life Lobby its right wing, there are several groups clearly on the left.

Prolifers for Survival was founded in 1979 to bridge, in the name of the sanctity of human life, the peace and prolife movements. It had a membership of about 2000 and opposed both legal abortion (but favored no specific legislation) and the arms race. Prolifers for Survival's membership included, among others, Quakers, Catholic Worker members, Jews, and Protestants.

Also on the left are Evangelicals for Social Action, JustLife, and Feminists for Life. These groups, if they must be characterized quickly, are religious "left" groups. They espouse a radical critique of American society that embraces most of the piecemeal reform efforts endorsed by political liberals but they include more searching criticisms of American foreign policy (which they describe as militarist) and critiques of the lack of generosity toward the poor they find in Democratic as well as Republican policies.

The number of active and independent pro-life groups is not easy to list with certainty. They include the Ad Hoc Committee in Defense of Life, started by James McFadden, associated with *The National Review* and editor of the *Human Life Review,* the U.S. Coalition for Life in Pittsburgh, Pennsylvania; Democrats for Life, Inc.; Families for Life in Southern Long Island, the independent National March for Life directed by Nellie Gray; Americans United For Life, a Chicago based pro-life legal aid organization: the National Pro-life Action League, started by Joseph Scheidler who promotes nonviolent direct action against clinics; Human Life International, run by Rev. Paul Marx; Libertarians for Life, directed by Doris Gordon, and many more. A direct action group called "Operation Rescue" came into prominence in 1988. These groups and their positions cannot be adequately described here but they illustrate the many independent centers of antiabortion activity and the wide variety of tactics and understandings of the issue.

Perhaps a significant aspect of the right-to-life movement is that it has, so far, no charismatic person who attracts a personal allegiance among most pro-life activists. Only the issue of the termination of fetal life is charismatic. For a proper analysis of social movements, this one at least and probably others, more attention should be paid to the organizing and binding power of deeply held moral conceptions among ordinary people.

THE ALTERED ROLE OF ROMAN CATHOLICISM

A word must be said about explicitly religious pro-life activity. At one time the Catholic Church occupied a singular position in the opposition to legal abortion, but its centrality has been considerably lessened and its role has changed over time. The strategies adopted by the Catholic Bishops, especially their emphasis on a "consistent ethic" approach to abortion, and their support of the unsuccessful 1983 "Hatch" amendment that would have returned the question of abortion to the state legislatures, have deeply divided the right-to-life movement. The Catholic Church retains its own internal structures in the right-to-life movement which include the Bishops' Pro-life Action Committee, which sponsors educational material as part of its "Respect Life" program. It also sponsors the separately incorporated National Committee for a Human Life Amendment (NCHLA) which is financed mainly through donations from individual bishops and which actively lobbies in support of various pro-life legislation. The NCHLA through its "Life Roll Card Project," the collection of names, mostly through parish organizations, of those favoring a human life amendment, has organized "congressional district action committees" in 217 of the approximately 435 U.S. Congressional Districts to lobby for antiabortion legislation on the local and state levels. In 1982 the NCHLA claimed that it had enrolled more than three million as members of these local pro-life action groups. From the start both the National Committee for a Human Life Amendment and the Bishops Pro-life Committee endorsed what came to be called the "consistent ethic" or "seamless garment" approach to pro-life issues, linking opposition to abortion with support for antipoverty measures, reduced military expenditures, higher welfare supports and opposition to the death sentence. In terms of this combination of ethical conservatism and progressive social teaching, the Catholic presence in the right-to-life movement has caused internal conflict (especially in Bishops' support of the unsuccessful 1983 Hatch Amendment). The Bishops have been particularly criticized by the American Life League and those who endorse only a human life amendment that prohibits all abortions. By returning the question of abortion to the state legislatures, the Hatch amendment in effect conceded, since not all states would prohibit all abortions, that an abortion law prohibiting all abortions is not achievable without major changes in American culture and society.

Protestantism and the Right-To-Life Movement

The relationship between Protestant denominational families and the right-to-life movement is not easy to summarize. While it is true that the theologically liberal denominations such as the Methodists, Episcopalians, United Church of Christ, and Presbyterians, favored Roe, they did so generally in the context of maintaining that abortion remained a grave moral matter but that in some cases, the "tragic" cases, abortion was the lesser of two evils. They also argued that respect for conscience and for pluralism called for the legal acceptance of abortion. More conservative denominations, such as the Southern Baptist Convention, the Missouri-Synod Lutheran, the Lutheran Church in America, and a great number of fundamentalist and evangelical churches, rejected Roe, but they became politically active only in the mid and late 1970s. In terms of numbers (Nelson 1981; Gallup 1981: "Catholic/Protestant Views are Similar") most Protestants oppose elective abortion and support some restrictions on abortion. An interesting fact about the right-to-life movement is that organized religious opposition to Roe has increased rather than decreased over time. In 1975 the first Evangelical Christian pro-life organization was founded, the Christian Action Council started by Billy Graham, Dr. Harold O. J. Brown, Dr. C. Everett Koop, Mrs. Edith Schaeffer, Dr. Harold Lindsell, and Mrs. Elisabeth Gren. Within each of the liberal Protestant denominations pro-life groups have emerged in opposition to their church's endorsement of Roe. In 1978 Episcopalians for Life reorganized nationally; it had begun in Arizona in the late 1960s. In 1978 Rev. Olga Fairfax formed Methodists for Life; and Lutherans for Life was formed in the same year; in 1979 Presbyterians for Life began; in 1982 Friends for Life began in the United Church of Christ. In no Christian tradition is there an absence of a formal pro-life group protesting the church's acceptance of Roe. Probably the most active grass roots evidence of the ecumenical movement is in the right-to-life movement, joining laity and clergy from across the spectrum of American denominationalism. Numerically, there is nothing comparable to it in the ecumenical movement. It can be said that the pro-life movement represents the most successful example thus far of ecumenism in that individuals of all religious traditions have sought each other out and actively seek to coordinate their activities in ways that the ecumenical movement rarely achieves, although *Bread for the World* and *Habitat for Humanity* represent noteworthy achievements. On October 31, 1985 nine of these groups met at the office of the National Committee for a Human Life Amendment (co-hosted by Candice Mueller of Lutherans for Life) to see how they might further help each other.

SOME OF THE SURPRISING DIMENSIONS OF THE RIGHT-TO-LIFE MOVEMENT AND WHAT IT SUGGESTS FOR SOCIAL MOVEMENT THEORY AND THE SOCIOLOGY OF RELIGION

An interesting aspect of the controversy over abortion is that both the acceptance of legal abortion and opposition to it have increased over time.

The legalization of abortion has brought about a great increase in the number of abortions and has not merely replaced abortions that before Roe were illegal. By the mid-1980s about 16 million abortions were performed nationally, whereas in 1973 there were 615,831. But the right-to-life movement has over this time strengthened and become more stable. The entrance of Evangelical Christians into abortion politics and the formation of pro-life groups within denominations whose leadership had endorsed Roe show social movement vitality rather than decline. So too does the appearance of new social movement organizations that emerged at the end of the 1970s decade, such as Prolifers for Survival, Feminists for Life, Women Exploited by Abortion and Just Life. Public opinion has shifted toward a greater acceptance of legal abortion, but here too opposition to elective abortion shows sustained strength. Those accepting elective abortion—the ruling of Roe—have remained at about 25% of those polled, while those opposed to all legal abortion have remained somewhere around 20%. Most Americans want neither the right-to-life movement nor the proabortion movement to succeed. They want something in between, probably something close to the original reforms recommended by the American Law Institute.[7]

Perhaps the most significant finding in terms of the staying power of the right-to-life movement is that most Americans continue to think of abortion as a moral issue. The 1981 the Connecticut Mutual Life Report on American Values found that 65% in a national sample described abortion as morally wrong. A Yankelovich, Skelly, and White poll for *Life Magazine,* November, 1981, found that 56% described having an abortion as morally wrong. Over 40% of Americans in some polls have even been found to agree that abortion is murder (Harris Poll of June 1970; ABC News/Harris Survey, March 7, 1977; Yankelovich, Skelly, and White poll of November 7, 1977; for a summary, see Adamek 1982) as opposed to weaker descriptions, such as the termination of developing life. Although their different wordings make them difficult to briefly summarize, polls show (see Adamek, 1982) that a large majority of Americans think that life begins either at conception or within the first trimester. The most obvious reason for the staying power of the right-to-life movement is that the principle it proclaims is widely believed: simply, that abortion stops a human life and that this is a morally grave matter. Moreover, this belief, especially when supported visually by pictures of aborted fetuses after the first trimester, when the human features of the fetus are unmistakable, and films such as "The Silent Scream" that show fetal pain during abortion, make it likely that opposition to Roe will not in time evaporate. But it does not mean that the right-to-life movement will achieve its stated goal.

WHY THE RIGHT-TO-LIFE MOVEMENT IS LIKELY TO REMAIN VITAL WITHOUT ACHIEVING POLITICAL VICTORY

A main reason why the right-to-life movement is unlikely to achieve a political victory is that the majority of political and cultural elites favor elective abortion. Polls show that the highest support for legal abortion comes from the affluent and the well educated. Elites generally favor legal abortion and the relationship between abortion and welfare costs are too obvious to ignore. It is not without significance that the Presidential Commission on Population Control and the American Future, chaired by Governor Nelson Rockefeller, recommended that elective abortion be considered as a means of birth control. The first known call for legalized abortion was made in 1915 in a publication of the Malthusian League that held that overpopulation was the chief cause of poverty (Francome 1984, p. 64). The first argument offered in Congress (June 24, 1976) against the Hyde amendments that restrict medicaid funding of abortion was that the amendments would cost the government between $450 and $565 million dollars a year in increased welfare payments. There is a receptive public for such arguments. A Newsweek Poll found that 70% thought that if abortions were made illegal "welfare costs would rise to pay for unwanted children of the poor" (*Newsweek,* January 14, 1985, p. 23).

While the first abortion law reformers made the case for liberalizing the laws in terms of the "tragic cases" and did not deny the traditional moral status granted the fetus as a developing human life, there have been ideological formulations that have dissolved this tension. Dominant feminist groups define abortion as an essential element of equality (Luker 1984, Chapter 7) and interpret opposition to legal abortion as opposition to women's equality. Another powerful ideological support comes from the congruence of arguments for elective abortion with what has come to be the basic tenet of liberalism. The tenet states that the state has no competence to mediate on questions of ultimate meaning or the good life and exists solely to protect an order within which individuals might define for themselves their conceptions of the meaning of life. The confluence of these powerful cultural and social forces—dominant feminist ideology, the individualism and agnostism of dominant philosophical liberalism, and the Malthusian explanations of poverty among economic elites—make likely the permanent defeat of the major goal of the right-to-life movement, a human life amendment prohibiting all abortions. There are also aspects of traditional moral thought that make a pro-life legal victory unlikely, especially arguments based on maternal health.

Legal abortion is consistent with the dominant ethos of liberalism and congruent with Malthusian conceptions of poverty. But legal abortion for those cases described as "hard" or "tragic," including the mother's health and rape and incest, have received moral analyses that are also congruent with traditional ethics. Simply put, these analyses argue that other values besides biological life are part of moral analyses, and that at least until the fetus is clearly a human being with some consciousness it need not to be accorded a moral claim equal to that of its mother's. But it should be noted that these claims are made with some disquietude, as the point when fetal consciousness of pain exists is difficult to establish, and even the point of viability is now somewhere at the end of the second trimester. The fact that some moral philosophers have openly acknowledged that the arguments for abortion are capable of extension to infanticide make many uneasy. In terms of traditional ethical categories, the most persuasive argument for opposing efforts to overthrow Roe is that abortions would simply continue and that some of them would be unsafe and cause maternal death. Finally, a law prohibiting all abortions would be unenforceable. While these factors make right-to-life success unlikely, they do not make the movement's declension likely. And this prompts the analyst to examine what sort of role a movement that persists without succeeding might have in society and culture.

A LIKELY ROLE OF THE RIGHT-TO-LIFE MOVEMENT IN AMERICAN SOCIETY

While the right-to-life movement is not likely to succeed in its stated goal of making all abortion illegal, it is likely to continue and with some vitality. It is also likely to make some contributions to American culture that can be characterized as progressive even by those who do not share its manifest goal of reversing Roe. Not to see these progressive elements leads not only to mistaken analyses of the right-to-life movement, but these distortions in turn undermine continuing efforts to think beyond abortion polarities and toward more constructive policy possibilities (Erdahl 1986).

It is hard to think of the right-to-life movement as a single issue movement as "progressive" in that it seems to exist solely to make abortion illegal and to return the law and public opinion about abortion to what it had been before the late 1960s, while explicitly challenging or directly changing no other part of contemporary society. This not especially likely accomplishment would thus seem to promise only to reinstate the protection of fetal life. But by solely retrieving a legal ban on abortion, or restricting some or many of them, pro-life success as commonly described would seem to represent a stride backwards toward a renewed evaluation of fetal life but no similar stride forward in terms of the classical motivating aspirations of Western life toward liberty, equality and fraternity. As it is usually presented, the right-to-life movement evokes enthusiastic response mostly from those who identify strongly with traditional Christian ethics and so to others seems to represent a movement of moral nostalgia, an attempt to return to an irrecoverable past. Indeed, if the right-to-life movement were to succeed it would, for the first time in our history, include the notion of moral retrieval in our notion of progress. Perhaps this above all separates pro-life moral impulses from classical liberalism which, in its notion of greater individual freedom, never explicitly included in its notion of progress the task of conserving moral tradition. Such a moral retrieval seems blocked by forces far stronger than whatever evocative power of moral traditionalism the pro-life movement can translate into political strength. After all, once invented and widely available the techniques of abortion are not likely to be lost even if legally prohibited. If women chose to use them rather than bring their unwanted pregnancies to term, there seems little that pro-lifers or government could do. Even in pre-Roe times no women who aborted, as opposed to the abortionist, was tried or convicted for a crime. Indeed, no pro-life organization has suggested that if a human life amendment were passed that women obtaining illegal abortions should be prosecuted under criminal law. Only the abortionist, they say, should be liable to criminal charges, just as it was in the past.[8]

The Latent Egalitarianism of Pro-life Arguments

Pro-life organizations most frequently restrict themselves to the claim that the principle they defend is foundational for any humane society. Typically they do not give much attention to showing how the illegality of abortion would specifically connect with other aspirations of the good society. To others, the right-to-life movement seems at best a defense of moral limits to technology. Yet a striking fact about the arguments of the right-to-life movement is that they are radically egalitarian, and it is this aspect of the right-to-life movement, not much commented on, that warrants closer inspection in terms of its strength as a social movement. There is a clear universalism in the right-to-life movement's objection to all abortions, whether by welfare parents, minorities, or white women, and pro-life objections to government funding of abortion includes foreign population aid even to countries commonly identified as ideological foes of American interests, such as China. On nationalist premises anything that reduces the population size of a potential enemy is a political good. Right-to-life activists place principle before national security or national affluence. This aspect of the right-to-life movement has some cultural and political significance.

THE EGALITARIAN BASES OF THE RIGHT-TO-LIFE MOVEMENT AND ITS PROGRESSIVE ROLE AS ASSERTING LIMITS TO TECHNOLOGY

The main argument of the right-to-life movement is strikingly simple and central to Western moral categories: Each human life is singularly important and cannot be morally subordinated to the self-interests of those who are more powerful. This principle resonates not merely with Judeo-Christian sentiments but also with putatively rational presentations of the foundations of the moral life, such as the Kantian imperative. This premise has far more radical implications than the principle of meritocracy that grounds the moral bases of capitalism and the principle of equal opportunity that largely defines contemporary liberalism. The contrary principle asserted in defense of elective abortion (as opposed to "tragic" case analysis that concedes the supremacy of the right-to-life as a moral principle, but not its universal priority, such as in cases of maternal health) is the "quality of life" standard, which is an unlikely egalitarian moral principle. The "quality of life" ethic, hardly as systematically reflected on as the "sanctity of life" with its rich historical casuistry of just war theory and the principle of double effect (to mention just two core refinements), is far more pliable to manipulation by elites than the principle of the sanctity of human life which has an inherent egalitarian thrust. Quality of life broadly states that the criteria of morality must include not simply questions of biological life but those things that make life worth living. As an ethical consideration, the quality of life emphasis in the abstract can be progressive or regressive. It is progressive when it is used to ground political arguments for raising the standards of living and health for citizens, although these arguments are far more likely to be based on considerations of human dignity than on "quality of life" premises. The quality of life ethic is regressive when used as a measuring device to determine who is worthy of societal interest and who is not, as when neonates with Down's syndrome are denied ordinary medical care because their prospects for a life of sufficient "quality" are judged to be poor. This is not a rare medical practice. Some isolated cases of withholding treatment from handicapped infants have received wide publicity, especially the April 9, 1982 death by dehydration of the Bloomington, Indiana "Baby Doe" case and the October 1983 "Baby Jane Doe" Case, Port Jefferson, Long Island, when the parents initially elected not to have their spina bifida child's hydrocephalus surgically treated. But the general public is probably unaware of the extent of the nontreatment of handicapped neonates including those with good chances of survival.[9]

The October 1981 report of The Hastings Center described passive euthanasia as a common practice in hospital nurseries. Turnbull (1986, pp. 363-389) describes the difficulty in data collection but concludes that there are sound reasons to think that the number of newborns denied life-saving medical treatment is "in the several thousands each year. . . it is common in the United States to withhold routine surgery and medical care from infants with Down syndrome for the explicit purpose of hastening death." The 1984 U.S. Commission on Civil Rights and the 1983 Senate Committee on labor and Human Resources reported that the withholding of life-saving medical treatment from infants solely because they are handicapped is "not isolated to one or two instances" (Turnbull 1986). It is worth noting that since legal abortion began philosophical justification for infanticide have appeared with some regularity (Tooley 1972, 1974; Singer 1983).

An attempt to formalize the reasoning used by physicians and others in quality of life decisions regarding the nontreatment of handicapped neonates has been attempted by Dr. Anthony Shaw (1977) and has been widely cited in pro-life publications. Shaw's formula is $QL = NE$ multiplied by $(H+S)$, where quality of life equals natural endowment (including physical and intellectual potential) times the sum of the contributions made to the child by his home and family plus the contributions made by society, namely the community's willingness to contribute to the costs associated with a handicapped citizen.

Any general application of "quality of life" as an ethical norm grants enormous power to those who make decisions and who calculate and weigh such intangible and class-influenced variables as "probable" family and social contributions and "natural" endowment. A quality of life ethic constrains the class biases of elites and professionals far less than a sanctity of life ethic, and thus immeasurably increases the amplitude of how the more powerful can treat the more vulnerable, including neonates, the incurably sick and the senile. Those who decide are those, obviously, in positions to decide and represent elites in the major institutional domains of society. In such calculations it is likely that criteria of efficiency will increasingly be dominant. A quality of life norm is likely to carry the modes of thinking representative of bureaucracy, that is, instrumental rationality (what works best to achieve the single goal of the organization, increased profits and market control), into domains that previously excluded it on the grounds that core values of human life precluded market criteria. It is not without significance that eugenics played an important role in the early stages of the population control movement (Kennedy 1976, p. 115; Francome 1984, pp. 64-65) and the contemporary use of eugenic arguments in the attempt to extend the logic of abortion to neonates is roughly similar. Two Nobel laureates, without using the term, have publicly promoted infanticide. In *Time* Magazine (May 28, 1973) James Watson declared that "if a child were not declared alive until three days after birth, then all parents could be allowed the choice only a few are given under the present system." In January 1978 Francis Crick was quoted in the Pacific News Service as saying that "no newborn infant should be declared human until it has passed certain tests regarding its genetic endowment and that if it fails these tests, it forfeits the right to live."

It is probably not simply coincidental that opponents of legal abortion and euthanasia are likely to be poorer and less educated (and therefore nonelites) than supporters of abortion rights and euthanasia. Elites are accustomed to thinking that they will make decisions or have the power to veto decisions, while the nonelite are those who have decisions made about them and which they are not likely to negate. The intrinsic egalitarianism of the sanctity of human life ethic—there are no gradations demarking lives as more sacred than others; they are simply "sacred"—is a safer principle for nonelites than is the quality of life ethic. The lives of nonelites have typically been characterized as possessing low quality and their children thought of as unlikely contributors to higher stages of civilization. The great numbers of unmarried minority women with children on welfare greatly reduces the likelihood that the "quality of life" ethic would be used as a premise grounding political arguments for improved welfare measures. The sanctity of life ethic, on the other hand, entails the promotion of human welfare after birth, as those in the right-to-life movement articulating a "consistent ethic" approach have emphasized.

Objections to the Argument that Pro-life Positions Contain Egalitarian Themes

It might be argued that while in principle the core arguments of the right-to-life movement are egalitarian and progressive, in practice to right-to-life movement is either repressive or regressive, seeking to criminalize abortion and constrain nontraditional kinds of sexual activity. Current criticisms of the New Right employ charges of this sort. The universalism and the egalitarianism of right-to-life positions are thus reduced to ideology, to fabricated ideals used to mask a deeper but not publicly acknowledgeable animus against women's equality and changing sexual mores. But such a dismissal of the actual positions of the right-to-life groups overlooks not merely the pro-life organizations that do espouse a consistent ethic approach (the Catholic Bishops, American Citizens Concerned for Life, Just Life, Prolifers for Survival, Feminists for Life) but it also ignores details of the history of the right-to-life movement. The first directly political venture (beyond lobbying) within the right-to-life movement was an attempt to influence not the Republican Party, where it was thought that economic conservatives would see abortion as a useful means of controlling minority births, but the Democratic Party. In 1976, to force a consideration of the abortion issue, Ellen McCormick of the "Women for the Unborn" in Bellmore, Long Island sought the Democratic Party's nomination for the presidency and ran in several state primaries. Interviews with right-to-life pioneers show that almost half were Democrats (Leahy 1982, pp. 67-68; Kelly 1981, p. 656). All right-to-life groups acknowledge that opposing abortion also requires efforts to help mothers and children, and the approximately three thousand emergency pregnancy centers show a recognition that sanctity of life arguments include quality of life dimensions. Right-to-life activists are also found to support social and health programs, such as medicaid, job training, and increased welfare measures, that promote the welfare of mothers and children. While the National Right-to-Life

Committee takes no position on these issues, and the conservative politics of the American Life League's directors probably limit their enthusiasm for such political "liberalism," other groups, including American Citizens Concerned for Life, the Catholic Bishops, Evangelicals for Social Action, Prolifers for Survival and Feminists for Life, actively support these programs. It is of some significance that no pro-life group or publication has ever criticized welfare payments or efforts to increase them, not even the American Life League.

While there were and are clear indications in the right-to-life movement that the egalitarian implications about the sanctity of life were taken seriously and not simply used to make a repressive and regressive ideology, no dominant secular left political or cultural constituencies opened themselves to right-to-life groups. Since 1980 the Republican Party dominated by Ronald Reagan courted right-to-life organizations in a successful attempt to attract voters who did not otherwise share the economic priorities of the corporate elites who largely shape Republican economic policies. And the Reagan and Republican efforts to nominate judges, and especially Supreme Court Justices who follow a legal philosophy entailing a "hermeneutic of original intent," and thus are likely to restrict the use of the 14th Amendment to extend the scope of constitutional protection, have further lessened the likelihood that the egalitarian implications of right-to-life arguments would explicitly link with the traditional concern of the American left toward more equal distribution of wealth and resources.

THE NOTION OF A PERMANENT STATE OF NASCENCE

In terms of the content of right-to-life arguments, the chronology of the right to life movement and the tendency of social movements—including the pro-choice movement—to seek "the establishment of a new orthodoxy" (Back 1986, p. 3), it makes empirical and moral sense to think of the right-to-life movement as one that most Americans wish neither to succeed nor to fail. Lacking convincing alternatives to the likely problem of noncompliance with any total ban on abortion and failing to persuade most Americans that the ethic of the sanctity of life applies to the "tragic" cases of rape, incest and fetal deformity, most Americans do not agree with the stated goals of right-to-life organizations—a human life amendment banning all abortions (save those exceedingly rare cases where a mother's life is at stake). But most Americans do not wish to see elective abortion viewed as a matter of moral indifference, as merely an issue of choice and technology, which is the goal of pro-choice groups. The majority of Americans, including many of those favoring its legality, continue to think of abortion as immoral. While right-to-life groups are not likely to attract widespread support from dominant elites in American society—the ethos of individualism coupled with the interest in controlling the births of the economically unproductive is likely to ensure this (Francome 1984,

p. 210)—they are very capable of continuing as a vital marginal force in American politics and culture. It should be stressed that marginal in this context means something stronger than "tangential." The practice of selective treatment of neonates—including passive euthanasia—and the fears that passive euthanasia for the incurable (especially the elderly) will be powerfully affected by institutional finances and market criteria will give increasing plausibility to the pro-life contention that the principle of the sanctity of human life requires in our culture specific groups that monitor political, medical, legal, and economic elites who assert the priority of a "quality of life" ethic. In these terms an appropriate way to place the right-to-life movement within social movement theory is that it is a countervailing movement whose unintended permanent nascency contributes to the progressive egalitarian and pluralism that its critics claim it undermines. Because the right-to-life movement is rarely analyzed in terms other than the stereotypes associated with abortion polemics and politics, the constructive role this movement plays in blocking the diffusion of the instrumental rationality of dominant economic and political elites is insufficiently noted. Perhaps the notion of a "permanently nascent social movement" will free more observers to inspect more clearly the cultural significance of the right to life movement.[10]

NOTES

1.   I have interviewed leaders of the Religious Coalition of Abortion Rights, but these interviews are not reported here. I do, however cite representative pro-choice literature.

2.   In 1979 the Planned Parenthood Association in Chicago and Denver distributed to editors of college newspapers cartoons that included a Catholic bishop holding matches and a can of gasoline and saying that "the church is not worried about abortion because we've got the faithful out burning down the clinics." The Planned Parenthood material explained the cartoons by describing the Roman Catholic Church as seeking "to control other people through sex" (Beck 1978).

3.   Leahy found only three of his sample had been solicited by a religious leader to join an antiabortion group. Kelly (1981, p. 659) and Luker (1984, p. 133) found that personal experience (the experience of pregnancy, a miscarriage) far outweighed religious teaching in the mobilization of pro-life activists.

4.   While it is often cited as showing that laws against abortion were an innovation, and prompted by the status interest of professionally educated doctors seeking a monopoly against competing self-educated doctors, James C. Mohr's widely cited *Abortion in America* (1978, p. 35-37) acknowledges that these efforts started when the biology of the time made it clear that human life began at conception and not, as folklore placed it, at quickening. The first American Medical Association Committee on Abortion, appointed in May, 1857, gave as the first reason for abortion the "belief even among mothers themselves that the fetus is not alive till after the period of quickening."

5.   On the back of the front cover of *Abortion II* (1973) Lawrence Lader, a founder of the National Association for the Repeal of Abortion Laws, wrote, "It came like a thunderbolt . . . (Roe) was even more conclusive than any of us had dared to hope."

6.   Judy Brown and her husband Paul, who started the Life Amendment Political Action Committee, are Roman Catholic.

7.   There have been hundreds of polls about abortion or which have included questions about it. In all polling the wording of the question makes a substantial difference in the response, and this is certainly true about abortion. For example, a New York Times/ CBS poll (*New York Times,* August 18, 1980) asked in a national survey "Do you think there should be an amendment to the Constitution prohibiting abortions" and only 29% said yes; but when the *same* respondents were later asked, "Do you believe there should be an amendment to the Constitution protecting the life of the unborn child?," 50% said yes. In her recent summary of these surveys Lamanna (Callahan and Callahan 1984, p. 1-23) described these poll results as "consistent across researchers and time periods." The 55% of the American people who neither oppose nor approve of all abortions are more likely to approve of legal abortion for reasons of physical and mental health, rape and incest, and deformed fetus; they are not so likely to approve of legal abortion for financial reasons or cases of convenience. Most Americans approve of abortion (except in cases of maternal health) only in the first trimester. The majority of Americans support abortion in the *second* trimester only when the mother's physical health is endangered. Lamanna interprets these data as indicating a consensus (Callahan and Callahan 1984, pp. 6-7) in that three quarters of the American public favor abortion in at least some circumstances. But, she adds, "it is not a consensus in support of *Roe* v. *Wade,* that is, of elective abortion . . . Only about 25% support abortion as defined in *Roe* v. *Wade.*" Moreover, the increase in approval for abortion that followed Roe ceased by the late 1970s. In particular, fundamentalist Protestant and Baptist groups became less favorable toward legal abortion (Blake and del Pinal 1980, pp. 29-56.)

8.   A constant dilemma for the right-to-life movement has always been the question of the likely noncompliance with any future prohibitions of abortion, and comparisons are often drawn with prohibition. The argument that laws that cannot be enforced are bad laws is a traditional one, and especially applies in the case of abortion where images of "back-alley" abortions are quickly introduced. (The standard pro-life answer is that the law will be, for the most part, respected, and that the deaths from illegal abortion had diminished to about 50 per year in the years preceding Roe, due to advances in abortion technology and antibiotics.) But abortion technology continues to advance and promises to make noncompliance with any possible future abortion ban even less enforceable than in pre-Roe times. For example, right-to-life spokespersons have recognized that "chemical" abortions by ingestion of progesterone-blocking pills are presently being tested (Richard D. Glasow, Ph.D., "Omen of the Future?: The Abortion Pill RU-486.) While these pills have received little clinical testing there is considerable expectation that they will eventually be developed and perhaps replace many if not most of the abortions currently being performed in the first two weeks of pregnancy—about 80% of all abortions. Pro-life activists have claimed some success in blocking American Companies from manufacturing prostaglandin suppositories (Willke, *NRLC News,* July 31, 1986, p. 3). A pro-life boycott of Upjohn products and a demonstration at the Kalamazoo, Michigan Upjohn headquarters in the Summer of 1986 were associated by pro-life activists with Upjohn's decision not to market its postaglandin suppository "Meteneprost." But newer products— such as the French Company Roussel-Uclaf's RU 486—differ from prostaglanding suppositories in major ways: it is a pill, its side effects seem less severe, and it causes abortion by creating a hostile environment for implantation rather than by causing uterine contractions which prematurely expel a fetus. They can be taken without knowing for certain if conception has occurred. The fact that the pills can be taken either once a month or simply when contraceptive failure is suspected means that a woman need not be sure that she is pregnant. And since opinion polls have long shown that early abortions are judged less seriously than late abortions-when the human features of the fetus are obvious-there might be a more receptive public response to these abortifacient pills than to protaglandin suppositories that expel fetuses by inducing labor. There are also therapeutic uses for some of these drugs (including treatment of breast cancer, brain tumors and a disorder of the adrenal gland called Cushing's Syndrome) which make likely their eventual production.

9.   There is a vast right-to-life literature that cautions about the extension of the reasoning involved in justifying legal abortion to new-borns and attempts to document the practice of

infanticide and selective nontreatment of handicapped neonates. (See, for example, "Primum Non-Nocere" 1982; Quay 1980; Horan and Mall 1980; Horan and Delahoyde 1982; Stanton 1982.)

10.   The description of pro-life activists as fanatic and absolutist is common and prevents a genuine analysis of their positions. I think anyone who reads their literature about euthanasia and infanticide, for example, will be impressed by the subtlety of their reasoning and the lack of any doctrinaire "biologism." These pro-life authors do not endorse a maximalist position on treating handicapped infants or babies born prematurely, or with less than 700 grams weight. They do not argue that everything possible be done to keep these infants alive as long as possible. They insist only that the medical treatment be based on the best interest of the infant rather than on criteria based on cost efficiency or parental desire. They point out that the "quality of life" formula suggested by Shaw—and widely followed—(quality of life equals natural endowment times parent and societal resources) includes the economic resources of the parents and the availability of social agencies, and thus discriminates against the children of poorer parents. Class bias in the diagnoses of the handicapped children of the poor need not be conscious and no cases of coerced nontreatment are recorded; but in terms of counselling and expert recommendations, poor parents are not likely to realize that nonmedical criteria such as their income and their intellectual capabilities, as judged by professionals, were taken into account. Given the great costs associated with the right-to-life position that every handicapped neonate be given the care that nonhandicapped children are given, one might expect that they also argue for a system of medical care, we would have to call it "socialized medicine," that removes medical care from the logic of the market place. But this connection is not drawn. Pro-life doctors and lawyers, thus far, represent the extension of the civil rights thinking of liberal democratic ideology into areas abandoned by mainstream liberalism.

REFERENCES

Adamek, R. 1982. *Abortion and Public Opinion in the United States*. The National Right to Life Educational Fund, Washington, DC.

Back, K. W. 1986. "The Logic of Socially Innovative Movements." Paper presented at the meeting of the American Sociological Association.

Beck, J. 1978. "A Tasteless Anti-Church Tirade." *Chicago Tribune*, March 1.

Blake, J. and J. H. del Pinal. 1980. "Predicting Polar Attitudes Toward Abortion in the United States." In *Abortion Parley*, edited by J. T. Burtchael. Kansas City, MO: Andrews & McMeel.

Burtchaell, J. T. 1982. *Rachel Weeping*. New York: Andrews and McMeel.

Callahan, S., and D. Callahan, eds. 1984. *Abortion: Understanding Differences*. New York: Plenum.

Connecticut Mutual Life Insurance Company. 1981. *Connecticut Mutual Respect Life Report on American Values*. Hartford, CT: CMLIC.

Erdahl, L. O. 1986. *Pro-Life/Pro-Peace*. Minneapolis, MN. Augsburg.

Francome, C. 1984. *Abortion Freedom*. Winchester, MA: Allen and Unwin.

Freeman, J. 1973. "The Origins of the Women's Life Movement." *American Journal of Sociology* 78:792-811.

Gallup, G. 1981. *Religion in America 1979-1980*. Princeton, NJ: Princeton Religious Research Center.

Glasow, R. D. 1986. *Omen of the Future?: The Abortion Pill RU-486*. Washington, DC: The National Right-to-Life Committee.

Granberg, D. and B. W. Granberg. 1981. "Social Bases of Support and Opposition to Legalized Abortion." Columbia: University of Missouri, Center for Research in Social Behavior.

Hall, E. J. 1986. "Religious Conservatism and Abortion Attitudes: Some Unexpected Findings." Paper presented at the meeting of the Eastern Sociological Society, April.

Horan, D. and D. Mall, eds. 1980. *Death, Dying and Euthanasia.* Frederick, MD: University Publications of America.

Jelen, T. G. 1984. "Respect for Life, Sexual Morality, and Opposition to Abortion." *Review of Religious Research* 25:220-231.

Kandermans, B. 1984. "Mobilization and Participation: Social-Psyhological Expansions of Resource Mobilization Theory." *American Sociological Review* 49:583-600.

Kelly, J.R. 1981. "Beyond The Stereotypes: Interviews with Right-To-Life Pioneers." *Commonweal,* November 20: 654-659.

Kennedy, D. 1976. *Birth Control in America.* New Haven, CT: Yale University Press.

Killian, L. M. 1984. "Organization, Rationality and Spontaneity in The Civil Rights Movement." *American Sociological Review* 49:770-783.

Lader, L. 1973. *Abortion 11: Making the Revolution.* Boston, MA: Beacon.

Lamanna, M. A. 1984. "Social Science and Ethical Issues: The Policy Implications of Poll Data on Abortion." In *Abortion: Understanding Differences,* edited by S. and D. Callahan. New York: Plenum.

Leahy, P. J. (1976) 1982. *The Anti-Abortion Movement.* Unpublished doctoral dissertation, Syracuse University.

Luker, K. 1984. *Abortion and The Politics of Motherhood.* Berkeley, CA: University of California Press.

Mohr, J. C. 1978. *Abortion in America.* New York: Oxford University Press.

Nathanson, B. N. 1983. *The Abortion Papers.* New York: Frederick Fell.

Nelson, R. J. 1981. "The Divided Mind of Protestant Christians." In *New Perspectives on Human Abortion,* edited by T. W. Marzen, D. J. Horan, and D. Mall. Frederick, MD: University Publications of America.

Primum Non-Nocere. 1982. 3, (2).

Quay, E. A. 1980. *And Now Infanticide.* Thaxton, VA: Sun Life.

Shaw, A. 1977. "Defining the Quality of Life." *Hastings Report* 7(2).

Simpson, J. H. 1985. "Status Inconsistency and Moral Issues." *Journal for the Scientific Study of Religion* 24:119-236.

Singer, P. 1983. "Sanctity of Life or Quality of Life?" *Pediatrics* 72:128.

Stanton, J. 1983. *Infanticide.* Chicago: Americans United for Life.

Tooley, M. 1974. "Abortion and Infanticide." In *The Rights And Wrongs of Abortion,* edited by M. Cohen, T. Nagel, and T. Scanlon. Princeton, NJ: Princeton University Press.

―――――. 1983. *Abortion and Infanticide.* New York: Oxford University Press.

Turnbull, H. R. 1986. "Incidence of Infanticide in America." *Issues in Law and Medcine* 1(5):363-389.

Willke, J.C. 1986. "From the President's Desk." *The National Right to Life News* (July 31): 3.

Wood, M. and M. Hughes. 1984. "The Moral Basis of Moral Reform: Status Discontent vs. Culture and Socialization as Explanations of Anti-Pornography Social Movement Adherence." *American Sociological Review* 49:86-99.

THE FALWELL ISSUE AGENDA:

SOURCES OF SUPPORT AMONG WHITE PROTESTANT EVANGELICALS

Lyman A. Kellstedt

ABSTRACT

This paper examines sources of support for the Christian Right by a focus on an issue agenda called the Falwell platform. The issue agenda is consistent with issue positions identified in the writings of Jerry Falwell and includes the so-called "social" issues (school prayer, women's issues, abortion, sex education, homosexuality) along with issues of national defense, and support for the State of Israel. Attitudes toward this platform are examined in data from a national sample of 1,000 evangelicals collected in 1983. Support among white Protestant Evangelicals is greatest among lower status groups, Pentecostals and Fundamentalists, frequent viewers of religious television, those for whom religion and politics are closely linked, and among ideological conservatives and Republican Party identifiers. Strong advocates of the Falwell platform are found to be active participants in the political process and Reagan voters in 1984. Some implications for further study of the Christian Right are explored.

Research in the Social Scientific Study of Religion, Volume 1, pages 109-132.
ISBN: 0-89232-882-7

INTRODUCTION

In the area of religion and politics, it has been the so-called Christian right that has occupied the attention of political pundits and more serious scholarly efforts in the past few years. Some academic attention has been given to its social/demographic base (cf. Liebman and Wuthnow 1983; Bromley and Shupe 1984). Other scholars have tried to evaluate its political impact (Brudney and Copeland 1984; Hood and Morris 1985; Johnson and Tamney 1982; Johnson and Tamney 1985; Johnson 1986; Lipset and Raab 1981; Miller and Wattenberg 1984; Pierard, 1985; Simpson 1985a; Wilcox 1986b). Less attention has been given to its policy base (but see Simpson 1983, 1984, 1985a, b; Yinger and Cutler 1984). Generally, it is assumed that issues such as abortion, school prayer, pornography, homosexuality, and women's rights form the core of the agenda of the Christian right—the so-called social issues.

This research begins with a related, but somewhat different, focus, with the writings of the leading figure of the Christian right, Jerry Falwell. An attempt is made to identify a policy agenda in his writings. Then a national sample of Evangelicals is used to investigate levels of support for that agenda, and to see if these policy positions are tied together in some coherent fashion. If such a set of consistent policy attitudes can be found to exist, what variables do the best job of predicting such attitudes? What about the impact of such political variables as ideology or partisanship, or the impact of various religious beliefs and practices? Are the policy attitudes linked to certain socio-demographic factors such as region, age, sex, income, or education? And are these policy attitudes related to levels of political activity and support for parties and candidates? These questions serve as the foci for this paper.

Jerry Falwell provides a blueprint of his plans in his speeches and writings. The latter provide a rather systematic exposition of his viewpoints (Falwell 1980, 1981). One scholar, in particular, has done a thorough analysis of Falwell's writings and has identified a sociopolitical platform he labels the "Falwell core" (Stockton 1984, 1985). The platform contains the following planks:

1. America is a covenant nation blessed by God, but it has strayed from its roots and must return to righteousness.
2. The family is God ordained. Any institution or program that is anti-family must be opposed; feminist ideology and organizations, and ERA are anti-family and, as a result, must be resisted.
3. The open expression of sexuality in books, magazines, movies and on television is a major problem and must be rooted out.
4. Homosexuality is wrong and its organizational supporters, the gay rights' movement, must be opposed.
5. Abortion is evil and efforts must be mounted to counter its legal status in the society.

6. The predominantly secular value structure of the public schools must be attacked. Prayer must be returned to the schools. Government support for private religious schools should be encouraged as an alternative to the public schools. Such assistance would include such things as tuition tax credits for parents who send their children to private schools. In addition, the treatment of sex in the public schools and the school curriculum must be monitoried carefully. Textbooks should reflect Godly values, including the creation story alternative in Genesis to the theory of evolution. Finally, in the school area, busing for purposes of racial integration is not desirable.

7. Government should play a minimal role in the economy and social welfare areas except crime, where it should punish criminals firmly and swiftly.

8. Government should provide a strong national defense, especially against the evil force of Communism.

9. The state of Israel should be strongly supported, for Israel is God's chosen people.

10. Racial injustice and world hunger must be opposed. Inclusion of such items on the Falwell agenda may seem surprising, but they are present in the Falwell writings and televison programming (see, for example, Falwell 1986).

11. Active political participation is an obligation for citizens in order to confront the evils previously noted.

Frankly, the Falwell agenda is massive. This paper examines attitudes of white Protestant Evangelicals toward a part of it.

DATA AND METHODS

In order to assess the Falwell platform and its base of support in American society, data was analyzed from a 1983 national telephone survey of 1,000 Evangelicals conducted by the polling organization, Tarrance and Associates, for scholars Stuart Rothenberg and Frank Newport for their book, *The Evangelical Voter* (1984). Random digit dialing techniques were used to select 1,000 respondents who met the following criteria: (1) registered voter; (2) Christian religious preference; (3) an affirmative answer to: "Do you personally believe that Jesus Christ is a real person who lived on this earth and was also the unique son of God?"; and (4) an affirmative answer to one of the following— "And in your opinion, does a person need to personally accept Jesus Christ as his or her savior in order to have eternal salvation and to be saved from eternal hell?" or "Would you call yourself a born-again Christian, that is, have you personally had a conversion experience related to Jesus Christ?"

These particular data are well suited for the proposed analysis for a number of reasons. First, a variety of questions pertaining to the religious beliefs and practices of the respondents are included as well as numerous items concerning their political attitudes and behavior. More important, however, this study contains a number of questions ideally suited as measures of the Falwell platform (see Appendix).

Another advantage of this particular data set is the large number of Evangelicals surveyed. In many national samples, the number of Evangelicals (if they can be identified at all) is often quite small. Here, the large numbers allow us to assess the homogeneity of the evangelical population in terms of its most controversial political manifestation—the Falwell phenomenon.

The proposed data set has limitations as well. First, the sample is restricted to registered voters and as a result to relatively politicized Evangelicals, not necessarily representative of Evangelicals as a whole. In addition, the conceptualization and measurement of "Evangelical" are somewhat limited. As previously noted, to be included as an Evangelical, respondents had to identify as Christians, believe in an historical Jesus, accept Christ as the Son of God, and either believe in Christ as Savior or have had a born again experience. Thirty-five respondents claimed to be born again but did not believe in the necessity of accepting Christ as Savior in order to obtain salvation. An appropriate Christology is believed to be central to evangelical faith; at a minimum this means the necessity of accepting Jesus Christ as Savior in order to obtain eternal life. As a result, these 35 respondents were classified as nonevangelical. Another conceptual difficulty is the failure to include items concerning Biblical inspiration as part of the defining characteristics of the concept "Evangelical" (Hunter 1983, p. 140). The authors include an item concerning the Creation story in the book of Genesis but do not use it to select evangelical respondents. Respondents could choose the Creation story as "literally true" or a "true" interpretation of how God created the world or a third alternative—"man's feelings about how the world may have been created." The latter response is clearly nonevangelical, for it assigns no role to God in the creation (Hunter 1983, p. 140). One hundred and eighty individuals gave this response, while 45 others answered "don't know" or gave "no answer." The white Protestants among these 225 respondents are included as nonevangelicals and are dropped from the bulk of the analysis reported in this paper. Finally, Rothenberg and Newport did not include a proselytizing screen in their definition because, in their view, many Evangelicals never attempt to witness to others (1984, p. 19). (Here, Rothenberg and Newport are in agreement with Hunter [1981, p. 366].) Central to the meaning of evangelicalism is a commitment to evangelism, to spreading the "Good News;" however, it can be concurred that such a commitment need to be conceptualized in terms of behavior or practice. Evangelicals, however, necessarily see the importance of evangelism in the life of the believer and the Church. At a minimum then, evangelicalism involves an appropriate Christology, a God-inspired view of Scripture, and a commitment to evangelism. Although *The Evangelical Voter* does not have multiple measures of these phenomena, its measurement of evangelicalism is better, on face validity grounds, than most other studies. For example, it does allow us to focus on at least one important subgroup within evangelicalism, fundamentalists, because of a fundamentalist self-identification measure that it includes. In sum, the strengths of the survey are greater than the limitations we have just noted. After an initial examination of the sample as a whole, 509 white Protestant Evangelicals are the focus of our attention in this paper.[1]

After brief consideration, Catholics and Blacks are excluded from the remainder of the analysis. Both groups have political, cultural, and religious traditions that are different from white Protestants (cf. Hunter 1983). In addition, the homogeneity of attitude, or lack of same, should be examined within white Protestant evangelicalism where the traditions may not be as diverse as between this group and Catholics and between Blacks and Whites. In particular, this will allow a better assessment of the effects of religious variables on the Falwell phenomenon within a white Protestant context. Next, the theoretical expectations that serve as the guiding focus for this study will be discussed.

THEORETICAL EXPECTATIONS

Although there is research support for a Moral Majority issue agenda (Simpson 1983, 1984) that includes attitudes toward homosexuality, prayer in schools, woman's issues, and abortion, the Falwell agenda is broader and includes such diverse matters as issues of national defense and attitudes toward the State of Israel. Attitudes toward both Jerry Falwell and the Moral Majority should distinguish respondents that support the Falwell issue agenda from those that do not. Thus, respondents that support Falwell and the Moral Majority should be more favorable to school prayer, tuition tax credits, defense spending, and the State of Israel and more negative to the nuclear freeze, ERA, the National Organization of Women, homosexuals, birth control materials in the schools, and abortion than opponents of Falwell and the Moral Majority among white Protestant Evangelicals.

Within white Protestant evangelicalism, where should the greatest support for the Falwell issue agenda come from? Simpson's research would suggest social location and religious denomination as the sources. He argues (1983, p. 195):

> Non-mainline Protestants throughout the land champion the platform of the Moral Majority. High levels of support are found among the aged, rural dwellers, the working and lower classes, and the poorly educated. . . . These results suggest that the farther one

is from the dominant center of American society and the less one possesses of the desiderata
of the society (education, youth, prestige), the more conservative one is in orientation to
the sociomoral platform of the Moral Majority.

Shupe and Stacey (1983, 1984) and Tamney and Johnson (1983, 1985) lean
more to "religious" explanations in trying to account for support for the Moral
Majority. Christian orthodoxy, religiosity (church membership, attendance,
financial contributions, and the like), and religious media attention were all
useful predictors.

In a somewhat different vein, the search begins for an explanation of support
for the Falwell issue agenda in the principle of consistency, congruity, or
balance (Heider 1958; Festinger 1957). The initial premise of this theoretical
approach is that individuals strive to reduce inconsistency and ambiguity in
their attitudes. Applied to this problem, the theory would suggest that doctrinal
positions, denominational or local parish practices, individual religious
practices, religious self-identifications (describing oneself as a fundamentalist,
for example), and social and political attitudes and behaviors should be in
balance. The more intense the commitments in these various areas, the greater
the likelihood of consistency. Thus, for example, the individual who accepts
fundamentalist doctrine (literalist views of Scripture), is a member of a church
that is fundamentalist in denomination, is actively involved in the church in
terms of attendance and voluntary church activity, watches religious televison,
and identifies as a fundamentalist is more likely to accept a Falwell issue agenda
than an individual who falls short in one or more of these areas. And, in
addition, the theory would expect strong supporters of the particular issue
positions to be involved in the political process and supporting candidates who
they perceive to be in favor of their issue agenda. Although the data set is not
ideal for testing the model with any degree of finality, these expectations will
be considered in the next section.

DATA ANALYSIS

The first question to answer in the analysis is whether we can identify a Falwell
issue agenda or platform. As previously noted, *The Evangelical Voter* data
set included numerous items that measure the policy positions that Falwell
espouses. (Exact wording of the items can be found in Appendix A.) As the
Falwell writings make clear on these phenomena: he is antiabortion, anti-ERA,
opposes birth control information in the schools, would probably agree that
AIDS is God's punishment for homosexuals, opposes a nuclear freeze, is pro
defense spending, favors school prayer, favors tuition tax credits, opposes the
aims and purposes of NOW, and is pro Israel (Falwell 1980, 1981).

In Table 1 we compare the mean scores of 509 white Protestant Evangelicals
to the Falwell platform items with nonevangelical Protestants, Catholics, and

Table 1. Comparison of White Evangelicals with White Non-Evangelicals,
Catholics, and Blacks on Items in the Falwell Platform

Falwell Platform Items	*Mean Scores*				Midpoint Score on Item
	White Evangelicals (*N = 509*)	White Non-Evangelicals (*N = 168*)	Catholics (*N = 222*)	Blacks (*N = 97*)	
School Prayer (Low scores favor)	1.35	1.46	1.51	1.49	3
State of Israel (Low scores favor)	3.41	4.16***	4.15***	3.64	5
Birth Control Information in Schools (Low scores oppose)	3.50	4.18	3.81*	4.07***	3
ERA (Low scores oppose)	3.10	3.77***	3.63***	4.52***	3
Tuition Tax Credits (Low scores favor)	2.79	2.78	2.30**	3.21***	3
National Organization for Women (Low scores favor)	3.05	2.57***	2.73*	2.24***	3
Defense Spending (Low scores favor)	2.71	2.74	3.23**	3.40***	3
Nuclear Freeze (low scores oppose)	2.98	3.01	3.33*	3.39*	3
Abortion (Low scores oppose)	5.67	7.20***	5.73	5.80	6
AIDS God's Punishment for Homosexuals (Low scores agree)	3.13	3.63***	3.78***	3.36	3

Notes: Exact wording and coding of each item is provided in Appendix A.
*p < .05
**p < .01
***p < .001

Blacks. The white Protestant Evangelicals differ from their nonevangelical
brethren in statistically significant terms on six of the ten items. On the school
prayer item, the differences are in the predicted direction, but the results are
not statistically significant (just about everyone in the sample favors school
prayer). On three items (tuition tax credits, defense spending, and the nuclear

freeze) there are no differences between Evangelicals and non-Evangelicals. Differences between white Protestant Evangelicals and Roman Catholics are significant on eight of the items. Only on school prayer and abortion are the differences not great. Blacks differ from white Protestant Evangelicals in the expected direction on all ten of the variables with the differences reaching the level of statistical significance on six occasions.

Substantively, what do the data in Table 1 tell us about the white Protestant evangelical community? First, they suggest that this group differs significantly from non-Evangelicals in terms of the so-called "social" issues. Second, they differ substantially from Catholic and Black respondents. (The data suggest that samples that include Catholics and Black Evangelicals should segregate these groups in the analysis.) Note, in addition in Table 1, that the white evangelical Protestants do not always agree with the issue positions taken by Jerry Falwell. They do agree on the items concerning school prayer, the State of Israel, tuition tax credits, defense spending, and abortion. But on the item concerned with making birth control information available in the schools, they favor this concept, whereas the group comes close to "neutral" or "undecided" mean scores on the other items. To conclude, the mean scores in Table 1 for the group presumably most favorable to Falwell issue positions, the white Protestant Evangelical, suggest strong but not overwhelming support for the Falwell issue agenda.

Are the diverse set of attitudes in the Falwell platform tied together? Is there an underlying unity amidst the content diversity in the items examined in Table 1? Table 2 answers these questions with a tentative "yes." What we are looking for here are consistent differences in the item responses between the proponents and opponents of Falwell and the Moral Majority. What the mean scores in Table 2 indicate is that this diverse set of Falwell platform items behave pretty much as expected when related to these two external variables. Falwell and Moral Majority supporters are more favorable to the Falwell issue agenda than opponents of the man and his organization. There is only one deviation from this pattern: Moral Majority proponents are more favorable to NOW than the opponents. In the case of the Falwell item, all 10 mean score differences between those who favor and oppose the man are statistically significant. Thus, in Table 2, there is strong supportive evidence that at least nine of the variables belong together (the NOW item is dropped from further analysis).

The data in Table 2 also puts to rest a persistent media myth about American Evangelicals. It is often assumed that Evangelicals are a united conservative political force. In fact white Protestant Evangelicals are diverse in their political attitudes and beliefs as has been noted recently by other scholars (cf. Hood and Morris 1985). But those that favor Jerry Falwell do have a set of attitudes consistent with those advanced in the writings of the man himself—attitudes that are conservative across the board except for the one item concerned with providing birth control information in the schools.

Table 2. The Falwell Platform Items Related to Attitudes Toward
Jerry Falwell and The Moral Majority
(White Protestant Evangelicals Only)

Falwell Platform Items	Moral Majority		Jerry Falwell	
	Favor (N = 112)	Oppose (N = 112)	Favor (N = 156)	Oppose (N = 149)
School Prayer	1.24	1.69***	1.14	1.62***
State of Israel	2.66	3.51*	2.48	3.79***
Birth Control Information in Schools	3.32	3.53	3.19	3.74***
ERA	2.60	3.08*	2.76	3.26***
Tuition Tax Credits	2.59	2.96	2.44	3.01**
National Organization for Women	3.09	3.29	3.23	2.91*
Defense Spending	2.28	3.04***	2.38	2.93***
Nuclear Freeze	2.61	2.97	2.71	3.12*
Abortion	5.26	6.39**	5.12	6.26***
AIDS God's Punishment for Homosexuals	2.82	3.39**	2.68	3.46***

Notes: Scoring for the Falwell platform items is identical to that in Table 1. Excluded from this table are
respondents that had not heard of the Moral Majority or Jerry Falwell, had heard of them but were
unable to give an opinion, or had a neutral opinion.

*p < .05
**p < .01
***p < .001

Table 3. Unrotated Factor Loadings of Falwell Platform Items

Attitudes Toward	Factor Loadings
Abortion	.631
AIDS God's Punishment for Homosexuals	.608
Birth Control Information in Schools	.528
ERA	.450
Defense Spending	.402
Nuclear Freeze	.361
Tuition Tax Credits	.337
State of Israel	.327
School Prayer	.301
Variance Explained: 58.3%	

The process of determining whether these nine items can legitimately be tied
together into a single index is continued in Table 3. Here unrotated factor
loadings for each of the variables are presented. We use unrotated rather than
rotated factor loadings because they provide us with the best linear combination

of the variables. The measures dealing with social issues have the highest loadings, with the defense variables falling into the middle range, and with the school prayer, tuition tax credit, and the Israel items contributing the least to the underlying pattern.

As a result of the analysis in Tables 2 and 3, we constructed a Falwell platform index that serves as the basis for the remainder of the data analysis for this paper. (Variables were added together using the factor scores multiplied by standard Z-score transformations of each item.) Is the index a valid one? The best way to answer the question is to see if the index behaves as expected when related to external variables—a task performed in Table 4. In particular, the variables in the social demographic package behave as expected: older, lower-status (less-educated, low-income) respondents are more likely to favor the Falwell issue agenda than their younger, higher-status counterparts. The regional variable does not show the strength of relationship that might have been expected. Southerners are somewhat more likely to support the Falwell issue agenda than non-Southerners, but the correlation is not statistically significant. Males are also somewhat more likely to favor the Falwell platform than women, but, again, the correlation is not significant. However, with a derived sex/employment measure, the results are more positive. Males are the most supportive of the Falwell issue agenda, followed by females who do not work, followed by women who are in the work force. No doubt the latter are influenced to some extent by a feminist agenda that would be anathema to strong supporters of the Falwell platform.

An overall glance at Table 4 reveals that the religious variables are closely related to attitudes toward the Falwell platform. Thus strong relationships are found between high scores on the issue agenda and denomination, doctrine, religious involvement, the perceived importance of religion to the respondent in political choices and the frequency of watching religious television. Moderate relationships were found between the Falwell platform and pastoral political activism. Although there is evidence of greater fundamentalist pastoral involvement in politics in recent years (Guth 1985), there still is a tendency for evangelical and fundamentalist pastors to steer clear of the political process (Beatty and Walter 1986). In addition, activist pastors supporting more "liberal" causes (anti-war, civil rights) are still around to counter the increased "conservative" pastoral thrust.

The stronger relationships between the religious variables and the Falwell issue agenda in Table 4 deserve further comment. In terms of denomination,[2] it is the Pentecostals that are the most favorably inclined to support the Falwell platform and not the Fundamentalists. Less supportive are the evangelical denominations, while least supportive are the remaining Protestant groups— Presbyterians, Episcopalians, Methodists, and Lutherans. Why would the Pentecostals be the most favorable to the Falwell agenda? It could be that the small number (27) of Pentecostals in the sample are unrepresentative. Equally

Table 4.   Correlations With The Falwell Platform
(White Protestant Evangelicals Only)

Social Demographic Items		Religious Items		Social/Political Attitudes	
Age	.14***	Denomination[a]	.30***	Billy Graham[b]	.08*
Socioeconomic Status[c]	-.16***	Religious Doctrine[d]	.30***	Sword of the Lord[e]	.09*
Region[f]	.07	Religiosity[g]	.32***	Dislike Roman Catholic Church	.21***
Sex[h]	-.05	Salience of Religion for Politics[i]	.45***	Conservatism	.27***
Sex/ Employment[j]	-.12**	Pastoral Political Recommendations[k]	.11***	Republican Party Identification	.27***
		Watch Religious TV Frequently	.25***		

Notes: The Falwell platform is coded from low to high. Explanations for other variables in the table are as
follows:

[a] Denomination: scored from low to high—Other Protestants, Evangelicals, Fundamentalists, Pentecostals.

[b] Billy Graham: low scores oppose while high scores favor.

[c] Socioeconomic Status: an index combining income and education with the higher the score the higher the
status.

[d] Doctrine: a measure combining belief in Christ, born again status, liberal to negative interpretations of the
Bible, and fundamentalist self identification. Low scores are nonevangelical; high scores are fundamentalist
and pentecostal in orientation.

[e] Sword of the Lord: attitudes toward a fundamentalist publication with low scores opposing and high scores
favoring.

[f] Region: low scores are Non-South; high scores are South.

[g] Religiosity: an index including church attendance, and the import of religion to the respondent; the higher
the score the greater the religiosity.

[h] Sex: low scores are male; high scores are female.

[i] Salience of Religion for Politics: an index of six items that asked respondents to indicate how important religion
was in their vote choices and other acts of political behavior. The higher the score, the greater the salience.

[j] Sex/Employment: low scores are male; midpoint scores are females who do not work; high scores are females
employed.

[k] Pastoral Political Recommendations: a two item index concerned with whether the pastor gave opinions about
and/or recommended candidates.

*p < .05
**p < .01
***p < .001

plausible, however, is a more substantive interpretation that suggests that
Pentecostal denominations are more conservative than other Evangelicals.
There is some support for this conclusion in the literature (Poloma 1982; Smidt
1984).

Next we turn to doctrine. Our measure combines responses to three items
of a doctrinal or experiential sort and fundamentalist self-identification item.
Briefly, the four items include: (1) the necessity for believing in Christ for

salvation; (2) born again status; (3) belief in a literal or true Creation Story account as told in Genesis or in an account that gives no place to God; and (4) self-identified fundamentalist status. The measure arrays respondents from top to bottom as follows:

1. Non-Evangelicals: Accept none of the four points.
2. Confessional Evangelicals: Belief in Christ for salvation only.
3. Born Again Evangelicals: Belief in Christ *and* born again status.
4. Biblical Literalist/Nonfundamentalist I.D.:   Belief in Christ, born again status, a literal view of Scripture, *but* no identification as a fundamentalist.
5. Non-Literalist/Fundamentalist I.D.:   Belief in Christ, born again status, a "true" interpretation of the creation story, *and* identification as a fundamentalist.
6. Pure Fundamentalists: Accept all four of the points above including a literal view of Scripture.
7. Pentecostals: No doctrinal or experiential questions were asked that would determine support for a Pentecostal perspective. As members of Pentecostal churches, the assumption is that these respondents give greater emphasis to the Holy Spirit than do other evangelical groups as well as experience modern day miracles such as healing and speaking in tongues in greater frequency than do their other evangelical brethren.

Non-Evangelicals are the least supportive of the Falwell issue agenda, while at the other end of the spectrum the Pure Fundamentalists (a group that holds all the doctrinal beliefs plus identifies as fundamentalist) and Pentecostals are the most favorable. The pattern is linear.

Next, religiosity is examined. Here the relationships are similar to those found by Shupe and Stacey in their Dallas-Fort Worth study (1983, p. 112). What is it about regular church atendance and identifying one's faith as important that bring about the strong relationship with the Falwell issue agenda? Involvement with fellow believers in the form of attendance and perceived salience of religion are likely to lead to attitudes and behaviors consistent with the dominant norms and behaviors of the local church. In evangelical churches, the dominant political values are likely to be conservative. The relationship between support for a Falwell issue agenda and an index that measures that salience of one's religion for political behavior is shown in Table 4. The relationship is the strongest in the whole table. Clearly, respondents that feel that their religion and politics are intertwined are more likely to accept the Falwell issue agenda than those for whom politics is less salient. It is reasonable to assume that Evangelicals that feel that the political process is an important and a legitimate avenue will find some outlet for these feelings. One way is to support a set of issue positions that seem related to one's faith commitments. Another is to involve oneself in the electoral process and to back parties and candidates that stand behind the issues that you support. At a minimum, the evidence in Table 4 suggests that politicized Evangelicals, those that see clear linkages between religion and politics, have adopted the strategy of identifying with a set of issues.

Finally, in the section of Table 4 titled Religious Items, we find a strong correlation between the frequency of watching religious television and the Falwell platform. The links between religious television viewing and political attitudes and behavior have been explored in numerous recent studies (Will and Williams 1986; Mobley 1984; Gaddy 1984; Tamney and Johnson 1984; Stacey and Shupe 1982). As in some of these studies, the data show a strong relationship between the frequency of watching and conservative political attitudes. The data suggest the possibility, then, that one source for mobilizing political attitudes of the type we are measuring in the Falwell issue agenda is religious television.

Table 4 examines three social attitudes and their relationships with the Falwell platform: attitudes toward the evangelist Billy Graham, the fundamentalist publication *Sword of the Lord,* and the Roman Catholic Church. It is often assumed that religious fundamentalists are separatist in outlook (Marsden 1980). Negative attitudes toward Billy Graham and the Roman Catholic Church would imply a separatist perspective. So would positive attitudes toward *Sword of the Lord,* a rather obscure publication that is not well known outside fundamentalist circles. The data in Table 4 support the hypotheses but in rather modest fashion except for the item concerned with the Roman Catholic Church. Dislike for the Catholic Church is strong among Falwell issue agenda adherents. Apparently the white evangelical Protestant component of the Falwell issue coalition still harbors some of the anti-Catholic sentiment that was so apparent in the 1960 presidential campaign. The social/demographic relationships in Table 4 provide us some clue to explain the negative views of the Catholic Church that emerge in these data. Note that Falwell platform advocates tend to be from older, lower status, and (to a somewhat lesser extent) southern segments of evangelical Protestantism, the very groups in which one would expect anti-Catholic sentiment to be strong. Finally, in Table 4, we find the expected strong relationships between conservative political ideology (a self-report measure ranging from strong conservative to strong liberal) and Republican Party identification and the Falwell platform.

To see which of the variables from Table 4 serve as the best predictors of the Falwell issue agenda, a multiple regression (Ordinary Least Square model) is presented in Table 5. Overall, the findings are gratifying; the multiple R and R^2 are fairly high. Among social location variables, older age and lower socioeconomic status are significantly related to positive attitudes toward the Falwell platform. This finding is similar to that found by Yinger and Cutler (1984) using a Moral Majority index (limited to "social" issues). The finding

Table 5.   The Falwell Platform: Best Fit Regressions
(White Protestant Evangelicals Only)

	BETA	Significance
Social Demographic Variables		
Age	.12	.002
Sex/Employment	-.10	.01
Socioeconomic Status	-.15	.001
Religious		
Denomination	.17	.001
Religiosity	.07	.07
Frequent Religious TV Watching	.11	.004
Political Religious		
Salience of Religion for Political Behavior	.33	.001
Pastoral Political Recommendations	.06	.12
Political		
Conservatism	.16	.001
Republican Party Identification	.13	.001
Multiple R .61		
R^2 .38		

that the younger, upper-status white Protestant Evangelical is not attracted to the Falwell issue agenda raises questions as to whether the platform is the wave of the future or a defense of the dying past. The results do suggest that attempts by groups to broaden the base of support for this particular set of issues to the young and upper status segments of the society will be difficult. Another growing portion of the society, women employed outside the home, are also opponents of the Falwell platform, as the sex/employment variable in Table 5 reveals.

Turning to the religious variables in the regressions in Table 5, it is interesting that only the doctrinal variable in Table 4 washes out as a significant predictor of the Falwell issue agenda. In fact, the denomination measure is the second strongest predictor in all of Table 5. It is in fundamentalist and pentecostal denominations that significant support emerges. Hood and Morris (1985) reach a somewhat similar conclusion; their research found a close link between fundamentalism and conservative political issues like those we have examined in the present research. In evangelical denominations, where conservative religious beliefs predominate, there is much less of a tendency to support the Falwell platform, although there is outright opposition to this political agenda in the remaining Protestant denominations. In addition, it is noted in Table 5 that frequent religious television watching is a significant predictor of favorable attitudes toward these conservative issue positions. The finding is similar to that of Tamney and Johnson (1984) in Middletown, although their dependent variable is support for the organization, the Moral Majority, rather than to specific issue positions. Our finding suggests that the Falwell issue agenda is, in part, a product of modern television. The measure of religiosity, which had a very strong bivariate relationship with the Falwell platform is explored in Table 5. Here, we find that the measure just fails to meet the standard criterion of the .05 level of statistical significance. In contrast, Yinger and Cutler (1984) find that religiosity is a significant predictor of their more social oriented Moral Majority index.

White Protestant Evangelicals that believe that religion is salient for political behavior are strong supporters of the Falwell platform. This finding from Table 4 is strongly reenforced in Table 5; in fact, the measure is the best predictor of all the variables in the table. In contrast, the measure concerned with pastoral political recommendations does not quite achieve the .05 level of significance. This finding may be due to the fact that pastors (even evangelical ones) are not giving cues on public policy and other social issues that are uniformly conservative in direction. Our data do not allow the content of the pastoral recommendations in terms of liberal or conservative tendencies to be differentiated, even if policy content is the focus of pastoral concern. Nonetheless, the results in Table 5 concerning the religious and political/ religious variables indicate that white Protestant Evangelicals that have strong beliefs in a Falwell issue agenda believe that religious values and politics *do* mix. Thus, these issue oriented Evangelicals are prime targets to be mobilized politically. The data suggest, not surprisingly, that Pentecostals and Fundamentalists are the groups within evangelicalism with the greatest potential for mobilization. In terms of strategies to reach these issue oriented Evangelicals, religious television appears to be a major source, while grassroots political activity on the part of pastors is a less likely strategic alternative to choose.

Finally, in Table 5, the predictive power of the political variables, conservative political ideology and Republican Party identification, is examined in terms of support for the Falwell platform. Both variables are significant predictors. These are not surprising findings given that the issues in the Falwell agenda appear, on their face, to be linked to conservative ideology. As for Republican Party identification, the links between the Republican Party and conservative political issues, like those in the Falwell issue agenda, can be observed in the party platforms adopted in both 1980 and 1984.

Does the Falwell platform affect vote turnout and other acts of political participation? Why is this a relevant question? First, the Falwell writings emphasize the need, in fact the duty, to participate. Second, organizational efforts were made by the Moral Majority to register voters and to encourage them to vote (Pierard 1985, p. 102). Table 6 examines the factors that affect turnout and participation rates. A number of caveats are in order. The rather low multiple R's and R^2s in this table are explained in part by the fact that the questionnaire did not tap such variables as levels of political information, interest in politics, political efficacy and citizen duty that are highly related to participation (Conway 1985). Second, the data presented are the end results of numerous multiple regressions and are the "best fit" in terms of explaining political activism. Turning to the results, first look at comparisons between vote turnout rates in 1980 and 1982. The pattern of predictors is somewhat similar for both years. Most important is the finding that the Falwell issue agenda has a significant independent impact on turnout in both 1980 and 1982. White Protestant Evangelicals that are predisposed toward the Falwell positions are more likely to vote than opponents of the platform. These findings are similar to those of other scholars (Brudney and Copeland 1984; Miller and Wattenberg 1984; Wilcox 1986b), although none of these works use an issue agenda as an independent variable in their analysis. What is significant about these findings is that an issue agenda with a strong religious basis (see Table 5) is able to serve as a significant predictor for voting turnout and not wash out in the analysis when pitted against standard predictors of turnout such as age, socioeconomic status and party identification.

Older age and higher socioeconomic status are both significantly related to turnout. What is significant here, however, is that for white Protestant Evangelicals turnout in the South, in 1980 and 1982, was not significantly lower than for their religious counterparts in the rest of the nation. In other words, region had no impact on 1980 turnout rates for these Evangelicals, although there is evidence turnout in the South in 1980 was lower than in the rest of the country for the voting age population as a whole (Asher 1984, p. 44). Denomination just fails as a significant predictor of vote turnout in 1980 and barely passes the same rather arbitrary level of significance in 1982. What is significant is that in 1980 the other Protestant category is the high turnout group, while the Pentecostals rank at the bottom. Hence the denominational grouping most favorable to the Falwell issue agenda is the least likely to vote or to engage in other conventional acts of political participation. In terms of the latter (which involve voting in a primary election, contributing money or volunteering time to a party or candidate), 30% of the Pentecostals were totally uninvolved in these acts as compared to 18% of the Fundamentalists, 16% of the Evangelicals, and 9% of the other Protestants. In addition, in Table 6 the Republican Party identification is found to be by far the most significant predictor of vote turnout in both 1980 and 1982 (particularly in the off year election). Other scholars have noted that Republicans are more likely to vote than Democrats and Independents, in good part due to their higher status characteristics (Abramson et al. 1982, p. 90). However, it should be noted that Republican Party identification is making an impact on turnout *independent* of socioeconomic status. Finally, with regard to turnout, a number of religious

Table 6.   The Falwell Platform, Other Variables, and Rates of
           Political Activity: Best Fit Regressions
           (White Protestant Evangelicals Only)

Other Variables	1980 Vote Turnout		1982 Vote Turnout		Political Participation[a]	
	BETA	Sig.	BETA	Sig.	BETA	Sig.
Age	.12	.01	.10	.02	.16	.001
Sex/Employment II[b]					.09	.03
Socioeconomic Status	.10	.04	.16	.001	.19	.001
Denomination	-.08	.06	-.09	.05		
Religiosity			-.09	.06		
Frequent Religious TV Watching			.10	.03	.10	.03
Salience of Religion for Politics[c]			.10	.05		
Republican Party Identification	.24	.001	.22	.001	.16	.001
Falwell Platform	.11	.03	.11	.03	.14	.001
Multiple R	.31		.37		.35	
R²	.10		.14		.12	

Notes:
[a] Political Participation is an index of three items: financial contribution to a party or candidate, primary election voting, and contributing time to a candidate or political cause.
[b] Sex/Employment II: a variable with the lowest score for males, a midpoint score for employed women, and the highest score given for women not in the work force.
[c] Salience of Religion for Politics: a shorter version of a variable used in Tables 4 and 5; this measure combines whether a repondent would raise religious/moral issues in a discussion with their congressman and with the perceived importance of the religious and moral views of candidates in making vote choices.

variables attain significance as predictors in 1982—religiosity (high church attendance/high salience of religion), frequent religious television viewing, and the perceived importance of religion for political activity. Of particular interest is the religious television variable. Although it achieves statistically significant status, the measure concerning pastoral political recommendations does not. Religious television, as of 1983, was a more important source of political mobilization than the grassroots activities of pastors of local congregations. The reason for this is due, in part, to the small number of white Protestant Evangelicals whose pastors ever talk about politics (26%) as compared with the larger number of religious television viewers within this segment of Christianity (once a week or more—41%).

Table 6 also examines factors affecting other forms of political participation. The results are similar to the vote turnout variables but note the much stronger loading for the socioeconomic status variable on participation rates. This confirms much prior research that links socioeconomic status to high levels

Table 7.   The Falwell Platform, Other Variables, and Vote Choice:
Best Fit Regressions (White Protestant Evangelicals Only)

	1980 Vote Choice		1982 Vote Choice		1984 Vote Choice	
Other Variables	*BETA*	*Sig.*	*BETA*	*Sig.*	*BETA*	*Sig.*
Socioeconomic Status	.13	.002			.13	.001
Denomination			-.14	.001		
Republican Party Identification	.48	.001	.67	.001	.44	.001
Conservative Ideology	.10	.03	.09	.03	.15	.001
Falwell Platform	.06	.21	-.03	.55	.09	.03
Multiple R		.55		.72		.54
R^2		.30		.52		.29

Note: High scores on the vote choice variables signifies a Republican vote. For the 1982 vote choice relationship,
denomination is recorded as follows: 1 = Fundamentalist; 2 = Evangelical; 3 = Other Protestant; and
4 = Pentecostal. For the 1980 relationship, denomination is coded in the same fashion as in earlier
tables.

of participation (Verba and Nie 1972; Conway 1985). In addition, the sex/employment variable is a significant predictor of these conventional forms of political activity. Males are the most participatory in these male dominated modes of activity followed by women in the workforce and then women at home. Frequent religious viewing is also significantly related to participation rates. Whether intentional or not, religious television viewing has an independent effect on conventional forms of participation; for many televangelists, no doubt, the impact is intended. Finally, Republican partisanship has somewhat less of an effect on conventional forms of participation than it does on vote turnout.

Vote choice in 1980 and 1982, and projected vote choice in 1984 is examined in Table 7. As expected, partisan identification, ideology, and socioeconomic status are significant predictors with Republican Party identification having by far the greatest impact (socioeconomic status washes out in 1982). When the relationships between denomination and vote choice are explored, some interesting patterns emerge. In 1980, 80% of the small Pentecostal category voted for Reagan, whereas the Fundamentalists, Evangelicals, and other Protestants were close together in the 58-59% range. As a result, in the regression analysis, denomination emerged as a significant predictor of vote choice. In 1982, a different pattern emerged—the few Pentecostals that voted gave 80% of their votes to the Republican Party. The Other Protestant group gave their support to Republicans by a five to four margin, whereas Evangelicals were evenly divided. Fundamentalists, however, returned to their Democratic Party roots (see Kellstedt [1986] for evidence of the historical links between evangelical denominations, including Fundamentalists, and the Democratic Party)—supporting the party by a margin of almost two to one. In the regression analysis, a recorded denomination variable (1 = Fundamentalist; 2 = Evangelical; 3 = Other Protestants; and 4 = Pentecostals) is significantly related to 1982 vote choice. In 1984, denomination does not achieve significance as a predictor of vote choice, because all four groups project support for Reagan without large differences between them.

Finally, the impact of the Falwell issue agenda on vote choice is examined in Table 7. Other scholars using other measures have talked about little or no impact for the Christian right (Lipset and Raab 1981; Abramson et al. 1982); others saw little role for the Christian right in 1980 but a greater impact in 1984 (Johnson and Tamney 1982; Johnson and Tamney 1985); although others saw at least modest influence for the adherents of the religious right (Brudney and Copeland 1984; Simpson 1985a; Miller and Wattenberg 1984; Hood and Morris 1985; Wilcox 1986b). (The differences in the studies are due more to conceptual and measurement differences and differing data sources than to anything else.) In 1980 the Falwell issue agenda had no significant impact; the beta is in the proper direction, but the variable is washed out by other measures. Substantively, this finding is easy to explain. The Falwell issue agenda was just beginning to make its impact, although other concerns—inflation, Carter's perceived lack of leadership—were no doubt more salient (cf. Abramson et al. 1982). In 1982, the Falwell issue positions were not the key concerns. In fact, in our data support for the Falwell issue agenda was related slightly, but insignificantly, to voting *Democratic* among the white Protestant evangelical sample. In terms of 1984 projected vote, however, this sample gave the Falwell issue agenda a prominent and significant place in their decision making. This is what one would expect among this audience at that time, for the period between 1980 and 1984 was one of intense activity on the part of the Republican Party and the Moral Majority, among other groups, to mobilize the evangelical audience to register to vote and to support Ronald Reagan because of his support for the Falwell issue agenda (cf. Pierard [1985] for discussion of these mobilizing efforts). Table 7 then shows a modest but not significant impact for the Falwell issue agenda in 1980, no effect on the 1982 midterm voting, and a significant impact on 1984 vote choice.

CONCLUSION

This paper has identified a series of policy positions that have been called the Falwell platform. Although not a perfect representation of the issue positions advanced by Jerry Falwell and the Moral Majority, they cover a significant part of the Falwellian agenda and divide the evangelical community. Empirically, however, the items tie together into a valid measure. In terms of predictors of this conservative issue agenda, such social/demographic variables as old age and low socioeconomic status are associated with the platform, while males were in support of the agenda with females in the work force opposed. Among religious variables, good predictors included Pentecostal and Fundamentalist denomination, frequent religious television viewing, and the perceived link between religious beliefs and political activity. Political conservatism and identification with the Republican Party served as the strongest political predictors. The Falwell platform is associated with levels of political activity (vote turnout and other forms of conventional political participation). In terms of voter preference, the Falwell issue agenda is closely associated with a projected Reagan vote in 1984, although having no relationship with Republican voting in 1982, and only a weak relationship to support for Reagan in 1980.

The results of the study provide some support for the consistency model developed earlier. Consistency or congruence among variables measuring social location, "religion," ideology, and partisanship was not the focus of the analysis conducted for this research, but the results do seem compatible with such a model. As previously noted, certain social/demographic, religious, and political variables did the best job of predicting the Falwell issue agenda. With the exception of male status, all of these variables seem congruent. And in an evangelical subculture, one would expect males to be more involved politically than females. Hence, it seems reasonable to suggest a hypothesis for future research— individuals that are intimately related to a fundamentalist or pentecostal subculture from less desirable social locations (in terms of the values of the dominant culture), that watch religious television frequently, and with conservative and Republican political identifications are the most likely adherents of Christian right political causes. And this support could take the form of issue advocacy, involvement in the political process, and voting for political candidates.

What are the implications of this research for future work on the links between religion and the conservative political agenda identified here as the Falwell platform? First, past research on this topic has neither conceptualized nor operationalized religion very adequately. Little attention has been given to denomination, although this research suggests that it is a promising area to examine. Certainly, improvements are needed in doctrinal measurement; little agreement exists as to how to measure evangelicalism, and almost no attention has been given to subgroup measurement—fundamentalist or charismatic, for example. Most studies lack a series of measures of religious practices as well, although it is reasonable to assume that most evangelicals that are involved in their church are more likely to have picked up conservative political cues than persons less involved. This research suggests that religious television plays a mobilizing role, but does not make clear the process. More careful attention is also needed concerning the role of the pastor and other church leaders in political socialization.

Second, the dependent variable focus has differed from one study to another—some research has examined support for the Moral Majority; other studies have looked at conservative political issues. The latter strategy is more appropriate. In the first place, organizations come and go (in fact the Moral Majority has been replaced by the Liberty Foundation). In addition, in data not reported in this paper, it was found that the *name* Moral Majority brought positive responses from some interviewees who strongly favored ERA and abortion and who self identified as liberals. Possibly, they were responding to a name that sounded good, not an organization that they knew anything about. If the future approach is to focus on an issue based dependent variable, more serious attention is needed as to what issues to include and how to measure them in a parsimonious and yet valid manner.

APPENDIX

Falwell Platform Items: Question Wordings

"Do you favor or oppose a freeze on U.S. and Soviet nuclear weapons at current levels, even if that means the U.S. has slightly fewer weapons?" [IF CHOICE MADE, ASK:] "And do you feel strongly about that?"

"Do you favor or oppose a tuition tax credit—where parents are given tax credits if they choose to send their children to private or parochial schools?" [IF CHOICE MADE, ASK:] "And do you feel strongly about that?"

"Are you personally for or against passage of the Equal Rights Amendment?" [IF CHOICE MADE, ASK:] "And do you feel strongly about that?"

"At the present time, prayers are not allowed in the public schools. Do you think that voluntary public prayer should be allowed in public schools?" [IF CHOICE MADE, ASK:] "And do you feel strongly about that?"

"Do you feel the U.S. should increase the amount of money we spend on defense, or should we decrease this amount of money?" [IF CHOICE MADE, ASK:] "And do you feel strongly about that?"

"In your opinion, should information on the availability and use of birth control methods be taught to teenagers in the public school system?" [IF CHOICE MADE, ASK:] "And do you feel strongly about that?"

"Abortion should not be legally available in the U.S. for any reasons." (PROMPT: "DO YOU AGREE OR DISAGREE WITH THIS STATEMENT?") [IF CHOICE MADE, ASK:] "And do you feel strongly about that?"*

"As you may know, there has been a lot of publicity recently concerning a contagious disease called A-I-D-S or 'AIDS.' A large percentage of those with this disease are homosexuals. Would you agree or disagree with the following statement: The fact that AIDS disease has struck largely in the homosexual community is evidence of God's punishment for homosexuals' immoral and sinful lifestyle." [IF CHOICE MADE, ASK:] "And do you feel strongly about that?"

"Now I'm going to read the names of some groups and people active in America today. For each one, please tell me if you recognize the group or person, and if so, whether or not you have a favorable or unfavorable impression of that group or person—N.O.W.—the National Organization of Women"

"Now I'd like to know how you feel about several types of people, countries, and religious groups. We'll use a scale which runs from 0 to 10, where "0" means you really dislike a group, and "10" means you really like a group. You can use any number from 0 to 10. First—Israel."

Note: *An abortion index was created from the three questions on abortion as follows: pro abortion—agrees abortion should be legally available for any adult who desires it; anti abortion—should not be legally available for any reason; all other responses are held to be middle ground positions.

ACKNOWLEDGMENTS

Revised version of a paper prepared for delivery at the Annual Meeting of the Society for the Scientific Study of Religion, Savannah, Georgia, October 25-26, 1985. The author is grateful to Stuart Rothenberg and Frank Newport, to Lance Tarrance and Associates, and to the Free Congress Association, for making the data available for this study. The author also acknowledges the assistance of Liz Morehead and Brent Hendry.

NOTES

1.   *The Evangelical Voter* began with 871 Whites. This number was reduced to 509 white Protestant evangelicals by eliminating respondents with the following characteristics:

   a.   Roman Catholics;
   b.   Non-Evangelical denominations—Mormons, Jehovah's Witnesses, Christian Scientists, Unitarians;
   c.   Respondents that did not accept the necessity of belief in Jesus Christ in order to obtain eternal life.
   d.   Respondents who felt that the Creation story in Genesis reflected "man's feelings about how the world may have been created"—a non-Evangelical response.
   e.   Respondents who identified as Fundamentalists but claimed not to have had a born again experience.

2.   We chose a conservative approach to defining fundamentalist denominations. If in doubt about a denomination, the approach did not assign it to a fundamentalist category. As a result, these denominations were coded as fundamentalist: Independent, Hard Shell, Missionary, Conservative, Fundamental, and other unaffiliated Baptists, Evangelistic Methodists, Church of God, Bible Church, Full Bible Church, and Congregational Evangelists. In addition, Southern

Baptists who believed in Christ as a man and yet the Son of God, believed in Christ as Savior, were born again, held a literal view of the Creation story, and identified as Fundamentalists were included as Fundamentalists. The Southern Baptist Convention is difficult to classify as fundamentalist or evangelical. Certainly, a substantial number of their congregations are fundamentalist in orientation. The assignment procedure here assigned the remaining Southern Baptists to the evangelical category. Other evangelical denominations included all other Baptist denominations not assigned to the fundamentalist grouping, Free and Wesleyan Methodists, Covenant Presbyterians, Church of Christ, Nazarenes, 7th Day Adventists, Salvation Army, Full Gospel, Unity, Dutch and Christian Reformed, Holiness, Church of the Brethren, and the nondenominational coding category. The latter were assigned as evangelical on doctrinal grounds. Pentecostals include all denominations with Pentecostal in their name plus Assembly of God members. All other denominations were labelled "Other Protestant." Most Methodists and Presbyterians, as well as all Lutherans and Episcopalians fit into this category.

Assignment of denominations into broader categories such as these is difficult and often arbitrary. Yet, there is no escape from the difficulty if such data are to be useful to social scientists.

REFERENCES

Abramson, P. R., J. H. Aldrich, and D. W. Rohde. 1982. *Change and Continuity in the 1980 Elections.* Washington, DC: Congressional Quarterly.

Asher, H. 1985. *Presidential Elections and American Politics,* 3rd ed. Homewood, IL: Dorsey.

Beatty, K. and O. Walter. 1987. "Social Groups and Religion: The Political Connection." Unpublished manuscript.

Bromley, D. G. and A. D. Shupe. 1984. *New Christian Politics.* Macon, GA: Mercer University Press.

Brudney, J. L. and G. W. Copeland. 1984. "Evangelicals As a Political Force: Reagan and the 1980 Religious Vote." *Social Science Quarterly* 65: 1074-1079.

Conway, M. 1985. *Political Participation In the United States.* Washington, DC: Congressional Quarterly.

Falwell, J. 1980. *Listen, America!* Garden City, NY: Doubleday.

_____. 1986. "The Gospel and Racial Equality." *Fundamentalist Journal* 5: 10.

Falwell, J., ed. (with E. Dobson and E. Hindson). 1981. *Fundamentalist Phenomenon: The Resurgence of Conservative Christianity.* Garden City, NY: Doubleday.

Festinger, L. 1957. *A Theory of Cognitive Dissonance.* Stanford, CA: Stanford University Press.

Gaddy, G. D. 1984. "The Power of the Religious Media: Religious Broadcast Use and The Role of Religious Organizations in Public Affairs." *Review of Religious Research* 25:289-301.

Guth, J. L. 1985. "The Christian Right Revisited: Partisan Realignment Among Southern Baptist Ministers." Paper presented at the meeting of the Midwest Political Science Association, Chicago.

Heider, F. 1958. *The Psychology of Interpersonal Relations.* New York: Wiley.

Hood, R. W., Jr. and R. J. Morris. 1985. "Boundary Maintenance, Social-Political Views, and Presidential Preference Among High and Low Fundamentalists." *Review of Religious Research* 27:134-145.

Hunter, J. D. 1983. *American Evangelicalism.* New Brunswick, NJ: Rutgers University Press.

Johnson, S. D. 1986. "The Christian Right in Middletown." Pp. 181-198 in *The Political Role of Religion in the United States,* edited by S. D. Johnson and J. B. Tamney. Boulder, CO: Westview.

Johnson, S. D. and J. B. Tamney. 1982. "The Christian Right and the 1980 Presidential Election." *Journal for the Scientific Study of Religion* 21:123-131.

————. 1985. "The Christian Right and the 1984 Presidential Election." *Review of Religious Research* 27:124-133.

Kellstedt, L. A. 1986. "Evangelicals and Political Realignment." Paper presented at the meeting of the American Political Science Association, Washington, DC.

Liebman, R. C. and R. Wuthnow, eds. 1983. *The New Christian Right.* New York: Aldine.

Lipset, S. M. and E. Raab. 1981. "The Election and the Evangelicals." *Commentary* 71: 25-32.

Marsden, G. 1980. *Fundamentalism and American Culture.* New York: Oxford.

Miller, A. H. and M. Wattenberg. 1984. "Politics From the Pulpit: Religiosity and the 1980 Elections." *Public Opinion Quarterly* 48:301-317.

Mobley, G. M. 1984. "The Political Influence of Television Ministers." *Review of Religious Research* 25:314-320.

Pierard, R. V. 1985. "Religion and the 1984 Election Campaign." *Review of Religious Research* 27: 98-114.

Poloma, M. 1982. *The Charismatic Movement: Is There a New Pentecost?* Boston: Wayne Publishers.

Rothenberg, S. and F. Newport. 1984. *The Evangelical Voter,* Washington, DC: Free Congress.

Shupe, A. and W. Stacey. 1983. "The Moral Majority Constituency." Pp. 91-100 in *The New Christian Right,* edited by R. C. Liebman and R. Wuthnow. Hawthorne, NY: Aldine.

————. 1984. "Public and Clergy Sentiments Toward the Moral Majority: Evidence From the Dallas-Fort Worth Metroplex." In *New Christian Politics,* edited by D. G. Bromley and A. Shupe. Macon, GA: Mercer University Press.

Simpson, J. H. (1983). "Moral Issues and Status Politics." In *The New Christian Right,* edited by R. C. Liebman and R. Wuthnow. Hawthorne, NY: Aldine.

————. 1984. "Support For the Moral Majority and Its Sociomoral Platform. In *New Christian Politics,* edited by D. G. Bromley and A. Shupe. Macon, GA: Mercer University.

————. 1985a. "Socio-Moral Issues and Recent Presidential Elections." *Review of Religious Research* 27:115-123.

————. 1985b. "Status Inconsistency and Moral Issues." *Journal for the Scientific Study of Religion* 24:119-236.

Smidt, C. 1984. "'Praise the Lord' Politics: A Comparative Analysis of the Social Characteristics and Political Views of American Evangelical and Charismatic Christians." Paper presented at the meeting of the American Political Science Association, Washington, DC.

Stacey, W. and A. Shupe 1982. "Correlates of Support for the Electronic Church." *Journal for the Sicentific Study of Religion* 21:291-303.

Stockton, R. R. 1984. "The Falwell Core: A Public Opinion Analysis." Paper presented at the meeting of the Society for the Scientific Study of Religion, Chicago.

————. 1985. "The Falwell Core." Paper presented at the meeting of the American Political Science Association, New Orleans.

Tamney, J. B. and S. D. Johnson. 1983. "The Moral Majority in Middletown." *Journal for the Scientific Study of Religion* 22:145-157.

Tamney, J. B. and S. D. Johnson. 1984. "Religious Television in Middletown." *Review of Religious Research* 25:303-313.

————. 1985. "Consequential Religiosity in Modern Society." *Reivew of Religious Research* 26: 360-378.

Verba, S. and N. Nie. 1972. *Participation in America.* New York: Harper & Row.

Wilcox, C. 1986. "Fundamentalists and Politics: An Analysis of the Effects of Differing Operational Definitions." *The Journal of Politics* 48: 1041-1051.

Will, J. and R. Williams. 1986. "Political Ideology and Political Action in the New Christian Right." *Sociological Analysis* 47:160-168.

Yinger, J. M. and S. J. Cutler. 1984. "The Moral Majority Viewed Sociologically." Pp. 69-90 in *New Christian Politics,* edited by D. G. Bromley and A. Shupe. Macon, GA: Mercer University Press.

SANCTIONING AND CAUSAL ATTRIBUTIONS TO GOD:
A FUNCTION OF THEOLOGICAL POSITION AND ACTORS' CHARACTERISTICS

Craig S. Smith and Richard L. Gorsuch

ABSTRACT

Attributions to God may reflect two distinct inference processes: (a) "sanctioning" leading to judgments of "responsibility" for an outcome; or (b) "causal inference" yielding causal judgments by explaining what produced the effect. Vignettes were used to identify sanctioning and causal attributions to God across several positive situations. Persons with a religious orientation attributed greater responsibility to God in general, as a causal agent and as a sanctioning agent. In addition, they attributed less responsibility to luck than did the nontheologically oriented people.

An important dimension of religious experience is the manner in which people interpret and explain personally relevant outcomes so as to consider them "religious." Such religious interpretations and explanations are often expressed through attributions of responsibility and/or causation to God for outcomes. That such attributions are central to religious phenomena is evident from

Research in the Social Scientific Study of Religion, Volume 1, pages 133-152.
Copyright © 1989 by JAI Press Inc.
All rights of reproduction in any form reserved.
ISBN: 0-89232-882-7

analysis of ordinary "God-talk" among lay Christians as well as from the language and imagery used throughout Scriptures. Thus, it would seem that the nature of religious attributions and their relationship to explanatory processes would be a fruitful area of investigation.

The phenomenon of religious attributions has received increasing attention from researchers over the past several years. Attribution theory, a conceptual formulation which deals explicitly with how people explain occurrences and make judgments in general has been proposed as a useful basis for exploring these religious phenomena (Proudfoot and Shaver 1975; Spilka, Hood, and Gorsuch 1985). However, relatively little is empirically known about religious attributional processes themselves. The available evidence does suggest that prior religious beliefs are associated with religious explanations (Gorsuch and Smith 1983; Ritzema 1979). Attributions to natural causes and to supernatural causes are frequently made concurrently, reflecting usage of a "multiple sufficient causes" schema (Ritzema and Young 1983). The nature of specific events and the contextual cues within events have been shown to relate to religious interpretations of events as well (Gorsuch and Smith 1983; Pargament and Sullivan 1981; Spilka and Schmidt 1983). Personal religiosity may provide a "cognitive map" that is used for event interpretation under certain conditions (Glock and Piazza 1981; Spradlin and Malony 1981). Finally, Pargament and Hahn's (1986) analysis of attributions to God in health-related situations suggested that God attributions relate to attempts at finding support and strength in stressful circumstances and to maintenance of a meaningful world view.

Only recently have there been attempts at developing a general attribution theory to organize existing data and to guide future research in this area (Spilka, Hood, and Gorsuch 1985; Spilka, Shaver, and Kirkpatrick 1985). This work has provided a helpful starting point by clarifying three basic attributional motives: the desire or need for meaning, control, and self-esteem. However, the inferential processes used in service of these different attributional motives remain unclear. Thus, it would seem that a useful approach to advance our theoretical development would be to clarify the types of explanatory processes involved when people make attributions to God. Developments within the field of attribution theory suggest that there are at least two types of inferential processes that can be used in event interpretation: (a) a *sanctioning* process which yields judgments of responsibility; or (b) a *causal inference* process which yields causal judgments by explaining what conditions or actions produced the event (Hamilton 1980).

The sanctioning process begins with two known starting points: an actor's behavior and an outcome (Hamilton 1980). This type of inference process involves evaluating the possible link between the behavior and the outcome in order to determine whether sanctions should be applied to the actor. The goal of the sanctioning process is assignment of responsibility for the effect that is being considered. A helpful example of sanctioning is seen through the reactions of the American public to the trial of Lieutenant Calley for the death of innocent victims in the "Mai Lai Massacre" during the Vietnam War (Kelman and Lawrence [Hamilton] 1972, cited in Hamilton 1978). A significant group in the national population approved of Lieutenant Calley's criminal trial on the grounds than an individual should be held accountable for the consequences of his actions. This group presumably attributed high levels of responsibility to Calley for the killings. However, another large group in the national sample disapproved of Calley's trial on the grounds that subordinates have a duty to follow orders that are given them by authorities. This second group apparently used a different model of sanctioning than did the first group and minimized Calley's responsibility for the outcome since his motivations and reasons for acting were determined by a role-relationship with his superiors. Thus, although the same outcome was being considered by attributors, sanctioning judgments of responsibility differed depending upon factors perceived as influencing the link between action and outcome (Hamilton 1978).

The above mentioned example illustrates how physical causality is often insufficient for establishing a person's responsibility for his own actions (or lack of action) and resulting outcomes. Mitigating circumstances such as an agent's role-relationship with an authority may either limit or enhance liability for sanctions (Fincham and Jaspars 1980, pp. 113-114; Hamilton 1978, 1980). The case of Lieutenant Calley also illustrates how perceptions of an actor's reasons or motivations for behavior are often instrumental in determining to whom responsibility is ascribed for outcomes. Individuals who tended to minimize Calley's responsibility presumably focused on such factors as the source of Calley's motivations for action, in contrast to the other group which tended to arrive at responsibility attribution by focusing on the direct consequences of Calley's physical behavior (Hamilton 1978). Thus, it is not only what a person does (i.e., his physical behavior) that determines his responsibility for outcomes, it is what he is expected to do from the viewpoint of the attributor that is often instrumental for establishing responsibility.

In contrast, the starting point for the causal inference process is some effect, and this process involves an attempt to explain the effect in terms of antecedent conditions or forces without which the outcome would not have occurred (Hamilton 1980). Although there is frequently no ambiguity regarding the direct causes of events in normal day to day affairs, certain outcomes will be "puzzling" at times, and it is under such circumstances that causal reasoning will be employed (Hamilton 1980). For example, consider the attempt of a police detective to make valid attributions of causation for someone's death. Assuming there is some ambiguity, the detective will evaluate all possible evidence to "uncover" how the death occurred (e.g., suicide versus a killing) and by what means it occurred (e.g., chemical poisoning versus asphyxiation).

In short, the detective will "explain" the outcome by making inferences that establish a link between the effect and pre-existing conditions. This process of causal inference is typical of all scientific investigation (Hamilton 1980) where the concern is for prediction of a future outcome or for replication of an effect by establishing the requisite conditions (i.e., "causes") determined to be necessary and sufficient for it to occur.

As Hamilton (1980) notes, the sanctioning process often follows the causal inference process since potential causes must be identified before responsibility judgments can be made. However, it is important to note that use of attributional language may, at times, be ambiguous with assignment of "responsibility" reflecting either a sanctioning logic or a causal inference logic (Fincham and Jaspars 1980, p. 104). For example, certain attributors may speak of Lieutenant Calley as "responsible" for the killings at Mai Lai because he was a direct cause, but they may not hold him liable for sanctions. Other attributors may speak of Calley as "responsible" both because he was a direct cause and because he is judged as liable for sanctions. Hence, careful consideration of language use needs to be made for a clear understanding of attributional logic within any given situation.

The foregoing review of types of explanatory processes suggests that interpersonal relationships between potential actors are often determinative of the types of explanations achieved for outcomes. A perceiver's understanding of the nature of interpersonal influence, if any, and his perception of locus of causation are instrumental variables governing attributional logic and resulting explanations.

TOWARD A MODEL FOR ATTRIBUTION TO GOD

Past research on religious attribution appears not to have addressed the possibility that attributions to God may reflect either or both the sanctioning and causal inference processes. For example, when Gorsuch and Smith (1983) asked persons to assign "responsibility" for outcomes, it is not clear whether responses were based on causal inference or liability for sanctions. Nor is the distinction clear in Pargament and Sullivan's (1981) study. These researchers asked subjects both about liability for sanctions and causality in a single dependent measure through ratings of the degree to which situations were "due to" (i.e., "responsibility" or "causal" ascription) or "caused by" (i.e., "causal" ascription) various forces. Similarly, in a recent study which investigated attributions to God (Spilka and Schmidt 1983), there was no attempt to clarify type of explanatory process since participants were asked simply to rate the extent to which various factors were "explanatory of what occurred" in vignettes. Hence, questions of responsibility versus causation have not yet been examined in relation to God attribution. It would seem that an important early step for understanding the meaning of religious attributions is to describe and investigate the use of explanatory processes underlying both causal and responsibility attributions to the deity.

Our preceding analysis of sanctioning judgments and causal inferences suggests that God may be viewed as "responsible" for outcomes through either explanatory process. For example, when causality is ascribed to God, the deity may be seen as either one of several necessary antecedent conditions or as the sole necessary and sufficient antecedent condition for the outcome. It is this later case that frequently leads to identification of an outcome as a "miracle" in lay language. In contrast, when God's "responsibility" is mediated through a sanctioning process, His relationship with direct causes (e.g., persons who are potential actors) are frequently determinative. For example, God may be ascribed responsibility for an outcome when an actor's motivations to cause an outcome are perceived as influenced by God. Thus, perceptions of locus of direct causation and perceptions of interpersonal influence between God and person are instrumental variables influencing attributional logic and explanatory process used by religious persons.

Both legal philosophy and empirical research suggest that perceptions of a potential actor's intent to act and ability to cause an outcome are instrumental for determining responsibility judgments and related inferences (Fincham and Jaspars 1980, p. 103; Weiner, Kun, and Benesh-Weiner 1978, cited in Fincham and Jaspars 1980, p. 93; Weiner and Peter 1973, cited in Fincham and Jaspars 1980, p. 93). For example, in situations where causes are ambiguous, establishing a person as possessing adequate ability to account for an outcome will be central to establishing him as a cause. The attributor would need to consider alternative causes when the person is judged as incapable of producing the effect in question.

In addition to perceptions of ability, inferences of intent to act would be expected to affect attributional processes. In ambiguous situations where a person is judged as desiring a certain outcome (i.e., possessing high intent), it may be inferred that he took action. In contrast, if intent is perceived as low, the person may be judged not to have taken action or to have been influenced in some way such that sufficient motivation to act was created.

Causal inferences and sanctioning judgments of responsibility in ambiguous situations where God and person are perceived would be expected to be influenced by interaction of the above mentioned factors. For example, if intent to produce an outcome is perceived to have been low before the outcome occurred, then either of two attributional patterns may result depending upon varying perceptions of the person's ability: (a) When the person is judged to have possessed insufficient ability to cause the outcome (in addition to possessing inadequate motivation to act, i.e., low intent), then alternative causes, such as God, would be sought since the person would not be judged as acting; (b) When the person is judged as having sufficient ability to cause the outcome but with low motivation (i.e., low intent), then he may either not be judged as acting, or may be seen as directly influenced by another agent (i.e., God) so that sufficient intent is gained to motivate behavior that subsequently causes the outcome.

In contrast, if intent to produce an outcome is judged to have been high before the outcome occurred, then two different attributional patterns may result corresponding to varying perceptions of the potential actor's ability: (a) With sufficient motivation to act, but with insufficient ability, the person may still be judged to have caused the outcome, but only with the "help" of other "causes" such as God; (b) When both ability and intent levels are perceived as sufficiently high, then the person would be expected to be seen as taking action and as being the direct cause. The presence of God as an authority who is inactive in the situation, but who sanctioned the action sometime in advance, would justify ascription of responsibility to the deity as well as possibly delimiting the person's responsibility (i.e., liability) for his own action and outcome.

A minor expectation involves attributions to luck. It is felt that attributions to luck would seldom be used by the highly religious.

PURPOSE

The purpose of the present study is to test characteristics of God and persons by varying levels of a potential actor's intent (high vs. low) and ability (high vs. low). Since there are wide individual differences in belief about God, we also hypothesize that religious belief will affect overall levels of attribution of responsibility to God across all models. Religious Conservatives are expected to make greater attributions to God than will persons with no religious commitment. Similarly, we expect that persons for whom religion is very important will attribute greater overall responsbility to God than will persons for whom religious beliefs are less important.

Finally, there may be individual differences in use of attributional models *within* groups of persons who subscribe to the *same* religious beliefs. A person's degree of commitment or "ego-involvement" (Sherif and Sherif 1967, pp. 115-136; 1969, pp. 295-297) in his theological position may be one such factor that would differentiate subgroups and have a corresponding influence on attributions. For example, it may be that a person with high ego-involvement in his own religious belief system will utilize only one model of responsibility attribution rather than flexibility employing different models when conditions vary. With less ego-involvement, there may be a corresponding flexibility in use of attributional model through which God's causation or responsibility is expressed. Since ego-involvement is generally uncorrelated with one's attitude, it may be an important additional factor for consideration in attributional research. It is, therefore, included as an exploratory measure in the present study.

METHODS

Subjects

The participants in the present study were drawn from four undergraduate institutions selected to provide a heterogeneous theological sample. The schools included a secular university, a small evangelical Christian college, a small private college affiliated with a moderate to liberal Christian denomination, and a third private college without religious ties. Questionnaires were administered to a total of 305 students in social science and religion courses. The classes ranged in size from approximately 20 to 130 individuals.

Vignettes

The study was introduced to participants as an investigation of how people form impressions given limited information. In the first section of the questionnaire, four brief vignettes were presented with a series of rating scales. All stories were constructed so that attributions of causality and responsibility were ambiguous. All vignettes described events with positive outcomes of high relevance to participants and were designed to vary levels of a potential actor's intent (high vs. low) and ability (high vs. low).

The levels of Ability and Intention between stories were presented in four counterbalanced orders. Each participant was placed under all possible conditions of the independent variables in a repeated measures format using one of the orders.

For example, one of the vignettes was about a person who might help another with directions to a place in the city. Four versions of the background information were created to vary perceptions of Intent (A = low; B = high) and Ability (C = low; D = high).

Background Information: Person J. (C: *does not know*/D: *knows*) where (C: *any*/D: *all*) of the hospitals are in the city. Person J. is an individual who (A: *very rarely*/B: *very often*) volunteers to help strangers, even in emergency situations. In the past, Person J. has (A: *very rarely*/B: *very often*) volunteered to help people who have asked for directions in the city.

Following presentation of the manipulation checks, participants turned to a new page where the same background information was presented along with a description of an event and outcome, similar to the one described in the manipulation check measures. For example, one of the events and outcomes was described as follows:

Event: Person J. was in a hurry. An adult approached J. on the street and asked for directions to a hospital in order to arrive on time for an important medical appointment. No one else was around other than Person J. The lost adult had tried all other possible ways of getting directions but was almost out of time. No one saw for sure if Person J. stopped to offer help.

Outcome: The lost person soon arrived at the hospital. The person was in time for the important medical appointment.

Measures

After reading each event and outcome, a series of 10-point rating scales (e.g., 1 = "Definitely Agree; 10 = "Definitely Disagree") were presented to assess agreement or disagreement with various attributional statements and responses to attributional questions. These were presented in four randomized orders across stories to minimize the possibility of a response set bias due to repeated exposure to the same questions after each vignette. The scales were:

1.   Person X intended to do what God wanted in the situation.
2.   To what extent is God responsible for the outcome?
3.   God directly gave person X the internal motivation/reason to be helpful in this situation.
4.   To what extent is Person X responsible for the outcome?
5.   God acted independently of Person X to cause the outcome.
6.   To what extent is luck responsible for the outcome?
7.   Person X is *a* direct cause of the outcome (even if there may be other direct causes).
8.   How hard did person X try to cause the outcome?
9.   God worked through Person X to cause the outcome.

After the participants read and responded to all four vignettes, they were asked to classify their own theological beliefs by selecting one of the following categories: Fundamentalist, Evangelical, Conservative, Orthodox, Neo-Orthodox, Liberal, Humanist, Agnostic, Atheist, or Other[1] (after Moberg 1969). Following the Sherif procedures for measuring ego-involvement (Sherif and Sherif 1967, pp. 115-136; 1969, pp. 295-297), participants were instructed to indicate all the terms from the above mentioned list representing theological beliefs that they found "objectionable" from their own position. The total number of these positions rated as "objectionable" (i.e., "Range of Theological Rejection") was identified as a measure of ego-involvement.

Finally, a measure of salience of religious beliefs was included. Participants were asked to rate the personal "importance" of their religious beliefs by selecting a number on a 10-point scale (1 = "Unimportant"; 10 = "Extremely Important").

Importance of Beliefs and Theological Self-Classification were combined to identify homogeneous groups of different theological positions. Three groups were predefined based upon logical multiple cutpoints on both measures with considerations of sufficient N in each group. "Conservatives" were defined as those reporting high on Importance of Beliefs (re, 8 to 10) and with theological self-classifications as Fundamentalists, Conservatives, or Evangelicals ($N = 104$). "Moderates" were defined as those also with scores in the range of 8-10 on Importance of Beliefs, but with theological self-classifications as Orthodox, Neo-Orthodox, or Liberal ($N = 52$). Finally, persons rating Importance of Beliefs in a lower range (i.e., 1-5 on the 10-point scale) and classifying themselves as either Humanists, Agnostics, or Atheists were labelled as having a "Non-theological" Position ($N = 33$).

Theological Self-Classification correlated significantly with Importance of Beliefs, but, as predicted, Ego-involvement was found to be uncorrelated with either Self-Classification ($r = .03$) or Importance (r also .03) in the sample of 284. Thus, it would seem that Ego-involvement is a construct which is independent of religiosity as commonly measured.

Ego-involvement measured as the number of theological positions rejected was divided to form two groups for purposes of statistical analysis. Persons with "low" Ego-involvement were defined as those rating three or fewer theological positions as "objectionable" from their own position ($N = 132$). Research participants with greater than three theological positions identified as "objectionable" were classified as "high" on this measure ($N = 57$).

ANALYSES

Manipulation Check Analyses

Due to the large number of tests computed in the analyses and the large N, the significance level was set at .01. (See Smith 1983 for .05 level results.)

Several questions were designed to serve as manipulation checks for Intent and Ability. An analysis of variance was conducted on each measure to verify the efficacy of the experimental manipulations. As designed, perceptions of motivation to act under low Intent conditions were found to be significantly lower ($M = 2.99$) than these perceptions under high Intent conditions ($M = 8.73$) ($F(1,186) = 600.03, p < .001$). Also, a main effect of Intent on Attributions of Effort to Persons ($F(1,183) = 109.98, p < .001$) showed that greater levels of personal effort were perceived under high Intent conditions ($M = 7.41$) as compared with these attributions under low Intent conditions ($M = 5.33$). However, an unexpected main effect of Ability on perceptions of Intent was found ($F(1,186) = 8.97, p < .01$) with slightly higher intent perceived under high Ability conditions ($M = 6.07$) than under low Ability conditions ($M = 5.64$).

As designed, perceptions of a potential actor's capability to produce outcomes under low Ability conditions were significantly lower ($M = 3.06$) than perceptions of this factor under high Ability conditions ($M = 8.99$) ($F(1,186) = 592.98, p < .001$).

These findings suggest that, overall, the experimental manipulations did create varying perceptions of Intent and Ability across experimental conditions.

Analyses of Dependent Measures

A series of four-way analyses of variance were conducted on each dependent measure. Theological Position (i.e., Conservative, Moderate, or Non-theological) and Ego-involvement were used as simultaneous blocking variables so that interaction effects among these grouping factors could be evaluated in addition to main effect analyses.

Attributions of Responsibility to God

It was hypothesized that religious Conservatives would attribute greater overall responsibility to God for outcomes than would persons with a Non-Theological Position. The analyses found the predicted main effect of Theological Position on Attributions of Responsibility to God ($F(2,138) = 60.28, p < .001$) with greater levels of attribution by the Conservatives ($M = 7.70$) and Moderates ($M = 6.68$) relative to persons with a Non-Theological Position ($M = 3.31$).

God's Interpersonal Influence

It was hypothesized that Moderates would see God's activity by providing reasons or motivations to act more than would Conservatives. A main effect of Theological Position was found for perception of Interpersonal Influence from God (i.e., God providing "reasons" or "motivations" to act) ($F(2,185) = 52.04, p < .001$) but contrary to prediction, Conservatives made greater attributions ($M = 7.34$) than did the Moderates ($M = 6.66$). Persons with a Non-Theological Position attributed the least amount of interpersonal influence to God ($M = 3.15$).

It was also suggested that religious persons would see God as inspiring action when potential actors' intent had been low rather than high. A main effect of Intent was found on perceptions of God's interpersonal influence ($F(1,185) = 7.83, p < .01$). However, contrary to prediction, there was greater perception of God providing reasons or motivations to persons under high Intent conditions ($M = 6.75$) relative to low Intent conditions ($M = 6.17$).

A significant interaction between Theological Position and Ego-involvement was also manifest on this dependent measure ($F(2,185) = 5.74$, $p < .01$) and is graphically presented in Figure 1 (see p. 144).

Inspection of Figure 1 reveals greater perceptions of God's inspiring motivation when Ego-involvement was high, but only for the Conservatives. For persons with a Non-theological Position, the relationship was reserved with greater amounts of attribution for those who were low on Ego-involvement relative to persons high on this measure.

God's Activity Through Persons and Independent of Persons

It was hypothesized that Conservatives would perceive God functioning independent of persons to a greater degree than would persons with Moderate or Non-Theological positions. As expected, a main effect of Theological Position was found on perceptions of God working independently of persons ($F(2,183) = 18.37$, $p < .001$) with greater levels of attribution being made by Conservatives ($M = 5.44$) and Moderates ($M = 5.06$) relative to persons with a Non-Theological Position ($M = 2.74$).

Essential to much theology is the perception of God working through human agency. It was hypothesized that Moderates would perceive God as "acting" in this way more than would Conservatives. Contrary to prediction, the Conservatives were found to perceive God working through personal efforts and actions to a greater degree ($M = 7.41$) than the Moderate ($M = 6.26$) and both to a greater degree than those with a Non-Theological Position ($M = 2.72$) ($F(2,183) = 62.65$, $p < .001$). A main effect of Ego-involvement on perceptions of God working through persons was found ($F(1,183) = 6.45$, $p < .05$) with greater attributions by persons with low Ego-involvement in their religious beliefs ($M = 5.91$) relative to those with high Ego-involvement ($M = 5.02$). But a two-way interaction of Theological Position and Ego-involvement on perceptions of God working through persons also was found ($F(2,183) = 6.84$, $p < .01$) and is graphically presented in Figure 2 (see p. 145).

Inspection of Figure 2 reveals that greater attributions of God working through persons were made by highly ego-involved individuals but only for those who were also Conservatives. For persons with Moderate or Non-Theological Positions, the relationship was reversed with greater attributions made by persons low on Ego-involvement.

The findings suggested that it might be instructive to look at correlations among these measures across experimental conditions. Correlations between Attributions of Responsibility to God and attributions of God's activity were computed separately for each condition, but differed little, hence the mean correlations are presented in Table 1. The positive and siginificant correlations among these measures across all conditions of the independent variables suggest that these judgments may be governed by related attributional principles.

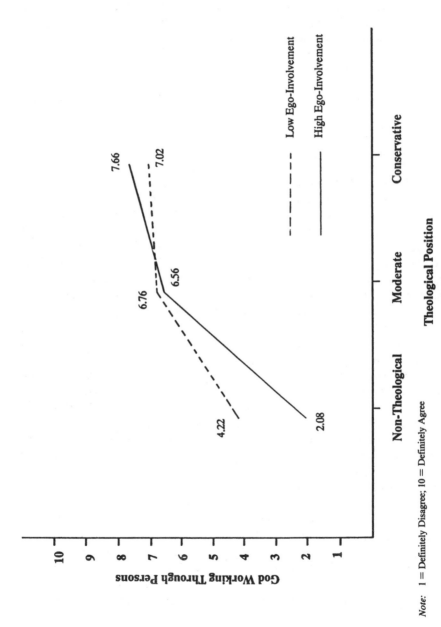

Figure 1. Attributions to God for Providing Reasons/Motivations to Persons

Note: 1 = Definitely Disagree; 10 = Definitely Agree

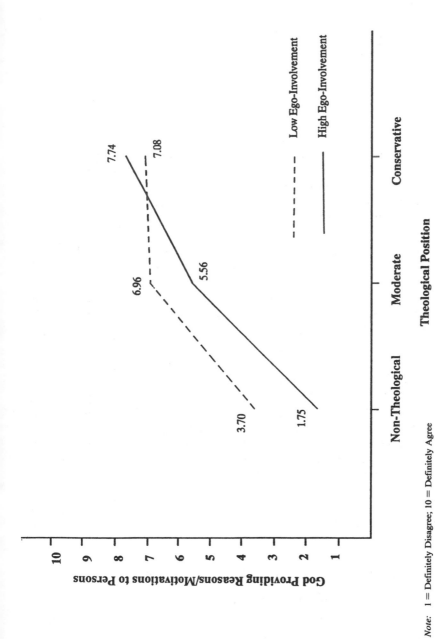

Figure 2.   Attributions to God for Working Through Persons

Table 1.   Means of Correlations Between Modality of God's
Actions and Attributions of Responsbility to God[a]

Measure	1	2	3	4
(1) Attributions of Responsibility to God	—			
(2) God Acting Independently of Persons	.43	—		
(3) God Acting Through Persons	.60	.40	—	
(4) God Providing Reasons/				
Motivations to Persons	.57	.35	.74	—

[a]$N = 279$. All correlations are significant at $p < .01$. Mean values were calculated across the four experimental conditions using Fisher's Z Coefficient.

The above mentioned findings do not support our hypothesis of an interaction between Theological Position and use of attributional model since God was judged as simultaneously active both through persons and independent of persons. The significant correlations among these attributional measures further suggests that when God is judged as responsible, he is seen as "active" through multiple channels simultaneously.

Attributions of Intent to Do God's Will

As previously noted, it was hypothesized that the Moderates would center more on the intent of the actors than would Conservatives. A main effect of Theological Position on judgments of Intent to Do God's Will was found ($F(2,186) = 28.50, p < .001$). However, contrary to prediction, the highest levels of this attribution were made by the Conservatives ($M = 6.92$), then Moderates ($M = 5.99$), and finally persons with a Non-Theological Position ($M = 3.96$).

A main effect of Ego-involvement was also found on perceptions of Intent to Do God's Will ($F(1,186) = 8.10, p < .01$). Greater levels of attribution were made by persons with low Ego-involvement in their beliefs ($M = 6.09$) compared with persons with high Ego-involvement ($M = 5.15$).

It was suggested that an actor may be judged as intending to do God's will either when his prior intent to act is seen as high or low, but with subsequent influence from God. Therefore, the obtained main effect for Intent on perceptions of motivation to do God's will ($F(1,186) = 60.87, p < .001$) was unanticipated. Greater perceptions of motivation to do God's will were made under high Intent conditions ($M = 7.12$) relative to low Intent conditions ($M = 5.47$).

Attributions of Responsibility to Persons

Our review of the attribution literature suggested that both perceptions of a person's intent and ability levels are determinative of personal responsibility for outcomes. As anticipated, statistical analysis revealed main effects for both Intent ($F(1,185) = 18.05$, $p < .001$) and Ability ($F(1,185) = 32.51$, $p < .001$) on this variable. Consistent with previous research, higher levels of attribution were made under high Intent conditions ($M = 6.51$) compared to low Intent conditions ($M = 5.76$). Similarly, greater levels of Attribution of Responsibility to Persons were found under high Ability conditions ($M = 6.52$) relative to low Ability conditions ($M = 5.75$).

Attributions of Direct Causation to Persons

It was suggested that when a person's intent and ability were both seen as low, then the persons would not be perceived as a direct cause of outcomes. As anticipated, main effects of Intent ($F(1,183) = 19.57$, $p < .001$) and Ability ($F(1,183) = 36.30$, $p < .001$) were found on Attributions of Direct Causation to Persons. Greater degrees of causation were attributed to persons under high Intent conditions ($M = 6.69$) compared with attributions under low Intent conditions ($M = 5.89$). Similarly, higher levels of causation were attributed to persons when Ability conditions were high ($M = 6.77$) rather than low ($M = 5.80$). However, the high levels of attribution across all experimental conditions suggest that persons were never perceived as inactive.

Luck

A main effect of Theological Position on Attributions to Luck was obtained ($F(2,183) = 5.99$, $p < .01$). Persons with a Non-Theological Position perceived luck to be a significant factor in outcomes to a greater degree ($M = 4.58$) than did Moderates ($M = 4.00$) and religious Conservatives ($M = 3.22$).

DISCUSSION

This study suggests that individual differences in religiosity mediate attributions of responsibility to God. As hypothesized, religious Conservatives ascribed greater overall levels of responsibility to God as compared with Moderates and persons with a Non-Theological Position. This finding supports previous research suggesting that attributions to God are influenced by various dimensions of religious belief (Gorsuch and Smith 1983; Ritzema 1979). In this study the Conservatives and Moderates resembled each other more than they resembled the Non-Theologicals.

These findings also suggest that attributions of responsibility to the deity follow attributional processes used in daily social interactions, but these attributions were found to be multiply determined when the attributors were religious Conservatives or Moderates. For these groups, the pattern of findings suggests that both God's inspiring of people and God's sharing in the causation are used simultaneously in determining responsibility ascriptions to the deity. In contrast, persons with a Non-Theological Position were found to attribute low levels of attribution to God across all measures. "Luck" was a more frequent attribution for the latter.

Conservative Theological Position

As predicted, Conservatives attributed the greatest overall responsibility to God of any group in the study. They also judged God to be more active in situations than persons with a Non-Theological Position. Conservatives saw God as acting through persons, as providing motivation and reasons for persons to act and as working outside of personal agency with all of these operating at the same time. Levels of these attributions were higher among Conservatives than among persons with a Moderate or Non-Theological Position. They also perceived more intent from the actors to do God's will in situations than did others, and rated luck as less responsible for outcomes than did persons with Moderate or Non-Theological Positions.

Beliefs in God's omnipotence or omniscience may have led the Conservatives in this study to see God as active through multiple channels simultaneously, rather than as seeing His activity limited to any single modality, such as either through persons or as independent of persons. Such beliefs in God's action through multiple channels may be reflected in the broad range of metaphors used by Conservative Christians to describe God's relationship to persons and events. For example, God may be seen as "Shepherd" when He is judged as working through persons, or when providing motivations to persons, since this metaphor emphasizes God's relationship to believers. Conservatives may also describe God as "sovereign King" since He is seen as determining events, independent of personal efforts and initiative. This tendency for believers to see God's responsibility mediated through multiple channels may also underlie their convictions that God is in absolute control of all events, while rejecting the control exerted by such factors as "luck." Thus, God may be perceived by Conservatives as insuring His sovereignty whether people participate with Him or not in producing favorable outcomes, consistent with God's purposes.

The highly religious persons in this study attributed high levels of responsibility to God even though they identified naturalistic causes, such as an actor's behavior. High levels of responsibility were attributed to both God and to actors by the Conservative subjects. It would seem that Conservatives saw the actors in vignettes as "agents" of God, and the actors' role-relationship with God may have provided the "normative context" whereby sanctioning judgments of responsbility were made to God for the outcome of the agents' behavior (Hamilton 1978). Persons with Moderate or Non-Theological beliefs may not have perceived actors as God's agents, and therefore may have used a different attributional logic for determining attributions of responsibility to God.

Moderate Theological Position

A similar overall pattern of God attribution was found across experimental conditions for Moderates as was described for the Conservatives, except that levels of attribution were lower. For example, Moderates attributed more overall responsibility to God than did those with a Non-Theological Position, but less than the Conservatives. Moderates judged God as simultaneously active through persons, in influencing persons, and in working independently of persons, but to less degrees than was found for Conservatives.

The above mentioned differences between Conservatives and Moderates— while not strong in this study—suggests that a different attributional logic may govern ascriptions of responsibility to God for each group. For example, it may have been that the Moderates saw some of the events as more "puzzling" than did the Conservatives, as when outcomes occurred despite an actor's low intent and low ability level. In contrast to the Conservatives, the Moderates may have used "causal reasoning" rather than sanctioning (Hamilton 1978, 1980) under these conditions to determine antecedent factors that accounted for outcomes.

The use of causal reasoning rather than sanctioning by Moderates is also supported by the findings that this group perceived less overall interpersonal influence from God than did the Conservatives, and less intent of the actors to do God's will than did the Conservatives. Thus, it would seem that the Moderates saw actors as functioning less as God's "agents" than did the Conservatives. Moderates may therefore see God as somewhat less "personal" than do the Conservatives and therefore acting mostly in situations involving outcomes that are not explainable through personal efforts and activities. Since the Moderates also attributed more responsibility to luck than did the Conservatives, they may tend to view God's activity as similar to luck in being more of an impersonal, unpredictable force.

Ego-involvement did function in a different manner for the Conservatives and for the Moderates. In past literature (Sherif and Sherif 1967, 1969) ego-involvement has been found to identify those who are more emotionally committed to the position, and hence show stronger effects. The results for the Conservatives are consistent with their interpretation, since the ego-involved Conservatives were like the other Conservatives only more so, seeing God as more active through persons and as motivating more human action. The ego-involved Moderates were, however, somewhat lower on these measures than were the ordinary Moderates. It seems that Moderates may look a bit more theologically conservative when they are less emotionally committed to their beliefs.

Non-Theological Position

Persons with a Non-Theological Position were found to attribute the least amount of responsibility to God of any group. Similarly, they judged God as less active in events through any means (e.g., through interpersonal influence or independently of persons) as compared with Moderates and Conservatives.

Implications

The multiple attributions of cause and responsibility to both persons and to God that were made by religious persons in this study corroborates past research in suggesting that the traditional dichotomy of causes into "personal" and "environmental" categories is inadequate for an understanding of God attributions (Gorsuch and Smith 1983). As discussed earlier, religious persons saw God as acting through multiple channels simultaneously. Rather than locus of causation determining responsibility attributions, this study suggests that it was the "interpersonal" context between God, persons, and event outcome that was determinative of attributional logic. The present findings therefore highlight the importance of making a conceptual distinction between attributions of responsibility (i.e., sanctioning) and attributions of causality (i.e., causal reasoning) in relation to God attribution. Since an interpersonal framework for attribution takes into account such factors as were found in this study to influence attributions of causation and responsibility to God, it would seem that this framework provides a useful theoretical basis for further investigation of factors determining attributions to God by religious persons and how such judgments relate to "secular" attributional processes.

Another model of attribution to God, not tested in the present study, is characterized by a person influencing God to cause outcomes through prayer. In this "Prayer" model, the person does not directly cause the outcome but God does. God is ascribed responsibility through a sanctioning process, particularly if a role-relationship (e.g., a "covenant") between God and the person is perceived. Highly religious persons who believe God to be acting independently of persons may use this model in ascribing responsbility both to God and to actors. This factor of personal influence from person to God would therefore be an important variable to consider in future research.

A more direct investigation of sanctioning logic for responsibility attributions, with "Prayer" and other models, could be made by manipulating factors associated with the relationship between God and actor as independent variables. For example, by directly manipulating perceptions of an actor's motivation to please God, and assessing effects on resulting responsibility judgments, we might further understand how sanctioning judgments function and how different religious beliefs influence this type of attributional process.

Research on God attribution might further explore the use of the attributional models proposed herein and how sanctioning and causal inference processes might be operative by different groups of persons. The attributional patterns found in the present study may have been limited since all events described positive outcomes within an interpersonal context where helping behaviors presumably could have occurred. Different types of events involving negative occurrences, and different types of interpersonal transactions might yield attributional patterns which fit more concisely to the demands of the different models of responsibility attribution in their "pure" form, as described in this study.

ACKNOWLEDGMENTS

This article is a portion of the first author's doctoral dissertation completed in the Graduate School of Psychology at Fuller Theological Seminary.

NOTE

1. Approximately 35 of the 305 research participants marked "Other" in designating their theological self-classification. These individuals used a variety of terms to describe their beliefs, including "Behaviorist," "Greek Orthodox (Armenian)," "salvationist," "Marxist," and "Latter Day Saint." The authors and two professors, all with graduate level training in theology, made independent ratings of each of these responses to reassign them to one of the nine other categories. These independent ratings were collated and consensual agreement among raters was used as the primary factor in final group assignment.

REFERENCES

Fincham, F. D. and J. M. Jaspars. 1980. "Attribution of Responsibility: From Man the Scientist to Man as Lawyer." Pp. 81-137 in *Advances in Experimental Social Psychology*, Vol. 13, edited by L. Berkowitz. New York: Academic Press.

Glock, C. Y. and T. Piazza. 1981. "Exploring Reality Structures." In *In Gods We Trust: New Patterns of Religious Pluralism in America*, edited by T. Robbins and D. Anthony. New Brunswick, NJ: Transaction Books.

Gorsuch, R. L. and C. S. Smith. 1983. "Attributions of Responsibility to God: an Interaction of Religious Beliefs and Outcomes." *Journal for the Scientific Study of Religion* 22(4):340-352.

Hamilton, V. L. 1978. "Who is Responsible? Toward a Social Psychology of Responsibility Attribution." *Social Psychology* 41:316-328.

_____. 1980. "Intuitive Psychologist or Intuitive Lawyer? Alternative Models of the Attribution Process." *Journal of Personality and Social Psychology* 39(5):767-772.

Moberg, D. O. 1969. "Theological Self-classification and Ascetic Moral Views of Students." *Review of Religious Research* 10:100-107.

Pargament, K. I. and J. Hahn. 1986. "God and the Just World: Causal and Coping Attributions to God in Health Situations." *Journal for the Scientific Study of Religion* 25:193-207.

Pargament, K. I. and M. Sullivan. 1981. "Examining Attributions of Control Across Diverse Personal Situations: A Psychosocial Perspective." Paper presented at the meeting of the American Psychological Association, Los Angeles.

Proudfoot, W. and P. Shaver. 1975. "Attribution Theory and the Psychology of Religion." *Journal for the Scientific Study of Religion* 14(4):317-330.

Ritzema, R. J. 1979. "Attribution to Supernatural Causation: An Important Component of Religious Commitment?" *Journal of Psychology and Theology* 7(4):286-293.

Ritzema, R. J. and C. Young. 1983. "Causal Schemata and the Attribution of Supernatural Causality." *Journal of Psychology and Theology* 11:36-43.

Sherif, C. and M. Sherif, eds. 1967. *Attitude, Ego-Involvement and Change.* New York: John Willey & Sons.

_____. 1969. *Social Psychology.* New York: Harper & Row.

Smith, C. S. 1983. "Sanctioning and Causal Attributions to God: A Function of Theological Position and Actors' Characteristics." Unpublished doctoral dissertation, Fuller Theological Seminary, Pasadena, California.

Spilka, B., R. W. Hood, and R. L. Gorsuch. 1985. *The Psychology of Religion: An Empirical Approach.* Englewood Cliffs, NJ: Prentice-Hall.

Spilka, B. and G. Schmidt. 1983. "General Attribution Theory for the Psychology of Religion: The Influence of Event-Character on Attributions to God." *Journal for the Scientific Study of Religion* 22:326-339.

Spilka, B., P. Shaver, and L.A. Kirkpatrick. 1985. "A General Attribution Theory for the Psychology of Religion." *Journal for the Scientific Study of Religion* 24:1-20.

Spradlin, W. and H. N. Malony. 1981. "Physiological State Deviation, Personal Religiosity, Setting Variation and the Report of Religious Experience." Paper presented at the meeting of the Society for the Scientific Study of Religion, Baltimore.

ADOLESCENCE AND RELIGION:
A REVIEW OF THE LITERATURE FROM
1970 to 1986

Peter L. Benson, Michael J. Donahue,

and Joseph A. Erickson

ABSTRACT

This review examines recent research on the religiousness of individuals aged 10 to 18. National profiles of religiousness indices for adolescents reveal a decline in most forms of religiousness over the adolescent years, and gender and race differences that correspond to those reported for adults. Research concerning cognitive processes in religious development indicate that this "adolescent apostasy" may be due in part to a rejection of the concrete religious images of childhood. Parental transmission of religious practices and values is found to be influenced both by the consistency and content of the parental messages. The impact of religious schooling, however, is less clear. Most social-personality research reflects interest in religion as a personal control against deviance, rather than the function of religion in the adolescent personality. An overview of the literature reveals a general lack of sophistication in measurement. The research in adolescent religiousness has tended to be the by-product of research in other areas, rather than an interest in itself.

Research in the Social Scientific Study of Religion, Volume 1, pages 153-181.
Copyright © 1989 by JAI Press Inc.
All rights of reproduction in any form reserved.
ISBN: 0-89232-882-7

The role of religion in adolescent development has been a focus of scientific research for decades. The most complete reviews of this literature were published between 1967 and 1977 (Bealer and Willets 1967; Elkind 1971; Havighurst and Keating 1971; Nelsen, Potvin, and Shields 1977; Potvin, Hoge, and Nelsen 1976). These reviews focus primarily on empirical literature published before 1970. Heretofore, the impressive volume of research studies generated in the 1970s and 1980s has not been systematically reviewed. The purpose of this review is to synthesize the empirical literature since 1970, with a focus not only on the high school years (9th to 12th grade) but also the years now commonly described as early adolescence (5th to 8th grade). Accordingly, the age span covered in this review is from 10 to 18.

The review is also limited to the literature published in the United States, with a few selected excursions into publications from other English-speaking countries. Only empirically- or theoretically-based publications are covered. The burgeoning literature on new religious movements is not reviewed for two reasons. First, most of the individuals involved in these groups are legal adults (18 or older) and therefore outside the range of our current concern. Second, thorough and recent reviews of the issues in this area can be found elsewhere (e.g., Barker 1986; Kaslow and Sussman 1982).

This review is divided into four sections: a national profile of adolescent religiousness, cognitive processes in adolescent religious development, psychosocial factors in religious development, and the relationship of adolescent religiousness to social-personality variables.

NATIONAL PROFILE OF ADOLESCENT RELIGIOUSNESS

Recent national opinion polls document that religious sentiments and practices typify the American adolescent. Gallup poll data on 13- to 18-year-old youth show that 95% profess belief in "God or a universal spirit, a proportion that closely parallels that for the adult (18 and over) population as a whole" (Gallup 1984, p. 69). Additionally, 75% believe in a personal God and 58% in life after death. Eighty-seven percent pray at least occasionally, and seven out of ten claim they are church members.

In this first section, we profile adolescent religiousness in more detail, documenting recent trends in survey data, and differences by age, gender, and race.

Historical Trends

Trends in adolescent religiousness vary by the decades under examination. Three reports published in the 1970s concluded that adolescent religiousness was more common in the decades prior to the 1970s. Dickinson (1976) reported declines between 1964 and 1974 in church attendance, frequency of Bible reading, and prayer among 10th to 12th grade adolescents in a small, northeast Texas community. In a 1977 follow-up study of "Middletown" (Caplow and Bahr 1979), significant changes in adolescent religiousness were documented, in comparison to data gathered 50 years earlier. Changes were particularly evident in the proportion affirming tenets the authors described as fundamentalist (e.g., in 1924, 94% agreed with the statement "Christianity is the one true religion and all peoples should be converted to it;" by 1977 only 38% reported agreement). Declines in religious importance and participation were less extreme. Because the demographics of Middletown changed significantly between 1924 and 1977, it is not clear to what extent these shifts reflect historical change.

Potvin et al. (1976) compared religious beliefs and practices for adolescents in 1951, 1961-62, and 1975. Decreases across time were evident in three areas: belief in a personal God, weekly attendance at religious services, and daily prayer. The three data collections, however, were not precisely comparable. For 1951, the authors used data from a study of 2,500 9th to 12th grade students (Remmers and Radler 1957), while the two later samples (1961-1962 and 1975) utilized a broader age range (13 to 18). Survey wordings also varied across the three data collections. In combination, these three studies suggest, but do not conclusively demonstrate, a decrease in some forms of adolescent religiousness between earlier decades and the 1970s.

The trends during the last ten years (1976-1985) reveal a more complicated picture. The most thorough, long-term examination of trends can be gleaned from the extensive data-base collected as part of the annual *Monitoring the Future* project conducted by the Survey Research Center of the Institute for Social Research of the University of Michigan (Bachman, Johnston, and O'Malley 1980a,b, 1981, 1984, 1985; Johnston, Bachman, and O'Malley 1980a,b, 1982, 1984, 1986). In each of these volumes, the authors present data on several religiousness indices from national representative samples of 16,000 high school seniors collected in the spring of each year, beginning with the class of 1976. Data for three indices ("how important is religion in your life," "how often do you attend religious services," "what is your religious preference") are presented in Figure 1. In all three cases, the 10-year pattern is slightly curvilinear, with a rise in religious expression between 1976 and 1980 and a decrease from 1980 to 1985. Essentially, percentages in 1985 return to the level of those found in 1976. Note, however, that weekly attendance rates in 1985 fall below those in 1976 (40.7% vs. 35.3%).

These data are in contrast to those presented by Gallup (1983) that reflect greater stability in religiousness between 1978 and 1983, based on pooled national samples of 13 to 18 year-old youth. However, because of the age range covered in the Gallup data, changes that might be evident with a particular

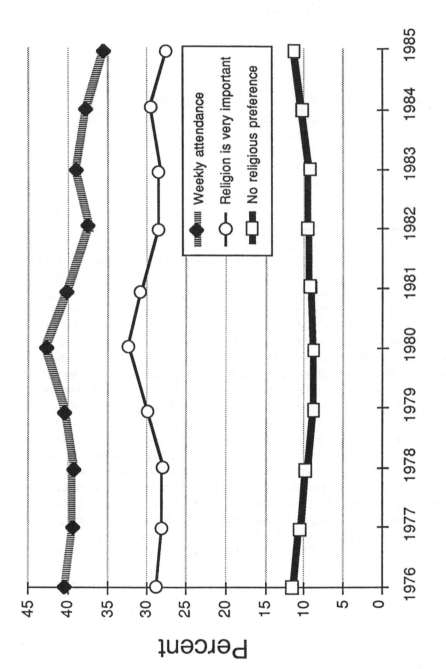

Figure 1

age-group, such as high school seniors, might be masked. Alternatively, the Gallup interviewers might have been more able to contact those who had dropped out of school, who are completely excluded from the *Monitoring the Future* data.

Age

Studies describing age changes in adolescent religiousness are universally cross-sectional in design. Accordingly, it is not possible to make conclusive statements about the amount of developmental change. Nevertheless, the constant finding across many studies is that religiousness and age are negatively related during the 10 to 18 age period. This holds for studies focusing on early adolescence (10 to 14) or high school-age youth (15 to 18). Because of the constancy of this finding in studies from 1970 to 1985, it is likely that developmental patterns toward decreasing religiousness are being evidenced.

Employing multiple-item indices of religion, Potvin et al. (1976) report significant declines between ages 13 to 15 and 15 to 18 in experiential religion (defined as closeness to God, frequency of prayer, and importance of religion), religious practice, and traditional orthodoxy. Gallup (1983) reported a similar difference between these two age groupings on a single-item measure of religious importance. Research on students enrolled in Catholic high schools demonstrated that 9th grade students (age 14 to 15) were more likely to view the church as important, to attend religious services, to read Scripture, and value religion than 12th grade students (Benson, Yeager, Wood, Guerra, and Manno 1986). In addition to these frequency or quantity measures, significant differences in religious orientations were also reported. In comparison to 9th graders, high school seniors score higher on measures of religious doubt and lower on measures of intrinsic religion (religion as an end in itself), extrinsic religion (religion as a means to other ends), vertical religion (religion understood as a relationship between the individual and God), horizontal religion (religion expressed as love of neighbor), and comforting religion (religion valued for support, comfort, and solace). No age differences were found for liberating religion (religion experienced as freeing and enabling). Ninth graders tend to exhibit higher restricting religion (religion experienced as supplying limits, controls, and discipline) than 12th graders.

Sloane and Potvin (1983) replicated the common overall negative correlation between age and religiousness, but they also reported a significant age-by-denomination interaction. Younger adolescents tended to be more religious than older adolescents among Baptists, Catholics, and mainline Protestants. Among sectarian groups (Pentecostal, Holiness, Mennonite), the reverse was true. No age-by-sex interactions were found.

Two studies of young adolescents demonstrate declines in several religiousness indices across ages. An investigation of 3,000 Minnesota 5th to

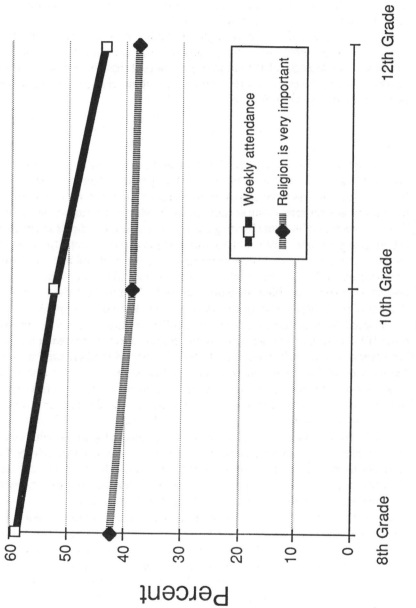

Figure 2

8th grade students reported declines in religious service attendance, daily prayer, and Biblical literalism (Nelsen et al. 1977). A national study of 8,000 5th to 9th graders indicated a grade-by-sex interaction for a multiple-item index of religious importance, with grade by grade decreases for boys but not for girls (Benson, Williams, and Johnson 1987).

One study spanned the junior high and high school years (Benson, Wood, Johnson, Eklin, and Mills 1983). Based on a random sample of 10,167 Minnesota 8th, 10th, and 12th graders, it reported that the decline in religious practice is considerably more pronounced than the decline in religious importance, as shown in Figure 2.

Gender

The literature on adolescents demonstrates similar patterns found among adults (Argyle and Beit-Hallahmi 1975): gender differences in religious behavior and attitude are consistently demonstrated, with females generally evidencing greater religiousness than males. This is particularly true when they focus in on religious behavior (e.g., worship attendance, prayer) or the self-reported importance or centrality of one's religious convictions. In all reviewed studies except two, females demonstrated higher levels of behavior and/or importance, and the effects held for both junior high and high school-age cohorts (Benson et al. 1987; Benson et al. 1983; Dickinson 1976; Gallup 1983; Johnston et al. 1986; Nelsen and Potvin 1981; Potvin et al. 1976). The two exceptions involved studies of students enrolled in Catholic schools. One found more Bible-reading by males, and no differences in worship attendance among high school students (Benson et al. 1986). The other found greater importance reported by males (Suziedelis and Potvin 1981). These latter authors noted these findings are consistent with research demonstrating that Catholic schools have more impact on males than females (Greeley, McCready, and McCourt 1976).

In their review of gender differences among adults, Argyle and Beit-Hallahmi (1975) argued that gender differences are more pronounced in private forms of religious expression than public forms (e.g., attendance). This distinction does not apply to adolescents. The difference between girls and boys is as pronounced for public behavior as it is for private expression.

Gender differences are more equivocal when belief content is considered. Two studies reported no gender differences in orthodoxy (Gallup 1983; Potvin et al. 1976). One reported higher orthodoxy for boys (Suziedelis and Potvin 1981). A study of high school students suggested that boys' belief patterns are more extrinsic than girls, while intrinsic, liberating, vertical, and horizontal themes are more prevalent among girls (Benson et al. 1986).

Four studies have sought explanations for reported gender differences in religious behavior and importance. Nelsen and Potvin (1981) found that girls score higher on a measure of experiential religion (as defined above) in those denominations that socialize girls to adapt to a traditional, feminine expressive role. Two studies (Benson 1986; Suziedelis and Potvin 1981) provided some evidence that differences in religiousness between boys and girls are partially explained by gender-related differences in sex-role orientations. And Nelsen (1981) showed that parental discord interfered more with the transmission of religious values to boys than to girls.

Race/Ethnicity

Differences by race and ethnicity have been infrequently studied. A synthesis of four studies reporting race differences yields these four differences between black and white adolescents:

1. Blacks attach more importance to religion than do whites (Benson et al. 1987; Benson et al. 1986; Johnston et al. 1986). Among high school seniors in 1985, 84% of blacks and 56% of whites report religion is "very" or "pretty" important (Johnston et al. 1986).
2. On a measure of intrinsic religion, black adolescents score significantly higher than whites (Benson et al. 1986).
3. Blacks attach more importance to church than do whites (Benson et al. 1986; Benson et al. 1987).
4. White adolescents are more likely to report weekly church attendance than blacks (Benson et al. 1986). The *Monitoring the Future* studies report this difference for every high school graduating class from 1976 through 1983, with no black/white differences for the classes of 1984 and 1985 (Bachman et al. 1980a,b, 1981, 1984, 1985; Johnston et al. 1980a,b, 1982, 1984, 1986). Dickinson (1982) reported a race-by-sex interaction, with white males attending more than black males, but black females attending more than white females.

We know of only one study comparing religion variables among blacks, whites, and Hispanics (Benson et al. 1986). In essence, Hispanic adolescents revealed religious patterns more like those of blacks than whites. Compared to whites, Hispanics placed more value on religion and church and were less likely to be weekly church attenders.

COGNITIVE FACTORS IN THE DEVELOPMENT OF RELIGIOUS THINKING

One of the dominant lines of empirical and theoretical inquiry in research on adolescent religiousness has to do with the role of cognitive factors. It is axiomatic in the developmental literature that a qualitative change occurs during the adolescent years. Based on the work of Piaget (1965/1932), the change is usually defined as a gradual shift from concrete operations to formal operations (often expressed as abstract thinking).

Since 1970, several researchers have extended inquiry about this shift into the religious domain. Drawing heavily on Goldman's (1964) work, researchers have looked at three interrelated issues: whether a qualitative change occurs during adolescence in religious cognition, how this change is related to other cognitive processes, and how this change is tied to religious commitment.

One consistent finding is that religious thinking between ages 12 and 18 becomes less literal and more abstract (Elkind 1971; Nelsen et al. 1977; Potvin et al. 1976). Goldman (1964) encouraged these investigations with his seminal work on the age-related sequencing of religious belief stages. Based on samples of British children, he postulated the occurrence of three stages: intuitive, concrete operational, and formal or abstract. The shift from concrete to abstract was placed in the 13 to 14-1/2 age span. Goldman concluded that the concrete-to-abstract shift in religious thinking requires that this shift had already occurred in general cognitive functioning; the shift to abstract religious thinking occurs more slowly than in other areas of cognitive functioning.

Peatling (Peatling 1974, 1977; Peatling and Laabs 1975) extended Goldman's work. Utilizing his Thinking About the Bible test, he reported that abstract religious thinking scores increased with age (9 to 18), as predicted by cognitive development theory. Abstract religious thinking correlated strongly with IQ, which is associated with abstract reasoning ability. Gender was unrelated to abstract thinking scores, but denomination was, with Missouri Synod Lutherans scoring less abstract than Episcopals (Peatling and Laabs 1975).

In a major contribution to the literature, Hoge and Petrillo (1978) sought to both replicate and extend this line of inquiry. This work documented three important findings:

1.   Abstract religious thinking among adolescents tends to be negatively related to creedal assent and religious practice, suggesting that the advent of abstract thinking is one factor accounting for the decline in adolescent religiousness documented earlier.

2.   Abstract religious thinking is correlated with the general cognitive ability to do abstract thinking.

3.   Contrary to Goldman's (1964) hypothesis, the discrepancy between level of religious thinking and overall cognitive capacity does not promote rejection of doctrine and church. The level of abstract religious thinking predicts rejection better than does the discrepancy.

Fowler's (1981) significant and creative theorizing about faith stages holds promise for understanding the cognitive structure of child and adolescent faith systems. He posits four stages in child and adolescent faith: primal faith (age

0 to 1), intuitive-projective faith (2 to 5), mythic-literal faith (6 to 12), and synthetic-conventional faith (13 to 18). Empirical work derived from these concepts could potentially refine the understanding of how religious thought evolves.

CONVERSION

No treatment of religion in adolescence, and most especially of religious development and religious cognition, would be complete without addressing the issue of religious conversion. It is included here because of the common assertion that conversion often corresponds with changes in adolescents' reasoning about self and world. Many contemporary treatments concentrate on alleged "brainwashing" or "coercive persuasion" by "cults" (see Bromley and Richardson 1983). But there is also a tradition stretching back to the very beginnings of American empirical psychology examining the phenomenon that is now popularly known as being "born again": "an abrupt, rapid change to an enthusiastic religious attitude, with highly emotional experiences and other conspicuous features accompanying it, whether lasting or not" (Neilson 1958).

Conversion may be the best-researched single topic in psychology of religion. Scroggs and Douglas (1967) estimated twenty years ago that there had been "at least five hundred publications dealing with the psychological dynamics of religious conversion" since the turn of the century (p. 206). Rambo (1982) lists more than 100 psychological and sociological studies on the topic from 1970 to 1981. Conversion is also probably the oldest topic in the empirical psychology of religion, as reflected by Starbuck's (1897, 1899) pioneering questionnaire survey on the topic. His findings, and the review of the literature presented by James (1902/1936) were to set the tone and foreshadow the findings of much of the research in this area for almost eighty years afterward: that "conversion is in its essence a normal adolescent phenomenon, incidental to the passage from the child's small universe to the wider intellectual and spiritual life of maturity" (James 1902/1936, p. 196, citing Starbuck 1899).

There also developed a standard "model" of the conversion process, that might be called the "four c's": conflict, crisis, conversion, contentment (cf. Batson and Ventis 1982; James 1902/1936; Meadow and Kahoe 1984). In this understanding, most conversions come about as a result of adolescent confusion in values and purpose in life, and these matters are simplified by making a "decision for Christ" or adopting some other religious system in toto.

More recent research, however, has challenged these somewhat simplistic explanations. Research reviewed by Meadow and Kahoe (1984) has demonstrated that conversions are frequently reported at ages both younger and older than adolescence, and that the frequently reported "adolescent" characteristic of the phenomenon was the result of relying on college samples for gathering data. "In every survey of individuals who had reached old age, the average age [of conversion] was raised sharply" (Ferm 1959, p. 210). Even the widely-held "crisis" theory of conversion has most recently been challenged by studies employing appropriate controls (Heirich 1977).

All of this having been said, it must also be admitted that virtually none of the recent research on religious conversion has been done on the 10 to 18 year-old age group that is being considered here. An examination of several recent psychology of religion texts (Batson and Ventis 1982; Meadow and Kahoe 1984; Paloutzian 1983; Spilka, Hood, and Gorsuch 1985) as well as a computer search of the topic "religion and adolescence" failed to uncover any significant body of research. Meadow and Kahoe noted national survey data indicating that one third of adolescents report a conversion experience; approximately the same number as in the adult population (see Gallup 1977-78, as presented in Paloutzian 1983). Meadow and Kahoe also noted a doctoral dissertation by Wilson in 1974 which involved a longitudinal study of 533 high school students. Eleven of the students experienced a religious conversion between the late fall and early spring of the 1971-72 school year. Wilson found that there was no evidence of a particular personality type susceptible to conversion, although conversion had generally positive personality effects on those who experienced it.

There is little doubt that, just as adolescents form many of the values and make many choices that will form their adult lifestyle in other areas, they make decisions about religion as well. The absence of research on this important topic with adolescents is a major lacuna in the field.

PSYCHOSOCIAL FACTORS IN RELIGIOUS DEVELOPMENT

As noted earlier, there is a steady decline in religious behaviors and attitudes during the adolescent years. This process of differentiation is ubiquitous and has remained relatively constant for over 30 years of research into adolescent religiousness. In addition to chronological age, a number of psycholosocial factors contribute to adolescent religious development. The focus of this section is to identify those factors which promote, influence, or inhibit adolescent religiousness. This literature is reviewed in five categories: parenting and family religious practice, parental values transmission, religious education (both school and church-based), peer influence, and other factors (geographic mobility, city size, and sibling structure of families).

Parenting and Family Religious Practice

Many studies have found that young people are more likely to remain affiliated with their parents' denomination or with some similar religious denomination than to convert to another religion or become religiously uninvolved (Spilka et al. 1985) and that parents are among the strongest influences on adolescent religious behavior (e.g., Potvin et al 1976; Hoge and Petrillo 1978; Benson et al. 1986). Argyle and Beit-Hallahmi (1975) found affiliation among adolescents conformed to parental affiliation in 40 to 90% of youth. Liberal Protestant denominations had lower rates of retention, while Catholics and Jews had higher rates.

Parental influence is manifested directly by socialization and indirectly by the way parents relate to their children and the forces in their environment (Potvin et al. 1976). Parents have their greatest influence on their children's church attendance, but peer influence may be more salient with regard to youth program attendance (Hoge and Petrillo 1978). In fact, Hoge and Petrillo found in their study of Maryland high school students that parents had almost no influence on their children's attitude toward church and church youth programs, suggesting the importance of peer influence. These researchers also found that consistency between parents with regard to their religious messages and behavior improved parents' success in communicating their values to their children.

Another issue has been whether parental influence is direct or indirect. Direct influence refers to behavior patterns passed on directly from parent to child, while indirect influence is the case in which parents' influence is filtered through the other socializing agents to which the parent introduces the child (i.e., church, school). Hoge and Petrillo's (1978) analysis suggests a direct parental effect, while later re-analysis looking at denomination effects on parental values (Hoge, Petrillo, and Smith 1982) found, "membership in one denomination or another predicted children's values more than did their parents' values," (p. 569) indicating a more indirect impact. Overall, the directness of parental influence is dependent upon the topic area being measured: parents are more influential in areas of observable behavior, especially ritual attendance, and peers' influence is more salient in youth group attendance and some forms of attitude formation.

Potvin et al. (1976) reported an overall correlation of .49 between parental and adolescent religious practice in their national sample of Catholic adolescents. Rosik and Gorsuch (1985) found that adolescents in the greater Los Angeles area generally resembled their parents on their level of intrinsic and extrinsic religiousness. But while parental and adolescent religious behaviors are undoubtedly related, this is not the only parental attribute which affects young people's religiousness, since neither parent's degree of religiousness prevents the decline in adolescent religiousness (Potvin and Sloane 1985).

A study of Mormon youth in Utah found that adolescents receiving high levels of both support (e.g., whether the parent "says nice things" about the child) and control (e.g., the parent keeps after the child to do well in school) tended to adhere more strongly to traditional forms of religiousness, have higher self-esteem, and were more likely to conform to parental expectations than others (Weigert and Thomas 1972). Nelsen (1980) also found a weak positive correlation between parental support and pre-adolescent religiousness in his data drawn from youth in grades 4-8 in southern Minnesota.

Benson et al. (1986) estimated several multiple regression equations predicting faith commitment (personal religiousness) and church commitment (institutional religiousness) from their national survey data of Catholic high school seniors. The three key factors predicting church and faith commitment were the student's perception of the importance of religion for mother and father, a positive family life, and the amount of religious activities in the home. The zero-order correlations between the predictors and the criteria were in the .20 to .30 range.

Hoge and Petrillo (1978) found that the variance explained by parental religiousness declined when other predictors were controlled (see also Acock and Bengtson 1978).

Taken as a whole, these studies seem to say that clear behavioral messages of love and support, consistency between mothers and fathers and between parental words and actions, and frequency of religious activities in the home seem to enhance overt religiousness on the part of adolescents.

Parent Value Transmission

For a number of years following Coleman's (1961) assertion that there was a separate youth culture with a separate youth-oriented value system, research in the area of religious value transmission focused on documenting the degree and nature of the "generation gap." For the most part, recent research has found mixed support for Coleman's notion. In their 1975 review, Argyle and Beit-Hallahmi asserted "there can be no doubt that the attitudes of parents are among the most important factors in the formation of (adolescent) religious attitudes" (p. 30). The work of Acock and Bengtson (1980) was influential in clarifying some of these crucial issues in values transmission research. They emphasized that youth are greatly influenced by the attitudes of their parents, "but it is the perceived, not actual attitudes which are influential" (p. 513).

A great deal of the research in the values transmission area has focused on which parent is more influential in determining youth's attitudes and values. Several studies report data showing the mother is more important (e.g., Acock and Bengtson 1978, 1980; Kelly, Benson, and Donahue 1986; Dudley and Dudley 1986), others have found the father to be more influential (e.g., Bengtson and Acock 1976), and still others have found mixed results (e.g., Hoge and Keeter 1976; Hoge and Petrillo 1978; Cornwall, Olsen, and Weed 1979; Nelsen 1980; Benson et al. 1987). Clark, Worthington, and Dauser (1986) reported differential results, with mothers having more influence on religious commitment and fathers having more influence on religious practice. Overall, which parent is more influential depends largely on what specific value one is measuring, and under what circumstances the child experiences the value.

Family tension has also been examined at as a factor in the transmission of parental religious values. Previous research had led Hoge and Petrillo (1978) to hypothesize that the amount of parent-child tension would influence values transmission. They found instead that parent-child tension was unimportant in their study of Maryland tenth graders. Hoge and Petrillo cited several studies (e.g., McCready 1972; Johnson 1973) suggesting that family tension, especially marital disagreement, adversely affects values transmission. They reported a positive correlation between parental marriage happiness and successful transmission of parental values to children.

Hoge et al. (1982) found that parental agreement on religious belief was one of the three most important factors associated with religious values transmission, the other two being younger age of parents and good parent-child relationships. Dudley and Dudley (1986) reported that when there was disagreement between parents as to religious values, adolescents were more likely to agree with the father.

Luft and Sorell (1986) found that fathers who practice a parenting style characterized by control and nurturance generated greater transmission of values, but that mothers maximized their influence by displaying a parenting style of control and communication.

In short, "the prevailing finding is that value transmission from parents to children is sometimes weak and sometimes strong depending greatly on the concreteness and saliency of the particular topic under study" (Hoge et al. 1982, p. 569).

Education

It was not until quite recently that religious schools and religious education programs have been studied with the sort of methodological rigor found in other areas of inquiry. This may be because of the complexity of the classroom situation as compared with laboratory and standard survey research, and because of the expense of drawing large representative national samples. Recent work (Benson et al. 1986; Kelly et al. 1985) has been able to draw large national samples of Catholic youth and educators in order to examine factors contributing to a full range of outcome measures, including adolescent religiousness.

The major finding in this area is that religious schooling does have a long-term impact on adolescent religiousness, especially during the high school years and if they involve at least 1,000 hours of classroom instruction in religion (Spilka et al. 1985). The initial suggestion of 1,000 hours as a "critical mass" was made by Bock (1977) in his study of Jewish young adults. Similarly, Greeley et al. (1976) found that the decline in adult religious practice was less for those with greater Catholic schooling (10 years or more).

Religious effects of schooling are also tied to certain school climate factors. For example, religious instruction can lead to rejection of religiousness when youth experience teachers as unapproachable, insincere, or uncertain about expressing their own beliefs (Hoge and Petrillo 1978).

Greeley and Gockel (1971) reviewed three previous studies on the effect of religious schooling (Erickson 1964; Johnstone 1966; Greeley and Rossi 1966). Their findings were mixed. Johnstone found the greatest impact of religious education was limited to youth with low parental religiousness, but Greeley and Rossi reported family religiousness interacted with religious schooling to create a "multiplier effect." There was a clear impact on the amount of biblical knowledge and overt religious behavior on the part of religious school students, but these studies were not able to identify what factors within the school led to these benefits. Greeley and Gockel also suggested that adolescence is the phase of development most likely to see a positive benefit from parochial schooling.

Greeley et al. (1976) compared the relative benefits of religious education (release time or Sunday school) to those of full-time Catholic schooling. Their finding was that part-time religious instruction is no substitute for the positive benefits associated with full-time schooling: an increase in religious behavior and favorable attitudes, a greater acceptance of change within the church, and higher levels of economic motivation.

In 1986, Benson et al. studied the effects of parochial education in schools with high concentrations (10% or more) of low-income students (below the federal poverty level), commitment and church commitment. They found that low-income-serving schools that stress academics and religion, possess high student morale, and encourage the centrality of religion and the development of community of faith tended to have higher student outcomes in terms of personal faith commitment and church commitment than similar schools without such emphases.

Kelly et al. (1986) studied the factors which account for positive outcomes in Catholic parish religious education programs. They found five: frequency of family religious discussions, program emphasis on an active faith life, program emphasis on promoting self-understanding, and how much the students like their program. As these findings illustrate, it is very difficult to separate the effects of religious education and parenting. While being enrolled in religious classes makes a significant difference in the prediction of adolescent religiousness, this should not be seen as causal (Potvin et al. 1976). Research examining these issues experimentally has yet to be pursued. Programs which consciously attempt to exploit the combined benefits of religious schooling and family involvement seem to be the most effective (Potvin et al. 1976; Kelly et al. 1986).

Peers

By and large, one would expect that peer influence would wax during the adolescent years, while parental influence would wane. This would be consistent with most theories of adolescent development. The research in this area does seem to demonstrate that both influences are important, but little research has investigated the relative effect of parents and peers on adolescent religious development (Spilka et al. 1985).

DeVaus (1983) found that while peers are important in the development of an adolescent's self-concept, there was no evidence that peers made any significant impact on adolescent religiousness. In this study of Australian youth, there was support for the notion that parents are more important sources than peers.

Peer groups probably do have some impact on religious variables such as youth group attendance and attitudes (Hoge and Petrillo 1978; Spilka et al. 1985), but "peer group impact is probably less overall than cultural folklore suggests" (Spilka et al. 1985, p. 92).

In a study of Catholic grammar school students, Carey (1971) found that high leadership males had a more significant impact on female peers than on other males in effecting religious behavior change (daily Mass attendance). Carey explains these findings in terms of differential influence exerted by males and females in the area of religious influence.

The major finding in this research is that while peer influence is important, and perhaps surpasses parental influence in the secular realm, it may not be salient to a number of central religious variables.

Other Factors

Denomination

The research looking at denomination has not yielded consistent findings, probably because the definition of religious practice and observance is so different between various groups. Sloane and Potvin's (1983) analysis of a national sample of over 1,100 adolescents yielded a very complex pattern of denomination, age, and gender interactions, suggesting that denominational practices have very different effects for male and female youth at different ages. We have already noted above the findings of Hoge et al. (1982) that denominational membership predicted adolescents' values more strongly than did parental values.

Social Class

Work by Potvin et al. (1976) tested the hypothesis that social class affected religious practice, but this hypothesis was not sustained for adolescents. They reported that lower class adolescents are more traditionally orthodox and fundamentalist, and tend to pray and "experience God" more. In their 1980 study, Nelsen and Potvin found significant interaction between denomination and occupation (white vs. blue collar used as a proxy for SES) in predicting the personal-experiential dimension of religiousness among non-southern adolescents. They found that higher levels of SES predicted more impersonal religiousness for mainline Protestant denominations, while higher levels of SES predicted more personal religiousness in Baptist and fundamentalist sects.

Sibling Structure

There are no conclusive findings about the effects on adolescent religiousness of siblings and other family members besides parents (Spilka et al. 1985). DeBord (1969) noted in his sample of Tennessee adolescents higher rates of church attendance for younger siblings who have older sisters who are church attenders. The lowest rates of attendance were found for younger siblings who have an older brother who is not a church attender. The crossover for gender is perhaps most interesting, suggesting that males may have a more significant leadership role in nonattendance, and females a more significant role in attendance.

City Size

In the Boys Town Survey (Potvin et al. 1976) a difference was noted in adolescent religiousness based on city size. Small town or city adolescents scored significantly higher on several religious measures than residents of large cities (50,000 residents or more). Small town youth were more conservative, orthodox, felt more personal closeness to God, and prayed more frequently.

SOCIAL-PERSONALITY VARIABLES

The research concerning the relation between religiousness and the personality and lifestyles of adolescents can be broadly characterized as being a by-product of the larger societal concerns regarding that stage in the life cycle. Thus there is ample research literature concerning "problem behaviors" such as sexual intercourse, delinquency, and drug abuse; there is very little research concerning the place of religion in the larger psychic economy of young people. At least in part, this reflects the difficulty in gaining access to public school samples for research on religion, and in turn why disproportionate amounts of research on religion in adolescence occur in Catholic schools.

This also may explain why the sophistication in measurement technique that has increasingly come to characterize research in psychology of religion

(Gorsuch 1984) is lacking in some studies in this area. Many religiousness measures in research with adolescents are single items included simply on the grounds that religion is one of those "sociodemographics" that are always included in good surveys. Use of such measures is all the more inappropriate in the case of adolescents, since measures such as church attendance and denominational affiliation are not under the personal control of many adolescents. Young people are taken to church by their parents, and are members of whatever denomination their parents belong to, so such measures may not reflect actual religious orientation. More recently, there has been work toward developing scales appropriate for younger respondents that will be helpful for further research in these areas. Relevant research is reported in Benson et al. (1987), Francis (1978), and Gorsuch and Venable (1983).

In spite of these methodological handicaps, research in this area has produced patterns of findings that indicate strong effects of religion in these areas. The areas that will be considered are problem behaviors (sexual intercourse, drug abuse, and delinquency); self-esteem; and altruism and compassion.

Problem Behaviors

Sexual Intercourse

The literature concerning the effects of religiousness on sexual intercourse is sufficiently large and consistent that one has the luxury of reviewing reviews. The major reviews available (Chilman 1980; Hayes 1987) and the major nationwide interview data collected by Zelnik, Kantner, and Ford (1981) all indicate strong constraining effects of religion on the likelihood of engaging in premarital intercourse. Spilka et al. (1985) in their review of this area indicate that religiousness may decrease the likelihood of engaging in intercourse by as much as 50%. These effects have continued into even the most recent data. An analysis by Donahue (1984) of the large-sample research reported by Benson et al. (1987) finds a correlation of -.31 between religious belief and frequency of intercourse in young adolescents. In addition, Dawson (1986) reports data from a national sample of women of childbearing age which indicates that church attendance has a strong negative impact on the likelihood of initiating intercourse for 15 to 18 year-olds.

Other recent studies, however, indicate that these conclusions may need to be qualified. A series of studies with black adolescents (Hendricks, Robinson-Brown, and Gary 1984; McCormick, Izzo and Folcik 1985; Roebuck and McGee 1977) have failed to find significant effects of religiousness on sexual attitudes and behaviors. A recent interstate analysis of adolescent pregnancy patterns by Singh (1986) found that adolescent birthrates for both black and white adolescents are positively correlated with the percent of state residents who belong to fundamentalist denominations, although the adolescent pregnancy and abortion rates were not significantly related. Jones et al. (1986) also report positive correlations between religiousness and teenage birth and pregnancy rates at the national level for several industrialized countries.

These findings indicate the possibility that there may be racial-cultural differences in the effects of religion on these behaviors, or that the general impact of religion on sexual behavior may be beginning to decline. However, these few studies are exceptions to the preponderance of evidence that religious adolescents are less likely to engage in intercourse.

Drug Abuse

A review of the literature concerning religion and drug abuse comes to rather unequivocal findings of a negative relation between the two. A recent example is the article by Hadaway, Elifson, and Petersen (1984). They first present a review of the literature that concludes that the constraining effects of religion on drug use is widely replicated regardless of drug or measure of religiousness used, a finding also reached in an earlier review by Gorsuch and Butler (1976). They then report data from a random sample of high school students in suburban Atlanta. They find that "even when controlling for other important influences, religion still has a significant effect on alcohol use, drug use, and attitudes toward drug use" (p. 109, abstract). These constraining effects were somewhat less strong for alcohol than for other drugs. Similar findings are also reported by Benson et al. (1987) in their study of fifth through ninth graders, and by Benson et al. (1986) in their nationwide study of students in Catholic high schools.

In this area, then, as in that of sexual intercourse, the preponderance of the evidence seems to speak with a single voice: religion inhibits drug use.

Delinquency

For the sake of the present discussion, delinquency will be defined as non-drug-related, non-sexual law-breaking such as vandalism, shoplifting, interpersonal violence and the like. The seminal article shaping current discussion in this area was undoubtedly Hirschi and Stark's (1969) "Hellfire and Delinquency," that in essence reported that there was no effect of religiousness on delinquency. That paper "quickly became the accepted word on the subject, frequently cited and widely reprinted" (Stark, Kent, and Doyle 1982, p. 5). This somewhat counter-intuitive finding sparked a spate of research on the topic. Reanalyses of the Hirschi and Stark data by Jensen and Erickson (1979) indicated that there were methodological problems masking the presence of a relationship between the two variables. The current state of the literature allows a number of conclusions to be drawn, but also indicates the necessity of some caution in interpreting the data.

First, when considered as a simple bivariate relationship, "a weak to moderate negative zero-order relationship does exist" (Elifson, Petersen, and Hadaway 1983, p. 522; see also Benson et al. 1986; Benson et al. 1987; Peek, Curry, and Chalfant 1985).

Second, Elifson et al. (1983) concluded that much, if not all of this zero-order relationship may be due to social environment—families and friends rather than religion per se. After accounting for whether they have friends who engage in deviant behaviors, the adolescents' closeness to their parents, and how important it is for them to do what their parents say, religion contributes little independent constraining effect.

Third, a recent analysis of a longitudinal study by Peek et al. (1985) raises issues that will be of importance to future researchers in the area. A consistent finding concerning religious development (see above) is that religiousness declines across the high school years for many adolescents, especially males. Peek and his colleagues replicated the constraining effects of religiousness on delinquency at each point in time, but found a curious and disturbing "deviance amplication" effect in their data. Students who started high on religiousness and then declined over time showed slightly *higher* rates of delinquency than was the case for those who had been low all the time; almost as if some of the adolescents were trying to "make up for lost time." While these findings are not strong, they are based on a large and representative sample of college sophomores (Bachman, O'Malley, and Johnston 1979), and should be of interest to future researchers.

Conclusions

The pattern of relations noted here, that religion constrains drug abuse and sexual behavior but has less effect on deliquency has been noted by a number of observers. The most frequent explanation for these findings is that religious values have their greatest effects when their influence is different from that of society at large. There is general societal rejection of vandalism, shoplifting, interpersonal violence and the like, and the locus at which these societal rejections are conveyed will be precisely in the interpersonal relations—family, friends—that "explain away" the effects of religion on these variables. Conversely, the areas in which parents have traditionally been portrayed as having the greatest difficulties in communicating with their children—sex and drugs—are those in which the children's personal value system—religiousness—has the greatest effect.

Self-Esteem

Research concerning the relation between religion and personality in adolescence has been relatively infrequent. One exception to this lack of attention has been a series of large-sample studies by Francis (1985) and his colleagues examining the relation between religiousness and mental health and personality in English secondary schools. In general, they find religion negatively correlated with extraversion and neuroticism.

Another area of concentration has been the relation between religion and self-esteem. The reason for this particular emphasis is probably twofold. First, a great many individuals concerned with adolescence view self-esteem as the key to a large number of important constructs—academic achievement, drug abuse, premature sexual involvement, suicide and the like. Second, there are theoretical concerns about the relation between the concepts with which religion deals—sin, salvation, guilt, confession—and their effects on the psychological processes of adolescence.

Of seven studies done with adolescents since 1970 (Bahr and Martin 1983; Benson and Spilka 1973; Benson et al. 1986; Buehler, Weigert, and Thomas 1977; Moore and Stoner 1977; Smith, Weigert, and Thomas 1979; Spilka and Mullin 1977) none showed evidence for a negative relation between religion and self-esteem. Two of the more recent (Bahr and Martin 1983; Benson et al. 1986), both using the Rosenberg (1965) self-esteem measure, showed essentially no relation between the two. Benson and his colleagues failed to obtain any notable relation in spite of the fact that they used eight separate measures of religion. Correlations in their study ranged from -.15 (for a measure of religious doubt) to .06 (for a measure of "comforting religion") and averaged .01. In contrast, Smith et al. (1979) in a major cross-cultural study of Catholics found modest positive correlations. In short, the relation between religiousness and self-esteem in adolescence is unclear.

Altruism and Social Compassion

It could be reasonably argued that altruism, (i.e., concern for the welfare of others), stands at the center of all religious ethics. Some form of the Golden Rule can be found in every major religious tradition. Yet research examining the relation between religion and altruism has been rather rare. A major exception to this lack of attention has been a programatic series of studies by Batson and his colleagues on the relation between various religious orientations and altruism (see Batson and Ventis 1982, for a review), but his research has concentrated on college students.

Two recent large-sample studies by Search Institute, however, have provided insight on this issue. The first involved a sample of 8,000 fifth through ninth grade students. Benson and his colleagues (1987) constructed a scale composed of students' self-reports of the amount of hours they spent "giving help to people *outside the family* that have special needs" and the likelihood that they would offer help in a variety of hypothetical situations (e.g., when a small child falls, or an old woman drops her groceries). They correlated these scores with a variety of religiousness measures. Overall, they found mild but consistent relations between the two—.20 to .30.

Similar but stronger relations were reported by Benson et al. (1986) in a nationwide study of more than 7,500 freshmen and seniors in Catholic high schools with high concentrations of poor students. A similar scale of self-reported altruistic actions correlated .20 to .30 with such measures of religiousness as orthodox Catholic beliefs, and the tendency to view religion as liberating. The measures of altruism also correlated .30 to .40 with the intrinsic, vertical, and horizontal religious orientations (as defined previously). A scale of "global concern" (i.e., willingness to change one's own behavior in order to help the less fortunate in other countries) formed basically the same pattern of relations with religion as the altruism measure. The altruism and global concern measures were correlated .41.

Interpretation of such research must always be tempered with concern over social desirability biases—the tendency to overestimate the likelihood of helping in order to "look good." But this, in turn, must be balanced with findings in Batson's research that religious people may be altruistic to a fault, pressing their offers of assistance even after they have been declined (Darley and Batson 1973). In addition, any observed effect of religiousness per se would have to have its impact over and above general cultural prescriptions in favor of altruism and compassion. In general, then, the initial findings with these large samples indicate evidence for a consistent positive association between religion and altruism.

Conclusions

By restricting consideration to research done with adolescents since 1970, we find that the major interest of researchers in adolescent religion has been its function as a social control mechanism. This function is certainly not trivial. Jessor and Jessor (1977), summarizing their longitudinal data on problem behavior and psychosocial development, have noted the crucial place of religion in the social control network of young people. The findings reported above for the impact of religion on sexual behavior and drug abuse are as strong as those displayed by any social-personality or individual difference variable in the social scientific tool chest.

But one is struck by what has been left undone. There has been little work on religiousness measures that might be uniquely appropriate for younger age groups. There is relatively little work on the relation of other areas, such as the development of prejudice or social skills, that are of interest to social scientists. The reason for this lack of attention is probably reasonably straightforward and can be summed up in a single word—money. Religion is not of interest, either as an independent or dependent variable, to many funders. A researcher cannot conclude an article by saying that the way to address drug abuse and teen pregnancy is by promoting religion in the public schools. And the religious organizations that should have strong interests in understanding and fostering religious development are only now beginning to sponsor serious research efforts to examine the effectiveness of their educational program (Benson et al. 1986; Kelly et al. 1986).

SUMMARY AND CONCLUSIONS

The evidence presented here indicates that religion has important and pervasive impacts on adolescents and their development. The large number of topics not reported here indicates that many important issues in this area remain to be explored.

Though research in adolescence and religion continues at a significant pace, the field continues to languish in a state of protracted infancy. Most publications are correlational in design and atheoretical in conceptualization. There is an almost complete lack of of longitudinal studies following cohorts of specific individuals. Neither are there significant efforts to employ experimental techniques, though some key questions are amenable to this. For example, certain religious independent variables could be manipulated, such as the kind and extent of formal religious instruction (see Yeats and Asher 1979; but see also Batson 1977, 1979).

The existing research is limited in scope. Considerably more work has been done on the constraining or preventative functions of adolescent religiousness (e.g., chemical use, intercourse, delinquency) than on its humanitarian functions. Research on prejudice, altruism, empathy, and volunteerism has been largely ignored.

Similarly, there have been few efforts to tie adolescent religiousness to the broader clinical/personality domain, including the areas of mental health, treatment outcomes, and help seeking. Research is also needed to tie religious development to other adolescent developmental issues, including sexuality, identity, autonomy, and affiliation. Perhaps most surprising is the failure to explore linkages with the burgeoning field of moral development (e.g., Kohlberg 1984).

Measurement continues to be narrow and constraining, with the focus primarily on quantity of religious activity, orthodoxy, and global assessment of importance. It would be fruitful to explore the development of more dynamic religious constructs. Most obvious here is intrinsic and extrinsic, one of the best-researched ways we have of thinking about religious orientation (Allport and Ross 1967). Donahue's (1985) review of the I-E literature revealed virtually no work with adolescents, aside from Thompson's (1974) data concerning religiousness and dogmatism. As research in adolescence and religion becomes more sophisticated, it is more likely that the religious dimension will receive due consideration from more academically-traditional social scientists. This, in turn, will fuel additional research, with the prospects that funding for this kind of research will improve.

Finally, research has largely failed to address how the meaning, content, interpretation, and application of religion change and develop during adolescence. Theoretical work is needed to tie the development of religious thought to changes in cognitive structures, and other significant transformations during this period. Such progress would in turn foster a considerable amount of both quantitative and qualitative research.

ACKNOWLEDGMENTS

The authors thank two anonymous reviews for their comments on an earlier draft of this paper.

Correspondence concerning this chapter should be sent to: Peter L. Benson, Search Institute, 122 W. Franklin, Suite 525, Minneapolis, MN 55404.

REFERENCES

Acock, A. C. and V. L. Bengtson. 1978. "On the Relative Influence of Mothers and Fathers: A Covariance Analysis of Political and Religious Socialization." *Journal of Marriage and the Family* 40:519-530.

_____. 1980. "Socialization and Attribution Processes: Actual versus Perceived Similarity among Parents and Youth." *Journal of Marriage and the Family* 42:501-515.

Allport, G. and J. M. Ross. 1967. "Personal Religious Orientation and Prejudice." *Journal of Personality and Social Psychology* 5:432-443.

Argyle, M. and B. Beit-Hallahmi. 1975. *The Social Psychology of Religion*. London: Routledge & Kegan Paul.

Bachman, J. G., L. D. Johnston, and P. M. O'Malley. 1979. *Youth in Transition: Vol. 6. Adolescence to Adulthood–Change and Stability in the Lives of Young Men*. Ann Arbor: University of Michigan, Institute for Social Research.

_____. 1980a. *Monitoring the Future: Questionnaire Responses for the Nation's High School Seniors, 1976*. Ann Arbor: University of Michigan, Institute for Social Research.

_____. 1980b. *Monitoring the Future: Questionnaire Responses for the Nation's High School Seniors, 1978*. Ann Arbor: University of Michigan, Institute for Social Research.

_____. 1981. *Monitoring the Future: Questionnaire Responses for the Nation's High School Seniors, 1980*. Ann Arbor: University of Michigan, Institute for Social Research.

_____. 1984. *Monitoring the Future: Questionnaire Responses for the Nation's High School Seniors, 1982*. Ann Arbor: University of Michigan, Institute for Social Research.

_____. 1985. *Monitoring the Future: Questionnaire Responses for the Nation's High School Seniors, 1984*. Ann Arbor: University of Michigan, Institute for Social Research.

Bahr, H. M. and T. K. Martin. 1983. "'And thy Neighbor as Thyself': Self-esteem and Faith in People as Correlates of Religiosity and Family Solidarity among Middletown High School Students." *Journal for the Scientific Study of Religion* 22:132-144.

Barker, E. 1986. "Religious Movements: Cult and Anticult since Jonestown." *Annual Review of Sociology* 12:329-346.

Batson, C. D. 1977. "Experimentation in Psychology of Religion: An Impossible Dream." *Journal for the Scientific Study of Religion* 16:413-418.

————. 1979. "Experimentation in Psychology of Religion: Living with or in a Dream?" *Journal for the Scientific Study of Religion* 17:90-93.

Batson, C. D. and W. L. Ventis. 1982. *The Religious Experience: A Social Psychological Perspective.* New York: Oxford University Press.

Bealer, R. and F. Willets. 1967. "The Religious Interests of American High School Youth." *Religious Education* 62:435-444.

Bengston, V. L. and A. C. Acock. 1976. "On the Relative Influence of Mothers and Fathers: A Covariance Analysis of Political and Religions Socialization." Paper presented at the meeting of the American Sociological Association, New York, September.

Benson, P. L. 1986. "Religion and Sex-role Orientations among Young Adolescents." Paper presented at the meeting of the American Psychological Association, Washington, DC, August.

Benson, P. L. and B. Spilka. 1973. "God Image as a Function of Self-esteem and Locus of Control." *Journal for the Scientific Study of Religion* 12:297-310.

Benson, P. L., D. L. Williams, and A. L. Johnson. 1987. *The Quicksilver Years: The Hopes and Fears of Young Adolescents.* San Francisco: Harper & Row.

Benson, P. L., P. K. Wood, A. L. Johnson, C. Eklin, and J. Mills. 1983. *1983 Minnesota Survey on Drug Use and Drug-Related Attitudes.* Minneapolis, MN: Search Institute.

Benson, P. L., R. J. Yeager, P. K. Wood, M. J. Guerra, and B. V. Manno. 1986. *Catholic High Schools: Their Impact on Low-Income Students.* Washington, DC: National Catholic Educational Association.

Bock, G. D. 1977. "The Jewish Schooling of American Jews: A Study of Non-Cognitive Educational Effects." *Dissertation Abstracts International* 37:4628A.

Bromley, D. G. and J. T. Richardson. 1983. *The Brainwashing/Deprogramming Controversy: Sociological, Psychological, Legal and Historical Perspectives.* New York: The Edwin Mellen Press.

Buehler, C. J., A. J. Weigert, and D. Thomas. 1977. "Antecedents of Adolescent Self-evaluation: A Cross-national Application of a Model." *Journal of Comparative Family Studies* 8:29-45.

Caplow, T. and H. M. Bahr. 1979. "Half a Century of Change in Adolescent Attitudes: Replication of a Middletown Study by the Lynds." *Public Opinion Quarterly* 43:1-17.

Carey, R. G. 1971. "Influence of Peers in Shaping Religious Behavior." *Journal for the Scientific Study of Religion* 10:157-159.

Chilman, C. S. 1980. *Adolescent Sexuality in a Changing American Society: Social and Psychological Perspectives.* (NIH Publication No. 80-1426). Washington, DC: United States Government Printing Office.

Clark, C. A., E. L. Worthington, and D. B. Dauser. 1986. "Family and Religious Values from Parents to First-Born Early Adolescent Sons." Paper presented at the meeting of the American Psychological Association, Washington, DC, August.

Coleman, J. S. 1961. *The Adolescent Society.* Glencoe, IL: Free Press.

Cornwall, M., J. Olsen, and S. Weed. 1979. "The Influence of Parents on Youth Religiosity." Paper presented at the meeting of the Religious Research Association, San Antonio, TX, October.

Darley, J. M. and C. D. Batson. 1973. "'From Jerusalem to Jericho': A Study of Situational and Dispositional Variables in Helping Behavior." *Journal of Personality and Social Psychology* 27:100-108.

Dawson, D. A. 1986. "The Effects of Sex Education on Adolescent Behavior." *Family Planning Perspectives* 18:162-170.

deBord, L. W. 1969. "Adolescent Religious Participation: An Examination of Sib-Structure and Church Attendance." *Adolescence* 16:557-570.

deVaus, D. A. 1983. "The Relative Importance of Parents and Peers for Adolescent Religious Orientation: An Australian Study." *Adolescence* 18:147-158.

Dickinson, G. E. 1976. "Religious Practices of Adolescents in a Southern Community: 1964-1974." *Journal for the Scientific Study of Religion* 15:361-363.

Dickinson, G. E. 1982. "Changing Religious Behavior of Adolescents 1964-1979." *Youth & Society* 13:283-288.

Donahue, M. J. 1984. "Correlates of Premature Sexual Intercourse: Technical Report." Unpublished manuscript, Search Institute, Minneapolis, MN.

———. 1985. "Intrinsic and Extrinsic Religiousness: Review and Meta-Analysis." *Journal of Personality and Social Psychology* 48:400-419.

Dudley, R. L. and M. G. Dudley. 1986. "Transmission of Religious Values from Parents to Adolescents." *Review of Religious Research* 28:3-15.

Elifson, K. W., D. M. Petersen and C. K. Hadaway. 1983. "Religiosity and Delinquency: A Contextual Analysis." *Criminology* 21:505-527.

Elkind, D. 1971a. "The Development of Religious Understanding in Children and Adolescents." In *Research on Religious Development,* edited by M. P. Strommen. New York: Hawthorn Books.

Erickson, D. 1964. "Religious Consequences of Public and Sectarian Schooling." *The School Review* 72:22-33.

Ferm, R. C. 1959. *The Psychology of Christian Conversion.* New York: Fleming H. Revell.

Fowler, J. 1981. *Stages of Faith: The Psychology of Human Development and the Search for Meaning.* New York: Harper & Row.

Francis, L. J. 1978. "Attitude and Longitude: A Study in Measurement." *Character Potential* 8:119-130.

———. 1985. "Personality and Religion: Theory and Measurement." In *International Series in Experimental Social Psychology: Volume 11. Advances in the Psychology of Religion,* edited by L. B. Brown. Oxford: Pergamon Press.

Gallup, G. 1983. "Teens Say Religion Very Important." *Emerging Trends* 5:4.

———. 1984. *Religion in America 1984.* Princeton, NJ: The Princeton Research Center.

Goldman, R. 1964. *Religious Thinking from Childhood to Adolescence.* London: Routledge & Kegan Paul.

Gorsuch, R. L. 1984. "Measurement: The Boon and Bane of Investigating Religion." *American Psychologist* 39:228-236.

Gorsuch, R. L. and M. Butler. 1976. "Initial Drug Abuse: A Review of Pre-disposing Social Psychological Factors." *Psychological Bulletin* 83:120-137.

Gorsuch, R. L. and G. D. Venable. 1983. "Development of an 'Age Universal' I-E Scale." *Journal for the Scientific Study of Religion* 22:181-187.

Greeley, A. M. and G. L. Gockel 1971. "The Religious Effects of Parochial Education." In *Research on Religious Development,* edited by M. P. Strommen. New York: Hawthorn Books.

Greeley, A. M., W. McCready, and K. McCourt. 1976. *Catholic Schools in a Declining Church.* Kansas City, MO: Sheed & Ward.

Greeley, A. M. and P. H. Rossi. 1966. *The Education of American Catholics.* Chicago: Aldine.

Hadaway, C. K., K. W. Elifson, and D. M. Petersen. 1984. "Religious Involvement and Drug Use among Adolescents." *Journal for the Scientific Study of Religion* 23:109-128.

Havighurst, R. and B. Keating 1971. "The Religion of Youth." In *Research on Religious Development,* edited by M. P. Strommen. New York: Hawthorn Books.

Hayes, C. D., ed. 1987. *Risking the Future: Adolescent Sexuality, Pregnancy, and Childbearing.* Washington, DC: National Academy Press.

Heirich, M. 1977. "Change of Heart: A Test of Some Widely Held Theories about Religious Conversion." *American Journal of Sociology* 83:653-680.

Hendricks, L. E., D. P. Robinson-Brown, and L. E. Gary. 1984. "Religiosity and Unmarried Black Adolescent Fatherhood." *Adolescence* 19:417-424.

Hirschi, T. and R. Stark. 1969. "Hellfire and Delinquency." *Social Problems* 17:202-213.

Hoge, D. R. and L. Keeter. 1976. "Determinants of College Teachers' Religious Beliefs and Participation." *Journal for the Scientific Study of Religion* 15:221-235.

Hoge, D. R. and G. H. Petrillo. 1978. "Determinants of Church Participation and Attitudes among High School Youth." *Journal for the Scientific Study of Religion* 17: 359-379.

Hoge, D. R., G. H. Petrillo, and E. I. Smith. 1982. "Transmission of Religious and Social Values from Parents to Teenage Children." *Journal of Marriage and the Family* 44:569-580.

James, W. 1936. *The Varieties of Religious Experiences: A Study in Human Nature: Being the Guilford Lectures on Natural Religion Delivered at Edinburgh in 1901-1902.* New York: The Modern Library. (Original work published 1902.)

Jensen, G. F. and M. L. Erickson. 1979. "The Religious Factor and Delinquency: Another Look at the Hellfire Hypothesis." Pp. 157-177 in *The Religious Dimension: New Directions in Quantitative Research,* edited by R. Wuthnow. New York: Academic Press.

Jessor, R. and S. L. Jessor. 1977. *Problem Behavior and Psychosocial Development: A Longitudinal Study of Youth.* New York: Academic Press.

Johnson, M. A. 1973. "Family Life and Religious Commitment." *Review of Religious Research* 14:144-150.

Johnston, L. D., J. G. Bachman, and P. M. O'Malley. 1980a. *Monitoring The Future: Questionnaire Responses for the Nation's High School Seniors, 1977.* Ann Arbor: University of Michigan, Institute for Social Research.

————. 1980b. *Monitoring the Future: Questionnaire Responses for the Nation's High School Seniors, 1979.* Ann Arbor: University of Michigan, Institute for Social Research.

————. 1982. *Monitoring the Future: Questionnaire Responses for the Nation's High School Seniors, 1981.* Ann Arbor: University of Michigan, Institute for Social Research.

————. 1984. *Monitoring the Future: Questionnaire Responses for the Nation's High School Seniors, 1983.* Ann Arbor: University of Michigan, Institute for Social Research.

————. 1986. *Monitoring the Future: Questionnaire Responses for the Nation's High School Seniors, 1985.* Ann Arbor: University of Michigan, Institute for Social Research.

Johnstone, R. 1966. *The Effectiveness of Lutheran Elementary and Secondary Schools as Agents of Christian Education.* St. Louis, MO: Concordia Seminary.

Jones, E. F., J. D. Forrest, N. Goldman, S. K. Henshaw, R. Lincoln, J. I. Rosoff, C. F. Westoff, and D. Wulf. 1986. *Teenage Pregnancy in Industrialized Countries: A Study Sponsored by the Alan Guttmacher Institute.* New Haven and London: Yale University Press.

Kaslow, F. and M. B. Sussman. 1982. *Cults and the Family.* New York: The Haworth Press.

Kelly, F. D., P. L. Benson, and M. J. Donahue. 1986. *Toward Effective Parish Religious Education for Children and Young People: A National Study.* Washington, DC: National Catholic Educational Association.

Kohlberg, L. 1984. *The Psychology of Moral Development: Essays on Moral Development,* Vol. 2. San Francisco: Harper & Row.

Luft, G. A. and G. T. Sorell. 1986. "Parenting Style and Parent-Adolescent Value Consensus." Paper presented at the meeting of the American Psychological Association, Washington, DC, August.

McCormick, N., A. Izzo, and J. Folcik. 1985. "Adolescents' Values, Sexuality, and Contraception in a Rural New York County." *Adolescence* 20:385-395.

McCready, W. C. 1972. "Faith of Our Fathers: A Study of the Process of Religious Socialization." *Dissertation Abstracts International* 33, 6472A.

Meadow, M. J. and R. D. Kahoe. 1984. *Psychology of Religion: Religion in Individual Lives.* New York: Harper & Row.

Moore, K. and S. Stoner. 1977. "Adolescent Self-reports and Religiosity." *Psychological Reports* 41:55-56.

Neilson, W. A., ed. 1958. *Webster's New International Dictionary of the English Language,* 2nd ed. Springfield, MA: G and C Merriam Company.

Nelsen, H. M. 1980. "Religious Transmission versus Religious Formation: Preadolescent-parent Interaction." *The Sociological Quarterly* 21:207-218.

————. 1981. "Gender Differences in the Effects of Parental Discord on Preadolescent Religiousness." *Journal for the Scientific Study of Religion* 20:351-359.

Nelsen, H. M. and R. H. Potvin. 1981. "Gender and Regional Differences in the Religiosity of Protestant Churches." *Review of Religious Research* 22:351-360.

Nelsen, H. M., R. H. Potvin, and J. Shields. 1977. *The Religion of Children.* Washington, DC: U.S. Catholic Conference.

Paloutzian, R. F. 1983. *Invitation to the Psychology of Religion.* Glenview, IL: Scott, Foresman and Company.

Peatling, J. 1974. "Cognitive Development in Pupils in Grades from Four through Twelve: The Incidence of Concrete and Abstract Religious Thinking." *Character Potential* 7:52-61.

————. 1977. "Cognitive Development: Religious Thinking in Children, Youth and Adults." *Character Potential* 8:100-115.

Peatling, J. and C. Laabs. 1975. "Cognitive Development in Pupils in Grades Fourth through Twelve. The Incidence of Concrete and Abstract Religious Thinking." *Character Potential* 7:107-115.

Peek, C. W., E. W. Curry, and H. P. Chalfant. 1985. "Religiosity and Delinquency Over Time: Deviance Deterrence and Deviance Amplification." *Social Science Quarterly* 66:120-131.

Piaget, J. 1965. *The Moral Judgment of the Child.* M. Gabain, Trans. New York: The Free Press. (Original work published 1932.)

Potvin, R. H., D. R. Hoge, and H. M. Nelsen. 1976. *Religion and American Youth: With Emphasis on Catholic Adolescents and Young Adults.* Washington, DC: United States Catholic Conference.

Potvin, R. H. and D. M. Sloane. 1985. "Parental Control, Age, and Religious Practice." *Review of Religious Research* 27:3-14.

Rambo, L. R. 1982. "Current Research on Religious Conversion." *Religious Studies Review* 8:146-159.

Remmers, H. and D. Radler. 1957. *The American Teenager.* Indianapolis: Bobbs-Merrill.

Roebuck, J. and M. G. McGee. 1977. "Attitudes toward Premarital Sex and Sexual Behavior among Black High School Girls." *Journal of Sex Research* 13:104-114.

Rosenberg, M. 1965. *Society and the Adolescent Self-Image.* Princeton, NJ: Princeton University Press.

Rosik, C. H. and R. L. Gorsuch. 1985. "Adolescent Religiosity in Relation to Parental Religiosity and Interpersonal Style." Paper presented at the meeting of the American Psychological Association, Los Angeles, August.

Scroggs, J. R. and W. G. T. Douglas. 1967. "Issues in the Psychology of Religious Conversion." *Journal of Religion and Health* 6:204-216.

Singh, S. 1986. "Adolescent Pregnancy in the United States: An Interstate Analysis." *Family Planning Perspectives* 18: 210-220.

Sloane, D. M. and R. H. Potvin. 1983. "Age Differences in Adolescent Religiousness." *Review of Religious Research* 25:142-154.

Smith, C. B., A. J., Weigert, and D. L. Thomas 1979. "Self-esteem and Religiosity: An Analysis of Catholic Adolescents from Five Cultures." *Journal for the Scientific Study of Religion* 18:51-60.

Spilka, B., R. W. Hood, Jr., and R. L. Gorsuch. 1985. *The Psychology of Religion: An Empirical Approach.* Englewood Cliffs, NJ: Prentice-Hall.

Spilka, B. and M. Mullin. 1977. "Personal Religion and Psychological Schemata: A Research Approach to a Theological Psychology of Religion." *Character Potential* 8:100-115.

Starbuck, E. D. 1897. "A Study of Conversion." *American Journal of Psychology* 8:268-308.

_____. 1899. *The Psychology of Religion.* New York: Charles Schribner's Sons.

Stark, R., L. Kent, and D. P. Doyle. 1982. "Religion and Delinquency: The Ecology of a "Lost" Relationship." *Journal of Research in Crime and Delinquency* 19:4-24.

Suziedelis, A. and R. Potvin. 1981. "Sex Differences in Factors Affecting Religiousness among Catholic Adolescents." *Jounral for the Scientific Study of Religion* 20:38-50.

Thompson, A. D. 1974. "Open-mindedness and Indiscrimination [sic] Antireligious Orientation." *Journal for the Scientific Study of Religion* 13:471-477.

Weigert, A. J. and D. L. Thomas. 1972. "Parental Support, Control and Adolescent Religiosity: An Extension of Previous Research." *Journal for the Scientific Study of Religion* 11:389-393.

Yeats, J. R. and W. Asher. 1979. "Can We Afford *not* to do True Experiments in Psychology of Religion? A Reply to Batson." *Journal for the Scientific Study of Religion* 18:86-89.

Zelnick, M., J. Kantner, and K. Ford. 1981. *Sex and Pregnancy in Adolescence.* Beverly Hills, CA: Sage.

THE HEBREW SCHOOL EXPERIENCE:
A PHENOMENOLOGICAL ANALYSIS OF
STUDENTS' PERCEPTIONS

Judith A. Press

ABSTRACT

This study uses phenomenological analysis to examine the perceptions of students attending a supplementary Hebrew School in a New England suburb. These students have ambivalent feelings about being Jewish. They equate being Jewish with being different, and they believe being Jewish has only a minor effect on their lives. They perceive the goals of Hebrew School on three levels: (1) The immediate level of learning prayers, learning about their religion, and learning Hebrew; (2) The long-term goal of Bar/Bat Mitzvah; and (3) The ultimate goal of transmitting Jewish traditions to future generations. Their perceptions about Hebrew School differ markedly and range from boring to fun. Positive aspects of Hebrew School mentioned by all students include socializing and informality of classes. A negative aspect was the inconvenience of the Hebrew School schedule. Implications drawn from this study are that the Hebrew School ought to strive to maintain practical goals and flexible curriculum, classroom environment, and school schedule.

Research in the Social Scientific Study of Religion, Volume 1, pages 183-196.
Copyright © 1989 by JAI Press Inc.
All rights of reproduction in any form reserved.
ISBN: 0-89232-882-7

INTRODUCTION

In America today approximately 165,000 Jewish youngsters attend two to three day-a-week supplementary schools, most often referred to as Hebrew School (Pollak and Lang 1979). While the number of students attending Hebrew School has declined dramatically in the last 25 years, Hebrew School remains the single most popular form of Jewish education. It outdistances its closest rivals, the one-day-a-week Sunday schools and the full-day Jewish schools, by a margin of two to one.

What is this Hebrew School experience all about? A review of the literature provides a striking in indictment of Hebrew School. Silberman (1976) characterizes Jewish education as a "disaster area;" Glazer (1971) describes it as "uniformly depressing," and Himmelfarb (1975) refers to Jewish students as victims of "cultural deprivation." In 1977 a task force of the American Jewish Committee reported that there was a prevalent sentiment that much of Jewish education in the United States has been a failure.

Yet, despite these sweeping indictments, the Jewish community places a high stake on education for the survival of the Jewish people. There is a widespread feeling that Jewish education can be an effective socialization agent maintaining ethnic group boundaries.

Studies conducted in the 1970s show that Jewish education has a positive effect only when it surpasses a certain quantitative threshold (Dashefsky and Shapiro 1974; Himmelfarb 1975; Bock 1977). Yet most parents and students are not willing to allow this amount of time. Thus, it becomes the responsibility of the researcher to determine not how much Jewish education is desirable, but, rather, how the limited number of available hours can be used to their maximum potential.

A limited number of qualitative studies in Jewish education have been undertaken. Ethnographic studies of Jewish Schools have been conducted by Schoem (1979), Himmelfarb (1980), and Heilman (1983). Schoem referred to the Jewish behavior of his subjects as "stepping out" of their normal routine. Heilman blamed the "flooding out" of his subjects on cultural dissonance. And Himmelfarb found that the day school he studied provided its students with more "belonging" than "meaning." In all three studies the most positive aspect of religious education was to be found less in the subject matter and more in the process of attending the schools.

This study takes the ethnographic model one step deeper to uncover how third and fourth generation American Jewish children perceive and interpret their Jewish education. The question it addresses is "What is it like to go to Hebrew School?"

To answer this question I turned to phenomenology, a philosophical and scientific research method that attempts to uncover the invisible driving force behind outward appearances. As a phenomenologist, I went directly to the students to obtain their first-hand observations and their in-depth testimony about the Hebrew School experience. Lofland (1971) distinguishes between this intimate, direct, phenomenological form of knowing and what he calls "knowing about." Buber (1958) refers to this experiential knowing as I-Thou, as opposed to I-It. Rist (1979, p. 20) explains that the task "is always one of learning how those involved interpreted and gave meaning to the situation."

METHODS AND DATA SOURCES

The sample for this study consisted of 18 students in the second through seventh grades who attend a modified open classroom, Conservative Hebrew School in a suburb of a New England metropolitan area. Although the sample size is small for purposes of drawing conclusions, it is as large a sample as is feasible for a phenomenological study. The students were chosen out of a total of 96 students in the Temple Israel School. (Temple Israel and all names used in this research are fictitious for purposes of anonymity.) Students were chosen according to the following three criteria:

1. students who represented the widest possible spectrum of perceptions about Hebrew school;
2. students who were best able to articulate their feelings, perceptions and attitudes;
3. students who, if taken as a whole, were considered by their teachers to be representative of the class.

In each class a conscious effort was made to include the student who was considered by the teachers and other students to be the "biggest trouble maker," "the lowest achiever," or "the most alienated student." Although some of these students were initially reluctant to be interviewed, they were coaxed into the study in the belief that, "the scrupulous fieldworker makes a conscious effort, and, if need be forces himself to talk to the people whom he dislikes, mistrusts, or despises" (Wax 1971, p. 272).

The most enthusiastic students in each class were also included in the final sample. These students were generally delightful to interview as they were cooperative, eloquent and full of vitality. A scrupulous effort has to be made not to include an overrepresentative number of these high achieving, super-motivated students in the final sample. The sample was not finalized until all of the teachers in the school reached a consensus of opinion that the sample was representative of the student body as a whole with regard to variety of achievement levels and ostensible attitudes toward Hebrew School.

Once the sample was finalized, several in-depth, semi-structured interviews were conducted with each of the students in an attempt to answer three research questions:

1.   What are these students' perceptions about being Jewish?
2.   What do these students see as the purpose of Hebrew School?
3.   How do these students feel about going to Hebrew School?

All interviews were taped and transcribed as manuscripts. The data were then analyzed according to the phenomenological attitude. This involved a three-step process:

1.   identifying what the informant considers to be the key issues in a given situation and uncovering feelings surrounding the issue, that is, the *noetic correlate;*
2.   stepping back from ordinary ways of looking at things, examining all the possible variations, causes and explanations for the concept being considered, that is, adopting an attitude of *Epoche';*
3.   searching for interconnections in meanings and identifying invariant themes, that is, *eidetic reduction.*

STUDENTS' PERCEPTIONS ABOUT BEING JEWISH

When this threefold phenomenological process was used to examine the first research question, three thematic elements recurred.

Theme of Being Different

For students in this sample, being Jewish was synonymous with being different and being non-Christian. The response of 10-year-old Hillel to the question, "What does it mean to be Jewish?" is typical:

> If you're Jewish you do a lot of things different. You celebrate Hanukkah. You don't have a Christmas tree. You light a menorah. And at Easter you don't have Easter eggs, you have Passover. And it's basically the same thing.

Eleven-year-old Linda gives a theological explanation: "I just believe that God was a god. I don't believe that Jesus was a god, too." To 12-year-old Noah the difference between Jews and other people is a statistical one:

> Only about four or five per cent of the people in the United States are Jewish. That is not very much. Therefore, we could be classified as different. We celebrate different holidays and have different customs.

Theme of Ambivalent Feelings

When students in the sample were asked how they felt about being Jewish they responded by denying negative feelings. Typical responses included: "I don't mind." "There's nothing wrong with it." "It doesn't bother me." "I'm pretty used to it." "It has it's problems, but it's fun." "It's okay. My friends don't make fun of me." With striking consistency, the students expressed their feelings about being Jewish by denying negative feelings. Although they all insisted that they were glad they were Jewish, they chose a decidely negative manner of expressing these positive feelings.

Among the problems of being Jewish mentioned by the informants most often were feeling jealous of their Christian friends, being singled out because of their Jewishness, and encountering incidents of anti-Semitism.

Despite these problems all of the students in the sample were "glad to be Jewish." The source of this gladness was often the enjoyment of being unique, the celebration of holidays, and the pride in their religion.

Theme of the Effects of Being Jewish

For most of the students in this study being Jewish is "no big deal." Eight-year-old Frank holds that "being Jewish doesn't really matter." To 10-year-old Ira "being Jewish doesn't really mean a lot." For 11-year-old Tammi "It's just my religion." Eleven-year-old Melissa holds that the whole issue is blown out of proportion.

> I think being Jewish is the same as being Christian or any other thing like that, because you do almost the same things. In school you don't go to a different gym or anything just because you're Jewish. It's no big deal.

This "no big deal" attitude is often reflected in the student's homes. Ten-year-old Katy is receiving double messages:

> I really don't think my father cares what religion he is. He always gets a headache when we have to go to services on Yom Kippur or something. . . My mother was raised in a kosher home. She wanted to keep kosher, but my father said not to keep kosher, it makes him sick, so they don't.

Ira describes a common phenomenon:

> Being Jewish is nothing really special in the house. On holidays we might do some things like make decorations for Hanukkah. We used to light candles on Friday night, but lately we haven't done it much.

THE PURPOSES OF HEBREW SCHOOL

Although sometimes begrudgingly, all the students in the study believe that they ought to go to Hebrew School. When explaining the purposes of Hebrew School they mention three distinct time zones—the present, the time of their

Bar/Bat Mitzvah, and the time they get married and have children of their own.

Immediate Reasons for Attending Hebrew School

The immediate reasons for going to Hebrew School are often expressed as learning about your religion, learning how to recite Hebrew prayers and learning Hebrew. Katy sums up the view of several students:

> If there wasn't Hebrew School, then what would be the point of being Jewish? Your religion wouldn't be the same. You wouldn't even believe in your religion.

To other students learning prayers is the most important part of Hebrew School. Hillel explains:

> Learning to pray is the main part of coming to Hebrew School. It's more important than learning to read or playing games. When I learn prayers, I know it's the most important.

While most students considered learning to read Hebrew a valid goal of Hebrew School, the legitimacy of learning to speak Hebrew was more controversial. Some students, like Linda, "enjoy learning another language that almost no one else knows unless you are a Jew." Others, like Frank, question the quality of their Hebrew language education. "The teachers just tell us what the words mean, and then we forget them." Ten-year-old Jodi muses:

> As everyone says, it's for our own good, but I don't see what's the point of learning Hebrew when you're never gonna go to Israel and you're never gonna speak Hebrew to anyone.

The Long-term Goal of Hebrew School— The Bar/Bat Mitzvah

All of the students mentioned the Bar/Bat Mitzvah as an important goal of Hebrew School. Eric, a third grader, thought it was important to go to Hebrew School "to learn so in five more years I can have a Bar Mitzvah." Predictably, as students got closer to the dates of their Bar/Bat Mitzvah they began to mention the event with increasing frequency. Recurrent themes relating to the Bar/Bat Mitzvah were a sense of responsibility and a feeling of honor or pride.

For almost all Bar/Bat Mitzvah candidates the main concept of becoming a Bar or Bat Mitzvah was that of assuming an increased sense of reponsibility. Tammi explains:

> A Bat Mitzvah is when you become an adult Jew. You're more responsible. You know more about being a Jew. You'll be trusted like a grownup because now you're more responsible.

Ultimate Goal—Transmitting Jewish Traditions

Several informants held that an important purpose of Hebrew School was learning about Jewish traditions in order to transmit them to future generations. Linda offers this commentary:

> I feel good that I've learned all this stuff in Hebrew School, and now I have more things to remember so that when I grow up I can tell my kids this.

Noah agrees:

> We're learning about religion in Hebrew School now so that we'll remember it and we'll keep passing this down to our children and our children's children and so on and so forth.

This sense of transmitting traditions is so prevalent that all but one of the students indicated that some day they will send their own children to Hebrew School "even if they don't want to go." The exception is Tammi who explains that she will give her children a choice about going to Hebrew School like her parents gave her. She hopes, of course, that they will choose to go as she has chosen to go.

The students are very much aware that this tradition they will be handing down was transmitted through many generations. Twelve-year-old Seth, who is having difficulty learning to recite the prayers in Hebrew, insists that he does not want to resort to an English translation. His argument is as follows:

> The first Jews prayed in Hebew, and it's important to keep up the tradition. It's something that's worth a lot. I'll give you an example. If my great-great-great-grandfather handed down a vase or something to his kids, I would keep passing it on. I wouldn't get it and just break it.

Noah is more theoretical:

> We have to keep our religion going strong because if we don't sooner or later we're going to come to an age where people who are Jewish don't take part and lose their religion and in time there will be no Jewish people left. So we have to take pride and we have to keep ourselves going.

FEELINGS ABOUT GOING TO HEBREW SCHOOL

As students described the Hebrew School experience, four invariant themes recurred.

Theme of Fun and Boring

When asked what it was like to go to Hebrew School, most students responded with the word "fun" or "boring." An examination of their responses revealed that they perceive Hebrew School as fun when they judge it to be meaningful, challenging or action-oriented. They become bored when they perceive the work as repetitive, uninteresting or irrelevant. A search for any one Hebrew School activity that all students found fun or boring was futile. For example, while several students referred to repeating prayers as boring or frustrating, some found that to be the most rewarding part of Hebrew School. Melissa and Jodi dramatically demonstrate this phenomenon. Melissa expounds:

> I don't see why we have to learn Hebrew prayers. When I pray, I pray in my own personal way. I don't pray in Hebrew, because I don't know what I'm saying, and I don't know if the words mean what I really feel.

To Jodi, on the other hand, studying prayers is meaningful:

> I think it's fun learning prayers. That's my favorite part of all of Hebrew School. Somewhere along the line I always hear the prayer and it's familiar to me. These are our prayers to God for ourselves or our friends, and so like to know them. It's kind of confusing to understand what's going on, but I don't know, once you know how to say the prayers and you know that tune you feel good.

Theme of Socializing

Although there was no consensus on what subjects, activities, and classes are interesting and which are boring, there was consensus on three aspects of Hebrew School life. All of the students mentioned that socializing was a positive aspect of the Hebrew School experience. For some students the social aspects of Hebrew School help to compensate for the more negative aspects. Katy rationalizes: "Sometimes I'm having so much fun studying with my friends that I forget that I don't see any purpose in studying Hebrew." Rebecca is more dramatic: "I don't think I could take it if I had to sit there for three hours and learn without having a little break to talk to someone." For Hillel, too, friends are a key aspect of his enjoyment of Hebrew School.

> One of the things I like about coming to Hebrew School is I have friends here that I wouldn't have if I didn't come. Like I met Greg here and now we're pretty good friends.

Some students mentioned that they feel more comfortable and relaxed in Hebrew School because everybody is Jewish. According to Ira:

At school everyone picks on you. It is not always that much fun. But when you get to Hebrew School and you are around all the other Jewish kids, it is fun. If kids pick on you in public school, you can discuss it with Rabbi Schwartz when you come to Hebrew School and sometimes when you let it out it feels better.

Theme of Open Classroom

Another area of their Hebrew School experience to which the students gave unanimous approbation was the informal classroom environment. The most frequent accolades were reserved for this aspect of their Jewish education. Nine-year-old Greg was among the most enthusiastic:

It's easier to get a choice like we do. We can do anything we want at any time. We might do a worksheet or do payers. We can pick which one we want. It's really neat when you have a selection of things to do.

Noah likes the sense of responsibility that the open classroom affords him:

They're not forcing you to learn like in regular school, and I like that. They don't have all the tests, but you're supposed to learn on your own. It gives me a feeling of responsibility.

An aspect of the open classroom that the students appreciate is the informal relationship with teachers and aides. Jodi remarks: "You get to know the teachers here better than the teachers in public school. The teachers here spend more time with you and you're less shy." Greg agrees: "These teachers aren't harsh on you. They don't yell at you a lot like they do at public school. These teachers fool around with you. I feel more comfortable here." Even Melissa, who is generally antagonistic toward her Jewish education, concurs: "The teachers are nice and they understand and they give you enough time to practice and everything so that you get to know it right."

Theme of Conflicting Activities

For all students in this study, the Hebrew School schedule presents conflicts. These conflicts range from minor inconvenience to outright distress. Even students who are enthusiastic about Hebrew School once they arrive, express displeasure at the prospect of going.

Jodi sums up the perceptions of several members of the study: "The worst thing about Hebrew School is coming. The best part is going home with a sense of accomplishment that you've achieved something." The most frequent complaints include being rushed, not being able to play with friends, missing soap operas on television, and forfeiting extracurricular activities. Beth and Greg, who are among the most enthusiastic students in the sample, both complain about being rushed. Beth, a second grader has to rush through her job of cleaning the school chalkboards in order to get to Hebrew School on time. Greg puts its way:

> I only have five or ten minutes after I get home from public school to leave for Hebrew School. I have to get a quick snack, nothing big. Then I have to get back into my coat and shoes and boots and then I have to leave.

Jodi is most dramatic about the conflict:

> It's a pain coming to Hebrew School when I have other activities I want to do. Like I wanted to go to Girl Scouts, but I couldn't because of Hebrew School. . .Hebrew School inconveniences everybody. My gym teacher organized the whole team around the fact that I can't play on Tuesdays. I felt pretty embarrassed because it's a lot of work for people to organize a whole team to play on special days just for me.

A few students talked about trying to avoid coming to Hebrew School altogether. When Melissa's carpool driver gets to her house, she remembers she has to feed the dog and do other errands. When the driver perseveres in waiting, Melissa then "walks very slowly to the car." Hillel has a devious plan:

> On Sunday morning if I get up early I say to myself, 'Don't wake Mom and Dad up maybe we'll miss Hebrew School.' And if I get up late, I say to myself, Maybe if I lay here, they'll forget." But once I get up I know I have to do it.

CONCLUSIONS AND IMPLICATIONS

The sample of this phenomenological study is necessarily delimited. In addition, no attempt was made to analyze the data according to the students' ages or attitudes toward Hebrew school. Rather, the data were utilized to gain a phenomenological understanding of the Hebrew school experience as seen through the eyes of a group of 18 students. Instead of drawing far-reaching conclusions and deriving general implications from the data, the study should serve as a springboard for those who want to examine the phenomenon of Jewish education on a broader basis. The conclusions and implications presented here are, therefore, subject to further study. It is hoped that they will encourage researchers to conduct the much-needed research in this area.

The findings of this study show that these 18 students have ambivalent feelings about being Jewish, and in their quest to understand their minority status they look to the Hebrew School for support and confirmation. The students in this sample, although not always enthusiastic about the process acknowledged that the Hebrew School served a legitimate and positive role in their lives. The Hebrew School appears to be a place where the child "is taught how to be Jewish—both behaviorally and cognitively" (Shapiro and Dashefsky 1974, p. 99).

The Need for Practical Goals

An implication derived from this phenomenon is that the curriculum of Hebrew School ought to address itself directly to the expressed religious and ethnic concerns of the students. The goals that the students perceived as most meaningful were those that had practical implications, such as learning to recite the blessings for the Hanukkah candles, studying for their Bar/Bat Miztvah ceremony, and explaining their religion to other people. Subjects that were lacking in realistic application, such as learning to speak Hebrew or "learning what happened 10,000 years ago," were often found to be unmotivating. It appears that the purpose of Hebrew School must be seen as practical in order to be accepted by the students as legitimate. Students must see a real purpose to what they are learning or they may reject it out of hand.

In accordance with this implication, the Bar/Bat Mitzvah ceremony should be encouraged as a practical outlet for a student's emerging identification with the Jewish people. Too often in Jewish education the Bar/Bat Mitzvah ceremony is assailed as a subversive element of Hebrew School, since it may signal the end of formal Jewish education. While this condition is, indeed, unfortunate, this rite of passage should not become a scapegoat. The students consistently described the Bar/Bat Mitzvah ceremony as a meaningful symbol of their emerging responsibility as young Jews. The Hebrew School ought, therefore, to encourage and capitalize on these positive feelings and welcome the opportunity to provide students with practical knowledge that they can display before a real audience.

The Need for Flexibility

The disparity of pupils' perceptions about Hebrew School leads to the conclusion that there is no one typical perception of Hebrew School and there is no such thing as an "average child." The Hebrew School ought, therefore, to strive toward more flexibility in order to accommodate the needs of the wide variety of students it serves. This flexibility is indicated on the following levels.

The Curriculum

Not all students should be required to study an identical curriculum. Accommodations should be made for students who find one or more areas of the curriculum irrelevant. Only a flexible curriculum can meet the needs of both Melissa, who found studying prayers irrelevant, and Jodi, who found them to be the best part of Hebrew School!

Furthermore, since students differ in their styles of learning, teaching approaches should take into consideration these various learning styles. In addition, to address recurrent students' complaints that material presented in class was too easy or too difficult, the curriculum of the Hebrew School should be individualized to meet the variety of abilities of the students in attendance.

Classroom Environment

Since socialization was found to be a key factor in the process of Jewish education, classrooms should be arranged so as to maximize rather than minimize socialization. The students in this study have demonstrated that the Hebrew School, and not the home, is the main source of information and skills necessary for Jewish living. Now that the responsibility of the home has been thrust upon the school, Hebrew Schools should be modeled more on the informality and flexibility of the home, and less on the rigidity of the typical public school. Teachers, like parents, should attempt to develop personal, long-term relationships with their students. Rather than "passing" students from class to class each year, team teaching, "family" groupings of mixed ages, sides, and volunteers can be utilized to approximate the conditions of an extended family which will contribute to the continuity of the curriculum and the values it aims to transmit.

School Schedule

Because all students pointed to the conflict that Hebrew School presented with other activities, a flexible schedule of Hebrew classes seems to be indicated. Just as the curriculum should be tailored to meet the needs of different students, so, too, should the schedule of classes be flexible enough to meet the conflicting schedules of individual students. Rather than demand that students meet the schedule of the Hebrew School at the cost of waiving such activities as sports, cub scouts, and snacks, an element of flexibility and a sense of cooperation with other community institutions should be built into the school program. Cooperation between the public school and the Jewish community, for example, could yield a plan whereby students are bused directly from public school to Hebrew School, thus eliminating the rush about which many students complained.

If the Hebrew School schedule were more flexible and convenient, perhaps it could have a positive rather than a negative effect on a student's time constraints. If, for instance, Hebrew schools were open after school every day they could provide a form of enriched day care which would combine recreation, socialization, and education. Students could then choose to attend on the days that were most convenient for them. Although this would necessitate taking a new look at present Jewish educational policies, it would eliminate one of the chief sources of resentment that students build up toward Hebrew School, and ultimately toward their Jewishness. Such flexibility would better serve the broadening role of Jewish education in Jewish identification, the escalating needs of working parents, and the increasing competition for young people's time.

The policy implications of this study suggest that Jewish educators strive to develop relevant, flexible, pupil-oriented curricula that will meet the expressed needs, goals and aspirations of their students. More qualitative and quantitative studies are necessary to test out in a controlled, comparative way the differential effects of rigid versus flexible curricula, classroom environments, and school schedules.

REFERENCES

Ackerman, W. 1969. "Jewish Education—for What?" *American Jewish Yearbook* 70:3-35.

American Jewish Committee. 1977. "Colloquium on Jewish Education and Jewish Identity." New York.

Atkinson, M. 1972. "A Precise Phenomenology for the General Scholar." *Journal of General Education* 23 (February): 45-53.

Bock, G. 1976. "The Social Context of Jewish Education: A Literature Review." Jewish Education and Jewish Identity. New York: American Jewish Committee.

————. 1977. "Does Jewish Schooling Matter?" Jewish Education and Jewish Identity. New York: American Jewish Committee.

Buber, M. 1958. *I and Thou.* New York: Charles Scribner's Sons.

Cohen, J. 1965. *Jewish Education in Democratic Society.* New York: Reconstruction Press.

Cohen, S. 1974. "The Impact of Jewish Education on Religious Identitication and Practice." *Jewish Social Studies* 36 (July-August): 316-326.

Dashefsky, A. and H. Shapiro. 1974. *Ethnic Identification Among American Jews.* Lexington, MA: Lexington Books.

Fein, L. 1972. "Suggestions Toward the Reform of Jewish Education in America." *Midstream* 18(February):41-49.

Fox, S. 1973. "Toward a General Theory of Jewish Education." Pp. 260-270 in *The Future of the Jewish Community,* edited by D. Sidorsky. New York: Basic Books.

Glazer, N. 1971. "The Social Background of Amcrican Jewish Education." Jewish Education and Jewish Identity. New York: American Jewish Committee.

Greeley, A. M. 1971. *Why Can't They Be Like Us? America's White Ethnic Groups.* New York: E.P. Dutton.

Heilman, S. 1983. *Inside the Jewish School.* New York: American Jewish Committee.

Himmelfarb, H. 1980. *The American Jewish Day School: A Case Study.* Unpublished manuscript, Ohio State University.

————. 1975. "Jewish Education for Naught-Educating the Culturally Deprived Child." *Analysis* 51.

Howe, I. 1977. "Limits of Ethnicity." *New Republic* June 25:17-19.

Lofland, J. 1971. *Analyzing Social Settings.* Belmont, CA: Southwest Laboratories.

Pollak, G. and G. Lang. 1979. *Jewish School Census 1978/1979.* New York: American Association for Jewish Education.

Rist, R. 1979. "On the Means of Knowing: Qualitative Research in Education." *New York University Education Quarterly* 10 (Summer): 17-21.

Sanua, V. D. 1964. "Jewish Education and Jewish Identification." *Jewish Education* 35 (Spring): 37-50.

Schoem, D. 1979. "Ethnic Survival in America: An Ethnography of Jewish Afternoon School. Unpublished doctoral dissertation. Berkeley: University of California.

Shapiro, H. and A. Dashefsky. 1974. "Religious Education and Ethnic Identitication: Implications for Ethnic Pluralism." *Review of Religious Research* 15 (Winter):93-102.

Silberman, C. 1976. "Where Are Our Children?" *Moment* 1 (January):7-12.

Sklare, M. 1971. "The Social Background of American Jewish Education—A Commentary." Jewish Education and Jewish Identity. New York: American Jewish Committee.

Stone, F. 1979. *Philosophical Phenomenology: A Methodology for Holistic Educational Research.* Storrs, CT: Multicultural Research Guides Series, University of Connecticut.

Wax, R. H. 1971. *Doing Fieldwork.* Chicago: The University of Chicago Press.

THE SECULARIZATION OF CANADA

Hans Mol

ABSTRACT

Various data about religion in Canada at first sight seem to confirm the "inexorable secularization" thesis. Church attendance in French Canada as well as elsewhere seems to have dropped considerably since 1965. The percentage of individuals putting "no religion" on the census form has also increased. And yet, some of the sects increase their membership much faster than the population. The evangelical/fundamentalist sections of the major denominations also seem to be doing very well as compared with the liberal ones. The conclusion is drawn that in an increasingly loosely woven society where many norms and values are optional, such as Canada, those sects and religious groups which manage to strengthen a boundary around themselves and to form clearly delineated pockets of meaning are doing well indeed.

INTRODUCTION

There is a long standing tradition in the social scientific study of religion that technical progress, rationalization and secularization go hand in hand. And as the first two are inevitable, so the thought goes, secularization is also

Research in the Social Scientific Study of Religion, Volume 1, pages 197-215.

inexorable. Religion will of necessity lose more and more of its influence and power.

Well known scholars favor this view of inexorable secularization. Max Weber (1946, p. 155) saw his German society becoming more and more rationalized and intellectualized and felt that therefore the ultimate and most sublime values had to retreat. Karl Marx (1974) also saw the demise of religion. To him it was a reactionary force which would disappear as soon as the proletariat would become aware of its real interest. The reason that religion nowadays is reluctantly tolerated in a variety of communist countries goes back to the old Marxist conviction that if left alone religious institutions will die a natural death. Sigmund Freud (1964) regarded religion as a crutch, the need for which would vanish when, as he hoped, rational consciousness were to prevail. Bryan Wilson (1985, p. 18), a modern exponent of this view, adds that the secularization process is slow "because religious dispositions are deep-laid in man's essential irrationality, which resists the rationalization of the external social order."

Canadian data appear to justify the inexorable secularization thesis. In what follows I will look at (1) emancipation of secular structures (welfare, education, political legitimation); (2) membership data of religious organizations; (3) religious practices; (4) the power of secular, competing ideologies; and (5) the power of secular values and symbols. All these seem to provide solid evidence for increasing secularization. And yet, on second inspection, each of these also gives rise to doubt. In the conclusion I will draw all observations together in order to arrive at the best possible notion regarding the place of religion in Canadian society in 1989.

THE ARGUMENT FOR SECULARIZATION

Emancipation

In the first half of the seventeenth century when there were fewer than 2,000 settlers, the Jesuits ran New France. Their power was so great that they could impose fines and punishments for blasphemy, drunkenness and nonattendance at church on religious holidays. The Catholic Church also looked after orphans, the sick and the destitute. It alone provided education at any level. It alone solemnized marriages and buried the dead. Although as recent as the first half of the twentieth century the Catholic episcopate in Quebec was consulted about major legislation, the power of the Church has been slowly, but surely, whittled away. It now has no monopoly in the areas of social welfare, education, civil or judicial administration.

The same applies to the Church of England. In the early beginnings of English settlement it looked after education and social welfare. The government paid for the building of churches and the salaries of clergy. Yet in Nova Scotia toward the end of the eighteenth century the sole right to perform marriages and keep the register of births, death and marriages had to be given up. In what is now Ontario the Clergy reserves (the source of income for the Church of England) were secularized around the middle of the nineteenth century. Here too the monopolies were broken. Secularization both here and in Quebec meant differentiation in the sense that functions of church and state became separated, political and administrative alignments severed. Differentiation went further in Protestantism in that schooling, hospital and social security provisions are now generally independent from ecclesiastical control. This is less true for Catholicism.

Membership

The Canadian census figures show that those with "no religion" are on the increase. As recently as 1961 only 0.5% of the population stated not to have a religion, but by 1981 the figure had risen to 7.4%. Yet even this percentage covers only a small proportion of the population whose membership in a denomination is rather nominal. In 1971 the actual membership of the United Church of Canada, according to its yearbook, was 1,016,706 which is only 27.0% of those who were entered on the census form as such (3,768,508). The comparable figure for 1981 is 24.0%. The corresponding percentages for Anglicans are 27.3% for 1971, 23.5% in 1981. This does not mean, however, that 76% of United and 76.5% of Anglicans are now nominal; unconfirmed children and churchgoing adherents are also hidden in these percentages. Yet it means that a majority of Canadians who think of themselves as United or Anglican at census time in actual fact have little or no contact with the churches to which they belong. They are hardly distinguishable from those who put "No Religion" on the census form. What is more, in the United Church, for instance, their percentage has slowly risen from 66.3% in 1931 to 67.5% in 1941, 70.8% in 1951, 71.7% in 1961, 73.0% in 1971, and 76.0% in 1981. Regarding Presbyterianism, only 20.6% of those who in 1981 were adherents on the census records were also on its membership rolls.

Religious Practices

Another way of measuring religious decline is to compare church attendance figures. The National Institute of Public Opinion (Gallup Poll) has, at regular intervals, asked a representative sample of Canadians whether or not they had attended a church or a synagogue within the last seven days.

Table 1 shows that since World War II weekly attendance dropped from approximately two-thirds of the population to slightly more than one-third. The decline was particularly severe for Protestants until about 1970 when it

Table 1.   Percentage of Individuals who had been to Church or
              Synagogue in the Previous Seven Days

	1946	1956	1965	1970	1975	1980	1984
Canada, total population	67	61	55	44	41	35	36
Catholics	83	87	83	65	61	50	50
Protestants	60	43	32	28	25	26	29

began to even out. Catholic decline began in the latter half of the sixties and evened out in the eighties. However, there is a difference between Francophone and Anglophone Catholics which the Gallup Poll figures cannot detect. A secondary analysis of the 1965, 1974, and 1984 Canadian National Election Studies provide us with more discriminating data. It shows that since the Quiet Revolution in Quebec and the Second Vatican Council in Rome in the early sixties, the mass exodus from the Catholic Church in French-speaking Canada was spearheaded by the young (see Table 2); in the 18-30 age group 90% were regular attenders in 1965, but only 30% in 1984. The decline was less severe among the English-speaking Catholics of that age group (from 66% to 38%, Anglicans (from 27% to 24%), United (from 33% to 15%), and nonexistent among "Others," primarily small denominations and sects.

The decline in church attendance over the period 1965-1984 is less dramatic for older age groups. In particular, those over 61 more or less remained loyal to their churches. In the age group 31-60, French-speaking Catholics dropped from 93% to 49%, and English-speaking ones from 75% to 54%, but Anglicans and United Church members remained at the same levels which had always been below Catholic ones.

If we look at changes of attendance patterns for the various levels of education, 89% of Francophone Catholics with at least some post-secondary schooling were regular churchgoes in 1965 as compared with 39% in 1984. Those with only elementary education remained more loyal: church attendance among them declined from 89% to 64% over the same period. As for English-speaking Catholics with at least some post-secondary education, the percentage of regular churchgoers dropped from 71% in 1965 to 36% in 1984. Comparable percentages for those with only elementary schooling were 69% and 57%.

Residence also made a difference: the percentage of regular Francophone Catholics dropped from 83% in cities with over 100,000 inhabitants from 1965 to 1984. Yet in rural areas (villages with less than 2500 inhabitants), the decline was less severe: from 88% in 1965 to 60% in 1984. Corresponding percentages for Anglophone Catholics were 59% and 45% in cities and 75% and 60% in rural areas.

Table 2. Percentage of Regular Churchgoers by Denomination and Age in the 1965, 1974, and 1984 Canadian National Election Studies[a]

Age	Year	Anglican	Catholic (English-speaking)	Catholic (French-speaking)	United Church	Other	Total
18-30	1965	27	66	90	33	34	60
	1974	13	48	38	14	32	33
	1984	24	38	30	15	37	31
31-60	1965	34	75	93	32	41	60
	1974	24	58	67	30	42	47
	1984	31	54	49	30	48	45
61 and over	1965	36	77	87	55	56	65
	1974	36	63	84	37	36	52
	1984	39	68	75	43	54	56
Total (n in bracket)	1965	33 (273)	73 (391)	92 (778)	37 (540)	43 (429)	61 (2411)
	1974	23 (304)	55 (544)	59 (611)	28 (491)	38 (461)	43 (2411)
	1984	31 (318)	51 (766)	48 (674)	30 (532)	47 (673)	48 (2963)

Notes: [a]"Regular defined as "at least twice a month."
Those respondents who stated not to have a religion or refused to answer the question were eliminated from the calculations. The percentage of individuals who attended church less than twice a month is in each instance 100 minus the percentage of regular attenders.

Secular Ideology

Emancipation from under the religious umbrella, decline in membership and church attendance are often attributed to a secular ideology pervading modernity. Some Catholics put the blame squarely at the feet of the Second Vatican Council (1962-1965) which opened its windows to the world, but in doing so introduced secular air inside its hitherto carefully preserved Catholic identity. It abolished the Latin mass and replaced it with the language of the people. (Archbishop Levèbre of France continued to say the mass in Latin and was consequently suspended by Pope Paul VI. In Canada, Father Yves Normandin and others continued to celebrate Latin masses, but they did so without the consent of the local bishops, and their communicants knew about it only through word of mouth or newspaper advertisements.) Vatican II also began to stress "collegiality" (rule by the college of bishops) at the expense of papal authority. When in 1968 Pope Paul VI published the encyclical *Humanae Vitae* (which condemned aritificial birth control), the Canadian bishops weakened its impact by stating that, in final resort, individual conscience was the arbiter of moral matters.

Yet it is a mistake to blame internal, organizational decisions on the weakening of Catholic boundaries. Pressures to use the vernacular for the mass and to relax proscriptions of artificial birth control existed long before the 1960s. The secular individualism of urbanized societies had infiltrated many Catholic circles, and Vatican II merely recognized the change taking place. In a survey of twelve parishes in Metropolitan Toronto, taken on behalf of Archbishop Pocock in the early 1970s, 73% of practicing Catholics favored the changes brought about by Vatican II. Yet in the exuberant opening of windows, the innate Catholic hankering for the stable frame of reference was underrated. Decline in church attendance shows a continuing disillusionment with the changes.

For at least some Canadian Catholics, "Catholicism is like a city destroyed by war" (Roche 1982, p. 10). In former days, when Catholic education depended on rote learning rather than on developmental psychology, external authority for one's actions was taken for granted. The confessional enforced the idea that evil was to be eradicated and forgiven rather than to be discussed and personally mastered. Good was excitingly demonstrated in the lives of the Christian martyrs in the beginning of the Christian era and was rewarded in heaven rather than regarded as variable with time and circumstance. The consequences of ambiguity for church-going are described by the example Roche (pp. 10, 16) gives of her father, who was a millwright in Newfoundland. She says:

> I was never so shocked in my life as when my father told me, several years before he died, that he was no longer going to Mass. . . My father, whose faith through the poor times,

> and through my mother's agonizing death, had remained so innocent, cheerful and trusting, who until then would have rather died than miss Mass intentionally, who took Holy Communion so seriously that he wouldn't receive it if he had so much as laughed at a blasphemous joke in the mill—now for him, the miracle had departed. They had taken away his Lord, and he didn't know where they had laid him.

She concludes (somewhat excessively) that the heart of Catholicism is broken. One cannot live the Catholic life unself-consciously anymore. One can go to church out of love, "but it is love among the ruins." Gutted Masses with antic priests, manufactured excitement, and cafeteria casualness are all she can see. Clearly her opinions are not shared by many other Catholics.

Yet the other mainline churches fought similar battles with secular ideology. In the Anglican Church the problem of secularization surfaced into consciousness in the middle-sixties when its Department of Religious Education commissioned Berton (1965) to write a critical book about the Church. *The Comfortable Pew* became a runaway bestseller. Berton had been raised as Anglican at Dawson City (Yukon) in the 1920s. He was confirmed in Victoria, B.C., but began to slowly drift away from the church. However, the Vancouver daily newspaper for which he worked appointed him church editor, and as such he had to report on Sunday sermons and other religious activities of the city. He was married in the United Church and had all his six children baptized there because he did not agree with the Anglican order of baptism which began with the statement that "all men are conceived and born in sin." He felt rather that children were innocent slates waiting to be written upon (Berton 1965, p. 24).

The Comfortable Pew had an effect far beyond the Anglican Church for which it was originally intended. It showed the thinking of well-educated, articulate Anglicans who had drifted away from the Church. Dogma clashed with science, Berton said, and he lashed out against the religious establishment, which cowardly attempted not to rock any boats, preached deadly dull sermons and condoned war and nuclear armament while condemning pre-marital sex and other pleasures of the flesh. The woof and warp of Berton's argument consisted of a secular ideology and open-minded pragmatism in which there was more room for enjoyment than for sin, activism than contemplation, performance than meaning.

In the United Church Crysdale (1965, p. 10) embarked in 1963 on a national survey in which he investigated the effect of "urbanism," an urban style of life with "openess to new ideas and readiness to question old norms" and with much emphasis on rational routines, plurality of customs, and a vast array of media choices. The survey consisted of a mail sample of 1,708 individuals on United Church lists of communicants and adherence. It found that an increasingly urban style of life went roughly together with an increasingly liberal theology for "beliefs and social situations area closely interrelated" (p.

78). By liberal theology Crysdale meant freedom of interpretation concerning the nature of God, Jesus and the Bible. The implication was that rationality had been a pervasive influence on both urbanism and theology.

The openess of the United Church toward its environment (rather than withdrawal from it) has led to a continued interest in social research. It backed another large national project in 1975 conducted by Bibby (1979), now a sociologist at the University of Lethbridge in Alberta. Like Crysdale, Bibby was interested in the phenomenon of secularization. In writing his report on *Canadian Commitment,* prepared for the United Church of Canada (1979, p. 4), he anticipated finding that the high level of industrialization in Canada would lead to an ever-decreasing minority of religious people and that even this minority would rationalize belief and delimit religious authority. And that is what he found. Religion is becoming more and more peripheral in Canadian society and maintains itself mainly through religious socialization in the home. Religion has little input in personal well-being and interpersonal relations. "Only in the sphere of personal morality and in one's response to death does religious commitment in Canada give evidence of making a significant 'difference'" (pp. 72-73).

Twenty percent of Bibby's sample was traditionally Christian in that they believed in God, the divinity of Jesus, life after death, prayed regularly, experienced God's presence, and knew the Bible. For the United Church this percentage was as low as 14%. The author blames this state of affairs on a pervasive industrial worldview which is propagated quite unconsciously in all institutions of Canadian society. It expresses itself, he says, in people's basic commitment to the senses and the observable world rather than to anything spiritual. And the United Church has adjusted itself so much to this outlook "that the commitment differences of United members and nonmembers—while existing—are consistently smaller than those found for other Canadian religious groups, suggesting that participation in local United congregations does not as readily foster a traditional Christian outlook" (p. 15).

Increasing ideological competition between secular culture and organized Christianity can also be surmised from the fact that even on the narrow "religious" level one can hardly speak about a monopoly any longer. Kilbourn (1968, p. 6), with tongue in cheek, calls Toronto's Maple Leaf Gardens the most important religious building in Canada because it is there that the religious cult of Hockey Night in Canada is celebrated. More seriously Edwards (1973, pp. 261-262) extends this argument by pointing to "saints" who have become immortal through their triumphs on the playing fields and to "gods," the superstars whose charisma enthused millions. "Scribes" (sports reporters and telecasters) similarly enhance the reputation and standing of the organization in the eyes of the public. "Seekers of the Kingdom" (the true believers, devotees, fanatics and converts) reinforce loyalty and commitment to the club, which keeps cups and other trophies in those places where religious organizations have their "shrines."

It is because of strong loyalties to sports organizations and adulation of god-like superstars that one can encounter Canadian clergyman who privately (or sometimes even publicly) denounce these commitments as idolatry (trespass on their terrain). The fact that nowadays they tend to do this privately shows a change in public opinion. About the turn of the century (when the Lord's Day Alliance was at the height of its power), scheduling training sessions in sports on Sunday mornings would have been out of the question. They now occur fairly frequently. If it is countered that there is nothing transcendental about this secular religion, one can point to organizations and practices entirely outside organized Christianity which maintain the transcendental element.

Every week in Canada there are roughly three to four thousand weekly gatherings of Alcoholics Anonymous. Although it allows the widest possible interpretation of who God is (if a member wants to define God as a rather vague power of some kind, that is fine with A.A.), it also insists in its twelve steps of recovery that members acknowledge that only a power greater than themselves can restore them to sanity and that only by turning their will "over to the care of God as we understand him" can they get well again. A.A. members are convinced that recognizing their powerlessness over alcohol, believing in a power beyond themselves, and submitting to this power with trust, are central to a successful recovery.

Secular Values and Commitments

In Moore's *The Luck of Ginger Coffey* (1972, p. 70), a fellow proofreader at the Montreal *Tribune* feels that he must acquaint Ginger (a newcomer from Ireland) with the major Canadian values: "Money is the Canadian way to immortality. . . Money is the root of all good here. One nation, indivisible, under Mammon that's our heritage." In Atwood's *Surfacing* (1973), p. 42), the heroine, reminiscing about her youth, says that glamour to her was "a kind of religion," and that the pictures of fashion models on her bedroom walls were the corresponding "icons." What both authors mean is that the prime motivating forces, the unifying commitments, can be quite different from the source of salvation in organized Christianity or Christian theology. Preoccupation with health, power, and fame are other commitments which the Canadian public at large associates with religious feeling.

Free enterprise and business success comprise the theology of George A. Cohon, who in a decade amassed a personal fortune of $50 million by peppering Canada with 400 McDonald's hamburger outlets. Peter Newman (1981, pp. 175-6) describes his commercial commitments as "born-again evangelism" and his personnel as "smiling, smiling not for Jesus, but for Big Mac." Cohon's chief operating officer, who left to start his own hamburger chain, has become a heretic, a non-person (". . . in my religion I forgot his name," said Cohon). Cohon actually admits "McDonald's is a religion with me."

The Canadian public at large often associates militancy with religion. A good example is the Women's Liberation Movement. Particularly in its early stages, its fervency (Stephenson 1977, p. 116) was its most conspicuous characteristic. It wanted to unite all women against oppression and discrimination. In the 1980s it began to mellow, while maintaining its beliefs in the necessity for greater equality and justice for women. It also continues to keep these goals in the forefront of attention through a strategy of consciousness raising and the ritual encouragement of feelings and emotions aroused by actual wrongs.

Another source of commitments bypassing organized Christianity has to do with horoscopes, palmreading, witchcraft, black magic, etc. Palmreaders sometimes have offices in shopping malls. Bibby (1979, Table A4) shows that as much as 15% of his Canadian sample read the horoscope daily, 62% consult it occasionally. The percentage of individuals who read their horoscope regularly goes up among Protestants who are merely members, affiliates (not formal members of a denomination): 22% for United Church affiliates as against 13% for members, 23% for Conservative affiliates as against 10% for members (Conservatives in Bibby's survey are Protestants belonging to the smaller, often evangelical denominations such as Baptist, Brethren, Pentecostal, Salvation Army.) Unfortunately, from the data published in Bibby (1979), it is not possible to discover more about the kind of people who consult their horoscope daily, but if Australian data are any indication, they tend to be the irregular churchgoers, the insecure, and the frightened (Mol 1971, p. 43).

One can find numerous other examples of Canadian society ignoring Christian values. For instance, President Alvin Lee of McMaster University said at a symposium on youth held at Oakville's Sheridan College on November 15, 1984:

> . . . society, or the "real world," as many critics of academic institutions like to think of it, provides no real standards or values. Many of the ordinary conventions of our society stand for immaturity and mindless expenditures of energy. Social values that surround a teenager today are rooted in the entertainment industries, and in the organized greed represented by advertising. The young person's erotic needs and other appetites are grotesquely exploited in dozens of ways.

> Consider by contrast a different set of conventions. The civilization we inhabit had for centuries as one of its dominant teachings the idea of seven deadly sins by which we, as creatures of free will, may choose to destroy ourselves or not. The seven were pride, avarice, envy, wrath, sloth, gluttony and lust. I invite you to consider the advertising messages of our society and how the value system they purvey is a total exploitation and celebration of precisely those appetites. One might almost say our economy is based on them.

The argument for the inexorable secularization of Canada is persuasive indeed. And yet it has feet of clay. Let us go over each of our sub-headings again, this time furnishing evidence for the counter argument.

THE ARGUMENT AGAINST SECULARIZATION

Emancipation

The advanced division of labor in modern societies (differentiation) has indeed freed many social functions from religious control. However, to assume that this has been a disadvantage for religious organization is wrong. Those religious denominations in Canada which in the middle of the nineteenth century favored voluntarism and separation of church and state, appeared to thrive under the independence which they assumed or acquired. And even for those who were reluctant to separate the ties and release control (Anglicans, Catholics and some Methodists and Presbyterians), having to stand on their own feet proved to be a blessing in disguise. The cohesion of religious organizations (as measured by church attendance) in countries where they have to compete with one another is nearly always greater than in those countries where they are or were the only state church. Anglican attendance in England, Catholic attendance in France, Presbyterian attendance in Scotland (see for figures the entry under church attendance in the index of Mol, Hetherton, and Henty 1972) is and was always much below attendance for the corresponding denominations in Canada. The exception of Ireland and Poland to this rule is caused by the fact that Catholicism in those countries set itself off against foreign rule and became the rallying point (as in Quebec) for endangered nationhood. In other words, denominations and churches which had to contend with other structures, always gained in terms of stronger organizational boundaries and increased loyalty by the membership.

The freedom accompanying independence has another consequence. The prophetic, critical role of religion is usually compromised when it is beholden to and responsible for forms of establishment. Of course this possibility exists at all times, as the survival of religion is linked with the contribution it makes to the integration of other units of social organization (persons, families, communities, etc). Yet concrete proposals and critical verdicts necessary for justice, wholeness and sanity suffer when religious organizations are bound to secular structures. The sharply critical notes about native rights and unemployment in Canada by the Anglican and Catholic hierarchies in the first half of the 1980s are difficult to imagine if the latter had been financially or otherwise dependent on those whose policies and ideas were opposed.

Membership

The mainline churches in Canada have obviously been getting a beating over the last 25 years. Yet not all Canadian denominations seem to share the decrease. In 1971 the Salvation Army (with 119,665 adherents) had grown 30% over the preceeding decade, by far outpacing the population increase of 18%

over the same period. Yet in the seventies it grew less rapidly than the population. The Jehovah's Witnesses increased their census membership even more spectacularly in the sixties. They grew by 157% from 1961 to 1971 when 170,810 Canadians stated on the census form that they belonged to the sect. But in the seventies their absolute numbers actually decreased to 143,485 by 1981. By contrast the Pentecostal Churches in Canada have grown by leaps and bounds also in the seventies. They grew 53% from 1961 to 1971 and 54% from 1971 to 1981 when their census membership had climbed to 338,790. So did the church of Latter Day Saints (Mormons) which grew by 33% from 1961 to 1971 and by 35% from 1971 to 1981 when it reached a census membership of 89,870.

An interesting clue comes from differences in growth within some of the mainline churches. A small, but vocal minority within the United Church (The United Church Renewal Fellowship) is growing while other sections are declining. Its membership consists of born-again and charismatic Christians for whom the Bible is literally inspired. Similarly within the family of Baptist churches, the fundamentalist Fellowship of Evangelical Baptists in Canada is growing faster than the less conservative Baptist Federation (Mikolaski 1982, p. 5).

Religious Practices

Moving to religious practices of the Canadian population, there are good reasons to doubt the inexorable secularization thesis here as well. Unfortunately so far I have not found detailed church attendance figures for Canada in the last century. However, if my Australian data are any guide (Mol 1985b, 53ff.) I have a hunch that from 1850 to 1950 the churchgoing of Anglophone Catholics went up as much as it went down from 1965 onwards. And while the Catholic rate went up, the Methodist one is likely to have gone down in the first half of this century. Although these are hunches, I am rather confident the historical variation has much less to do with the rationalization of culture than the proponents of the inexorable secularization thesis assume.

On the other hand there is good evidence for religious practices thriving in some pockets of the Canadian population, according to Crysdale (1965). Regular church attendance goes up with theological conservatism. In his sample 46% of the respondents were liberals in theology, but this percentage drops to 40% of those who attend regularly, 35% the core members, and as little as 14% for those with a high religious commitment (measured by regular prayer, biblical knowledge, religious experience, etc.). In other words, religious practices appear to be undiminished in pockets of theological conservatism.

Bibby (1979, p. 4) also adheres to the inexorable secularization view and links the high level of industrialization in Canada to an ever-decreasing minority of religious people. This may be true for the population as a whole, yet his own figures show that high levels of religious commitment are maintained in some sections of the population that offer strong resistance to the secularization trend. Sixty-five percent of the conservatives, but only 26% of the population prays daily and privately. Sixty-one percent of the former, but only 22% of the latter has had a definite feeling of being somehow in God's presence.

Hamm (1987, p. 251) studies patterns of secularization among the Mennonites of Canada and came to the conclusion that the sacralizing components (such as beliefs, attendance, experiences, etc.) more than stemmed the tide of secularizing elements (through secular education, urbanization, etc.).

All this seems to show that secularization in Canada is pervasive and yet also meets strong resistance in some quarters. Obviously the jury is still out on the inexorable character of secularization. Large sections of the population seem to be unable to stem the tide, but then other, smaller sections do. It is obviously too early yet to render a verdict.

Secular Ideology

The pragmatic hedonism of Berton's (1965) *The Comfortable Pew* has been and still is, a redoutable force in North American culture. It is realistic about the power of the senses, the urge of physical well-being and economic security. And yet, the very people who were on the margin of that culture and who were more likely than the comfortable middle classes to run health and financial risks, have felt all through the centuries a remarkable attraction to the sects preaching about sin and restraint. I suspect that the appeal of conservative, evangelical Christianity lies in its capacity to address itself to the entire realm of human experiences (not just economic deprivation and ill health, but also family conflicts, alcoholism, death, birth, marriage, divorce, frustration, stress, tension, depression as well as elation, pain as well as happiness, adultery as well as faithfulness, plain human cussedness as well as undeserved care, evil as well as good, greed as well as generosity, fortune as well as misfortune, diffidence as well as confidence).

Not that the mainline churches in Canada do not address themselves to these issues, but somehow it is easier for those who are better off to rely on their possessions, guaranteed securities and enjoyments than to take the flawedness of their most inner being seriously. Consequently they do not see society or the culture which provides them with these comforts as an ideological adversary. Actual reconciliation of secular and Christian ideologies is the innate and natural reaction of those millions in the mainline denominations who feel embarrassed about the "Jesus saves from sin" theology, as they don't feel squashed by sin and are too honest to fake the born-again experience. The result has been that those Christian theologians who justify secular ideologies with biblical sugarcoatings (such as Harvey Cox and the "God is dead" theologians) have acquired international recognition. Closer to home, Baum (1967, p. 164) similarly fitted in with the narcissistic beliefs of the me-generation and the individual rationalism of the scientific establishment by proclaiming that "while there may at times be tensions between fulfillment and the requirements of community, we must never make the mistake of realizing the human person in principle as vis-à-vis society."

The real problem, of course, lies with the fact that academics as well as others with secure positions in society have their worldview colored by their situations. Inexorable secularization and the necessity of Christianity to fit in with "the world come of age" therefore become part of the outlook. And so they don't ask themselves any more why it is more respectable to be obsessed with ecology, feminism or nuclear disarmament than with being saved by Jesus. They take it for granted. And yet the born-again Christians do not disappear because their views are less congenial to the secularized masses within the mainline denominations.

The vitality of those segments of the Canadian population which resolutely reject secularization can also be illustrated from the recent debate about a national survey (by Posterski and Bibby), Project Teen Canada (*The Hamilton Spectator,* 16 and 23 March 1985). The survey points to the massive estrangement of young people from the churches. Typically the mainline churches react to this alienation by turning within and finding fault with their ignorance of young people's needs. They cry mea culpa and humbly and earnestly try to be more in tune with the younger generation. The implication is that the secular world should not be condemned but accommodated. By contrast, the evangelical sects fault secular society and attempt to protect their young membership from the death-dealing effect of the surronding culture. Their stance takes the theological form of the saving remnant rather than the grieving parent (the usual mainline position). If private observations in the Hamilton area are accurate, those churches which condemn modern culture as mired in sin also appear to have the most vital youth organizations. On the other hand, those who just as realistically see some good in their surroundings and prefer patient appeal, have trouble holding on to their young people. It is as though those sects and churches which resolutely and unambiguously separate themselves from the secular, non-Christian iedology of their environment are organizationally more viable.

Now it may be sad that black/white thinking has greater appeal than refined awareness of moral complexity, but the fact of the matter is that clarity about values seems to be at a greater premium in modern Western societies than moral muddle. And this greater capacity for clear delineation within time and culture has given the least secularized religious bodies in Canada an advantage over those who traditionally have listened carefully to the stirrings and musings of the social environment. And maybe the reason this is so stems from the increasingly looser weave of that society evoking the protest of the many whose security (economic or psychological) is precarious. Exclusivity, digging a deep moat around bastions of meaning and morality, significantly relieves this precariousness. By contrast inclusivity prolongs the path and can be tolerated only by those who are sufficiently well off to feel rewarded by the kudos of fame, wealth, power and competence which that society continues to bestow in spite of looser weave and moral muddle.

Secular Values and Commitments

There is good evidence that many Canadian values and commitments have little do do with Christianity. Yet they also disprove at least one fact of the inexorable secularization thesis, namely that secularization is bound up with the increasing rationalization of Western society. If society is becoming more rationalized, how then can we explain the obvious vitality of the enthusiasms, loyalties for "secular" commitments, whether hockey, women's liberation, the power beyond the control of A.A. members, money, glamour, health, fame, free enterprise, or beliefs in horoscope and tarrot cards? One can actually build a good argument against the inexorable rationalism of modern society by pinpointing the numerous nonrational elements (such as morale, dedication to one's job, respect for authority, rituals of coffee breaks, office gossip, small talk smoothing out personal relations) at the heart of the so-called rational bureaucracies which are the examples par excellence of the "rational order" which impressed Max Weber and still impresses Bryan Wilson so much.

Actually one can build a pretty convincing argument about the importance of "irrationality" for whatever integration exists on a variety of other levels apart from bureaucracies. Sentiments of loyalty, mutual understanding and affection are indubitably more important for the integrity of a family than adequate income. Similarly the wholeness of a person hinges much more on emotional stability than on capacity for logical reasoning and rational competence. Traditionally, religious institutions have emphasized sentiments and values, such as love, faith, trust, and care for others, rather than procedures of efficiency, rational competence and economic achievements. And we can therefore be sure whatever else may be wrong with religious institutions, it certainly has little to do with the irrationality of the values they advance. After all these values seem to be at a premium precisely in those societies which are most advanced and suffer most from the breakdown of families and individuals.

Accepting that even in the most industrialized, urbanized societies human needs for emotional support, understanding, love, commitment, and forgiveness are undiminished, do the churches insufficiently provide for them? Let us take the *Book of Common Prayer* of the Anglican Church as an example. It has been central to worship throughout its entire history in Canada. It contains the thirty-nine Articles, agreed upon in 1562, which Anglicans have always regarded as their unique summary of what the Christian religion is all about. It formulates in detail its view of man as corrupted by sin and worthy of damnation. Yet this same man is also made whole through Christ, and therefore the Anglican community thinks of itself as part of an imperfect world of disorder and pain, but also protected under the wings of God's order and salvation.

The *Book of Common Prayer* has gone through various revisions, for instance, in 1918 and more recently in 1959, yet it continues to address itself to the widest possible range of human predicaments and blessings, whether on the personal (sickness, suffering, death, birth, prosperity, health) or on the communal level (war, discord, adversity, corruption, pride, adultery, peace, altruism, goodwill, harvest, charity). It puts all these human experiences, social tensions, and concords in a framework of meaning by relating them to God's covenant. In the Anglican services, the same point is made over and over again in a variety of forms: existence may be joyful or hard, full of peaks and valleys, accomplishments and failures, yet, in final resort, it receives its balance and purpose from God in whom everything connects. He represents the unity of all that is.

Yet this universality strikes a chord only with a minority of Anglicans or, for that matter, of Canadian Protestants in general. Why? The riddle increases when we consider that the *Book of Common Prayer* does more than putting existence into perspective. It deliberately, though latently, advances the integrity of families, communities, persons, countries, and the religious organization itself. Honoring parents, considering neighbors, obeying authority, disciplining appetites, paying homage to the sovereign, exalting the Church are all part and parcel of the commandments and prayers and are constantly reiterated. And if worshipping Christians have not fully lived up to expectations (as they are unlikely to), the prayers of confession and the assurances of pardon wipe the slate clean and offer a fresh beginning. One would therefore expect the Church's contribution to social and personal well-being to be highly appreciated. Generally clergymen go out of their way to put their messages in easily digestible form, and the saints of the Church exemplify the values to be followed.

It is fair to conclude that the Anglican Church and all the other Canadian Churches contribute more than amply to the personal and social need for integrity. Secularization therefore may consist not so much in commitments and values becoming obsolete through rationalization and urbanization or in the inadequate provision of them by religious institutions, but in other institutions and segments of society catering for them as well. And even here the situation is anything but hopeless for Christianity. It has a major advantage not shared by the others. It has a comprehensive intent and cosmic frame of reference which allows it to deal with all human experiences. By contrast, commitments to various causes, however necessary, can almost never deal with predicaments and changes in other areas, be they frustration, death or a win in the lottery.

CONCLUSION

The predicament of the religious institutions in Canada may ultimately and essentially be the predicament of society. In its present stage it may be so poorly integrated that it is even hard to find beliefs, commitments, and values which the population or, for that matter, local communities have in common. If this is so, then the real problem of the Canadian Churches may not be that they are not up to the job of mending social fences, but that they have illusions about the fences being mendable. As in other Western societies, differentiation in Canada may have gone too far—so far in fact that any repair job may be like illusionary tinkering. Basic surgery or fundamental reconstruction may be necessary when a high standard of living rather than common beliefs, commitments and values hold a tottering structure together. All viable societies and cultures have struck some kind of balance between differentiation and integration. When differentiation goes too far, alienation, anomie, and wholesale spurning of standards demoralize and corrupt that society. When integration goes too far, ossification and stultifaction prevent change and adaptation.

If religion and religious institutions (and they are two rather separate things) are rejected in a particular society and cultural secularization is taking place on a large scale, differentiation of that society may have gone dangerously far. This is what the figures and illustrations of the first half of this article appear to show. Yet sections of that society may also despair of the major religious institutions being capable of healing that culture. They may avoid the mainline churches because they do not see any solution of reinforcing Christian beliefs, commitments and values in organizations which do not radically separate themselves from what they regard as a lost cause.

Of course, this is the core of the appeal of the sects in Canadian society, such as Pentecostals, Mormons and others which grow much faster than the population at large. Through separation rather than accommodation they tend to create enclaves of belonging, care, and commitment to Christian beliefs and values which are perceived as antidotes to the strains and stresses of what they think of as cold, godless, rudderless culture. Apart from providing moral clarity and specific beliefs, these groups usually also clearly delineate the future (Armageddon, the Second Coming, etc.), thereby securing that future and imbuing the present with meaning from that vantage point.

More importantly they may also be the groups from which the reconstruction and revitalization of a defunct society ultimately may stem. They may be small, but so were the communities of Christians in the first century A. D. All universal religions started out originally as small, insignificant groups of individuals, too uneducated and ignorant to even imagine that one day their beliefs and commitments would regenerate entire civilizations. To those who believe in secularization inexorably steamrolling the modern West, this must sound like palpable nonsense. And yet I want to submit that the swelling tide of evangelical conservatism and charismatic zeal around the globe may be the harbinger of a new age in which the balance between differentiation and secularization, on the one hand, and integration and sacralization, on the other, is being restored. If I am wrong and the "inexorable secularization" scholars are right, the future is likely to be miserable indeed.

SOURCES

The material on church attendance comes from a secondary analysis of the 1965, 1974, and 1984 Canadian Election Studies. The first study was carried out by Philip Converse, John Meisel, Maurice Pinard, Peter Regenstreiff, and Mildred Schwartz; the second by Harold Clarke, Jane Jenson, Lawrence LeDuc, and Jon Pammett; the third by Ronald Lambert, Steven Brown, James Curtis, Barry Kay, and John Wilson. All three samples are stratified probability samples of Canadians eligible to vote. They were carried out with funding from the Canada Council and its successor, The Social Sciences and Humanities Research Council of Canada. The original collectors of the data and the granting agencies bear no responsibility for the analysis and interpretations presented here. The secondary analysis was carried out by the author of this article. Other materials used for this article come from Mol (1985, 1985a).

REFERENCES

Atwood, M. 1973. *Surfacing.* Don Mills, Ontario: General Publishing.
Baum, G. 1967. "Man in History: The Anthropology of Vatican II." Pp. 157-173 in *The New Morality,* edited by William Dunphy. New York: Herder and Herder.
Berton, P. 1965. *The Comfortable Pew* (A Critical Look at the Church in The New Age). Toronto: McClelland and Stewart.
Bibby, R. W. 1979. *Canadian Commitment.* Toronto: United Church Research Office.
Cox, H. E. 1965. *The Changing Church in Canada* (Beliefs and Social Attitudes of United Church People). Toronto: United Church of Canada, Board of Evangelism and Social Service.
Crysdale, S. 1965. *The Changing Church in Canada: Beliefs and Social Attitude of United Church People.* Toronto: United Church of Canada, Board of Evangelism and Social Service.
Edwards, H. 1973. *Sociology of Sports.* Homewood, IL: Dorsey Press.
Freud, S. 1964. *The Future of an Illusion.* Garden City, NY: Doubleday.
Hamm, P. 1978. *Continuity and Change Among Canadian Mennonite Brethren.* Waterloo, Ontario: Wilfrid Laurier University Press.
Kilbourn, W. 1968. "Prologue." Pp. 6-24 in *Religion in Canada,* edited by W. Kilbourn. Toronto: McClelland and Stewart.
Marx, K. 1974. *On Religion* (arranged and edited by Saul K. Padover). New York: McGraw-Hill.
Mikolaski, S. J. 1982. "Baptists on the March." *The Canadian Baptist* 128 (7): 4-5.
Mol, J. (Hans) J. 1970. "Secularization and Cohesion." *Review of Religious Research* 11:183-191.
————. 1971. *Religion in Australia.* Melbourne: Nelson.
————. 1985. "Secularization and the Canadian Churches." *Theodolite* 7(5).
————. 1985a. *Faith and Fragility* (*Religion and Identity in Canada*). Burlington, Ontario: Trinity Press.

———. 1985b. *The Faith of Australians.* Sydney: Allen and Unwin.

Mol, J. (Hans), J. M. Hetherton, and M. Henty, eds. 1972. *Western Religion. A Country By Country Sociological Investigation.* The Hague: Mouton.

Moore, B. 1972. *The Luck of Ginger Coffey.* Toronto: McClelland and Stewart.

Newman, P. C. 1981. *The Acquisitors (The Canadian Establishment),* Vol. 2. Toronto, Ontario: McClelland and Stewart.

Roche, A. 1982. "Love Among the Ruins." *Today Magazine,* April 10, p. 8-16.

Stephenson, M. 1977. "Housewives in Women's Liberation." Pp. 109-125 in *Women in Canada,* edited by M. Stephenson. Toronto: General Publishing.

Weber, M. 1946. *From Max Weber: Essays in Sociology,* edited by H. Gerth and C.W. Mills. New York: Oxford University Press.

Wilson, B. 1985. "Secularization: The Inherited Model." Pp. 9-20 in *The Sacred in a Secular Age,* edited by P.E. Hammond. Berkeley: University of California Press.

POPULAR RELIGIOSITY AND THE CHURCH IN ITALY

Roberto Cipriani

ABSTRACT

Studies of popular religiosity have tended to avoid concrete investigation of what the "popular" basis of religiosity consists. Researchers have tended to consider religiosity mainly in terms of conflict with, or judgments from, the side of established, institutional religion. This article considers various approaches to the study of popular religiosity in Italy (especially Southern Italy). It argues that one must examine such variables as the material-conditions of existence of the people, changing religious practices and ecclesiastical policy, social change, and connected forms of popular belief. A study of magic illuminates the intersection of popular belief, changing social practice, and changes in the role of sections of the clergy. However, a key element of popular religiosity is political, and the article concludes with references to the experiences of the base communities, Catholic dissent, and the "Christians for Socialism" movement.

INTRODUCTION

There has been a long discussion of secularization, and more recently of the return of the sacred, undertaken more by way of theoretical approaches than on the basis of precise empirical studies. So it is that what in various contexts

Research in the Social Scientific Study of Religion, Volume 1, pages 217-237.

seem to be the most widespread forms of religious experience at the popular level have remained in the background of many diatribes which have been as lively as they have been groundless. Even when quite accurate surveys have been carried out, the subject of popular religion has not emerged to the extent its real significance demands. This deficiency has been repaired to some extent by the important contribution supplied by anthropological or historical studies (cf. Burke 1978; Thomas 1971) which more carefully brought out qualitative aspects, rather than statistical data related to the faithful. In fact, there are not many studies in the field of sociology on the phenomenon of popular religion. This area of inquiry thus remains largely unexplored as is shown unequivocally by the absence of monographic chapters and specific treatments of the argument in almost all the basic texts covering the sociology of religion (cf. Pizzuti 1985).

Moreover, the definition of popular religion itself (cf. Greinacher and Mette 1986) involves a certain difficulty, in that the various viewpoints generally reflect an ideological perspective. On the one hand, there is a tendency on the part of the religious institution to distinguish "true" religion from the less "true" religion experienced by the "people," while on the other hand there is a tendency to stress the alternative nature of the "popular," to the point of seeing it as different from the ecclesiastical, "official" one (cf. Vrijhof and Waardenburg 1979). In reality, the continuum between the two models does not appear to have drastic interruptions. The effects are interconnected, and become complex, but without absolute breaks or categorical separations. Within the wider religious phenomenology, the convergences and differences alter case by case, context by context. In other words, there seems to be a reciprocal fertilization which gives rise to developments which are unforeseen at times, but remain within pre-existing limits. The antistructure is counterposed to the structure, the conventional acts as counterpoint to the informal. Old and new re-adapt, sometimes in original syncretic forms, and already well-established frameworks of orientation are integrated with different contents (cf. Prandi 1983). The regular also contemplates the exceptional. In this perspective, the understanding of the religious-popular phenomenon must come to terms with the weight of tradition, the opportunities for innovation, the changing fortunes of the relation with the transcendental, and the encounters and clashes between exponents of officialdom and representatives from the base. So, what may seem contradictions at the level of common logic must then be connected to a wider frame of reference which is never solely religious but involves the principal spheres of politics, economics, and law. The very survival of some religious groups and movements (cf. Kokosalakis 1982) is conditioned by the concessions of time and space adequate for the free expression of their own ritual natures, as well as by the financial resources available for undertaking initiatives and demonstrations, not to mention tolerance as an essential, indeed legal, prerequisite for maintaining and developing ways of existing differently from the dominant or more favored ones.

Mention has been made of the difficulty of clarifying terminology. Indeed, at the outset, the distinction between religion and religiosity needs some explicit explanation. To speak of religion rather than religiosity may in practice lead to incorporating into one particular, historical religion all those specific aspects of behavior which can be found in the "popular" context. This choice would lead indirectly to the need for a comparison, and a tendentiously negative value judgment of the institutionalized and codified form. Furthermore, one would be led to examine the theoretical, ideal contents of social action, rather than its results, at the expense of an organization of thought in a popular framework which does not achieve the completeness and refinement of a doctrine to whose formulation the most capable and (in a Gramscian sense) organic intellectuals in the apparatus of formalized religion, have lent a hand.

In the English-language sociological literature, the term most frequently used is "religion" instead of "popular religiosity." However, because of the difficulty in defining "religion," one is inclined to define religiosity as a measurable, evident phenomenon, which can be established on the basis of concrete, visible actions such as pilgrimages (Makky 1978; Oursel 1978; Sartori 1983). Yet there is not a clear separation between the two definitions of religion since the one evokes the other, and each to some extent has the same meaning, and implies the other. But as the sociologist's task has its limits too, it is convenient to stop at the threshold of the significance perceptible empirically both through participant observation and other qualitative methodologies.

Another awkward problem in the term "popular religion" is connotations of the term "popular." One should at once clear the way of another current formula: folk religion (Leslie 1960). Scholars of cultural or social anthropology disagree enough on what constitutes folklore and the folkoristic (Bronzini 1980) so that true scientific communication is impeded. Then, there is the risk of confusing the practical range of the concept, given that it carries with it all the preceeding influence of studies of popular traditions of a literary, artistic, musicological, and theatrical kind. Moreover, "popular" in English has connotations of something being well-known, famous, recognized, or widespread, not always suitable for religious forms. Thus, an explicit clarifying warning, so as to avoid unnecessary misunderstanding, is essential.

Others prefer to speak of the religion of the people, or the people's religion (cf. Guizzardi, Prandi, Castiglione, Pace, and Morossi 1981), usually alluding to people in the lower socioeconomic strata (Prandi 1977). Therefore, this religion would have to be understood as one specific to the poor or to the economically more dependent classes (Ginzburg 1979). At any rate, it is true that various features of a people's religion are also found where problems of survival do not seem to have much importance.

The linguistic confusion is further complicated by the use of the word "people" in various official documents. For example, in the case of Catholicism, the conception of the church as the "people of God" lumps together all the faithful under a single label. If this is legitimate on a doctrinal level, it does not facilitate the identification of specific categories of believers, who in reality have quite stratified and at times contrasted characteristics. The Ecumenical Council, Vatican II, never dealt with or covered in its official pronouncements, the subject of popular religion, which nonetheless marks out the existential cycles of large majorities of believers, especially in countries distant from the center of catholicity.

Essentially, to speak of popular religiosity seems a compulsory choice intended to get around the obstacles and pitfalls connected with the polyvalency of neighboring terms. Still the problem of popular religiosity remains. One should thus propose a suggestion for purposes of giving direction, which can tentatively describe the characteristics and contents of popular religiosity. First, popular religiosity does not spring up out of nothing, but is situated in a cultural framework which deeply conditions it (Nesti 1983) both in creating the most favorable conditions for its development and in providing terms of reference, modes of observance, ritual procedures, examples of hierarchy, norms of behavior, and basic values.

Second, popular religiosity generally inserts itself in a profile already furnished by individual historical religions, re-working certain aspects, bringing out others, and again in practice mistaking yet more. Thus there is established a connecting fabric which gathers together consensus and membership through the same channels as the mother organization. The latter in turn is persuaded to make working concessions so as not to lose contact with its members, and this behavior is duly reciprocated, given that even the protagonists of popular religion tend not wholly to break off their relation with the organization of origin.

Third, one observes a marriage of *reciprocal legitimation* between institutional forms and popular ways of behaving, even beyond manifestations of conflict, the taking of divergent positions, and mutual recriminations. The interest of both parties is too interrelated to give in too often to the temptation of definitive, destructive criticism.

Finally, the symbolic patrimony (Prandi 1984) is the ground where the most conspicuous exchanges between the parties take place. Indeed, this is a unifying reason, which prevents summary transfers to one side or the other, given that both are clustered about the same referents of meaning (religious objects, images, sounds, offerings, ornaments, fetishes, prayers, liturgical calendars, sacred places, and dogmas). Many of them attend and practice more or less in the same way. The diversity is little more than an addition. However, it is precisely on this difference that popular religiosity is based. It flows into the common channel of a given religious experience, but takes on what is needed to satisfy demands not fulfilled in the context of more rigorous observance, more orthodox and more lenient in the church-organization.

Without the possibilities offered by popular religiosity, many would perhaps have abandoned their condition as believers by seeking solutions outside the customary environment. But it is not solely institutional religious socialization that demonstrates its efficacy in prolonging and reinforcing membership in a particular confession. Rather, it is the totality of family education and the cultural context in which one lives which confirms some convictions and suggests systems of behavior, including religious ones. So it is that often the conditioning of the environment takes over from the elusive or unsatisfying activity on the part of the church apparatus. This conditioning directs one toward formulations long experienced and suitable for the most frequently recurring demands, which are not always entertained by the church tradition (cf. Lambert 1985).

This failure to entertain them is generally justified by the will to maintain the "purity" of religious faith. In this regard, the purpose with which this turns to popular religiosity is that of wanting to "purify" it of heterodox waste materials, to convert it to official orthodoxy. However, this concerns statements of principle not always accompanied by consistent measures, so that popular religiosity is enabled to proceed along its customary path of *parallel divergence*.

Then, too, a certain element of ambiguity, of ambivalence, is not absent from the popular, at times giving it a push toward innovation and at other times to conservatism (Lanternari 1975). Because of this, forecasts about the future developments of phenomena in progress are always difficult as there are insufficient data to grasp the tendencies under way, or because a large part of the most profound dimension of the religious phenomenon escapes even the sharpest observer. The nature of the link, the relationship with the transcendent, is of such a complex and inscrutible character that it destroys many investigative claims at birth. However, this cannot be a valid reason for avoiding an analysis of it.

Institutional religion itself has not failed to concern itself with the phenomenon (Secondin, González Novalin, Pacho, Moretti, López Gay, Castellano, Valabek, Rovira, Pigna, and Macca 1978), making use of the principal studies, but with slender scientific results. This is due primarily to the self-legitimating spirit of many approaches of this type. Furthermore, the most immediate objective is almost never the scientific knowledge of the facts but rather the provision of harmonizing contributions aimed at carrying out effective pastoral action to recover the strays, strike down the abuses, and limit the counter-productive effects of an overly-permissive tolerance. So one arrives at a somewhat reductive view of the facts under examination, and all is explained in the light of theological theorizing very distant from the spirit and practice of popular religiosity.

MAGIC AND RELIGIOSITY

When one speaks of popular religiosity one often implies that there are present in it phenomena of a magical kind. Socio-anthropological research has contributed much to the difussion of this idea. In Italy the overwhelming weight has undoubtedly come from the work of Ernesto de Martino (1958, 1959, 1961), who has often brought out the close tie between magic and Catholicism by asserting, among other things, that

> in reality, the magical "survivals" in Lucania, or generically in Southern Italy, do in some way "live" and in that society perform their function; and so long as they "live," even if only for restricted human groups, they maintain a certain coordination with the hegemonic forms of cultural life, beginning with the hegemonic religious form—Catholicism, with its often emphasized Southern touches of "outwardness," "paganism," and "magic." This will provide us with the awareness that "Lucanian magic" is not limited to a few, slight relics as it appears they are for someone who is more or less a prisoner of confessional polemics, and who sees as pure magic the spell for making mother's milk flow, and pure religion in the reciting of the rosary (de Martino 1959, pp. 87-88).

After thirty years, one might imagine the magical "relics" have almost disappeared, swept away by the rationalization circulated through the means of mass communication and a broader process of making the younger generations literate. In reality, even if some forms have changed and the old formulas have also been forgotten, some models remain in the background, and those direct the attitudes and behavior of large segments of believers. Because the conditions of material precariousness of existence have not changed (despite the palliatives of the Welfare State, the rates of unemployment remain high, especially in the Italian South, where incomes are generally still among the lowest in the country), it follows that expedients and inventions of a more or less "magical" kind, such as soothsayers, sorcerers and magicians, still find numerous customers and believers today, no longer and solely in rural areas, but mainly in urban and metropolitan centers. The influence and persistence of these cultural patterns are moreover sufficient to point even those whose socioeconomic conditions have changed toward well-known destinations. Therefore, it is not surprising that even now some

> connections between magic and the hegemonic form of religious life are evident in popular Catholicism, in private, extra-liturgical prayers, in the worship of reliquaries, in pilgrimages to Marian sanctuaries . . . in miraculous cures . . . : and yet here too one should not forget that this "magic" is at least potentially a mediator of Christian values . . . (de Martino 1959, p. 89).

It is sufficient to recall the cult of San Gennaor's blood in Naples, or the millions of annual visitors who frequent Italian sanctuaries, as witness of an obvious continuity with the past and indeed, possibly, an accentuation of religious-popular phenomena as a personal search for a more rewarding experience of faith than that provided in an institutional context. However, the most significant form which nourishes behavior of a magic-sacral kind is the appearance of forms of pathology hard to diagnose and treat. Given the impossibility of making use of the highest levels of medical science, generally there is a preference for listening to the advice of the local healers who are closer at hand and more involved than the medical luminaries too "different" with their knowledge and interpersonal relations.

In fact, magic refers back to "official" religion, which in turn uses similar instruments and rites.

> Through the connections and nuances mentioned, Lucanian magic thus communicates with the basic themes of the Catholic religion, with the sacramentary and the sacraments, and ultimately with the sacrifice of the mass itself, through a continuity of instances which, always potentially, mark a gradual alignment with the heart of the Catholic religion. At this point the specifically popular or downright "Southern" overtones partly dissolve and partly thin out and are sublimated to the stage of reaching that which characterizes Catholicism as a specific Christian confession. And yet, the "magic," however attenuated and made the mediator of elevated values (at least for those capable of re-living them), never wholly disappears. This is because—to consider the matter from the general theoretical viewpoint, and outside every confessional polemic—however "exalted" religions are (and if they really are religions and not just moral life, or knowledge or poetry, unrolled and made autonomous in consciousness), they always enclose a mythicoritual kernel, an "outwardness" or "showiness" which are public, a magic technique in action, however refined and sublimated" (de Martino 1959, p. 89).

Thus, there is no break in descent here between popular magic and religious experience, between propitiatory techniques and ecclesiastical rituals. Many live one or other experience without seeing possible contradictions between them. On the other hand, the theological and doctrinal knowledge adequate to grasp their differences of intentionality, their nature and their historico-evangelical model is lacking. Undoubtedly too, as de Martino himself recalls, Catholic liturgy has a much higher degree of effective and symbolic refinement.

Up to this point one can share the outlook of the author of *Sud e Magia* (*South and Magic*). The idea of a *de-historification of the negative,* a kind of exorcism of evil through a process of temporal negation of adversity, seems less convincing, now even more than in the past. It is probably still harder to come to terms with a reality one increasingly knows in its true forms, its dynamics linked to various forms of power. The very *crisis of presence* today perhaps conveys better the connotations of a search of identity.

De Martino (1959) rightly disagrees with Trede (1889-1891) regarding a series of very hasty judgments which describe as pagan a certain type of magical religiosity to which the whole of Catholicism is supposed to be reduced. But on the other hand, he himself lets drop some not wholly scientific expressions when he constantly calls Lucanian magic "crude." However, it is probable that this use of the adjective occurs mainly in relation to the elaborate *mise en scène* of Catholic ritual. Or else this conceals a reproof, typical of the intellectual in dispute with his colleagues or predecessors, directed against the educated class of Naples which did not employ rationality in order to confront magic.

Belief in the evil eye had basically shown the same characteristics as religious fanaticism. In other words, the high culture of Naples is held to have lacked that "civil energy" sufficient and ready to grasp the proposals of Anglo-French Enlightenment. As a reflex, but also for historico-cultural reasons, popular Catholicism is supposed not to have had the moral force to shrug off its debt to magic, to which the illusion of miraculous solutions remained tied. There derived from this an essential inability to think in innovative terms, on the part of the masses trapped in pagan-Catholic syncretism. And de Martino's conclusion, in hectoring style, has basically the function of hiding the reality of a disconsolate vision, which sees no way out. As we shall be able to see later, in reality, flashes of a "higher and more modern heroic future" were to appear in those same Southern regions, and in particular in Lucania (de Martino 1959, p. 139). But at the same time it was not to be equally the case that "the fictitious glow of magic will also fade," in that it was to be the longings for novelty which were once more to be extinguished.

Almost as a counterpoint to de Martino's studies, the historian Gabriele De Rosa has maintained the view of a more elastic relation between church and popular religion. First, De Rosa (1971) has showed what commitment some enlightened bishops really exercised in opposing presuress of a magic-sacral type at the popular level, and following that, he has tried to refute the "identification of magical practice with the religious practice prescribed by the Church, and also with the forms of specific, local, authentic religiosity" (De Rosa 1978, p. 6).

Here one sees some emphasis on the distinction between "'prescribed" religion and experienced religion, in order to demonstrate that the former does not always correspond to the latter, so that the gap exists, but is also repaired at the personal level. In other words, if the official church condemns certain manifestations of magic, it is not automatic that these instantly diminish among the faithful, since one usually finds a way of making the various modes of religious experience coexist.

On the other hand, some habits have profound cultural roots which no proclamation, edict, or excommunication easily manages to eliminate. Here one should recognize the existence of a *double contingency*: the observance of the basic teachings of religious orthodoxy, but also resource to more normal, culturally stratified and learned solutions. In essence, from my point of view, it is possible to attest to the presence of magical or paramagical aspects in experiences inspired within the norms prescribed in a church context. This is particularly true in categories of behavior less encroaching in official teaching: on the one hand in popular religiosity of the traditional type (as seems obvious), and on the other hand in popular religiosity with an innovative tendency (as would appear less obvious). The fact is that the subject under discussion within popular religiosity is almost never clear. Therefore, according to De Rosa's version, there is never a precise correspondence between popular religion and church religion; but it is not the case that the latter is not also experienced in forms belonging to the magico-sacral world. To speak of essential differences is as misleading as to talk of an identity taken for granted.

In essence, popular religiosity is a mediation between the morphology championed by ecclesiastical teaching, and the personal and cultural demands of the "people of God" (an expression of conciliar origin, which not by chance has had a great resonance and good fortune in current religious ideology, as well as in the experiences of Catholic dissent with a popular base—"the church is the people").

Furthermore, there is a question regarding the identification and delimitation of membership in the area of popular religiosity. For example, the category of persons who belong to the priesthood is not automatically classifiable from the perspective of prescribed religion: Differentiation, attenuation, and disagreements should all be taken into account. Indeed, priests and bishops may be more, or less, sensitive to appeals and requests of a popular type, even in the shape of adherence to the requests of the faithful of the base. This occurs in connection with very well attended ceremonies, popular pilgrimages, and major festivities; some moderate concessions are useful just to interest people in dialog, people not otherwise approachable outside such events. Thus there is no shortage of priests and bishops who adopt a certain tolerance or a balance in their approach to the devout. In general, an open clash is avoided, as they have learned from past negative experiences.

Until a few years ago, this could be seen above all in relation to behavior linked to religiosity with magico-sacral features. More recently, once the acute phase of ecclesiastical contestation was past, these same base communities, at one time strongly opposed by the official church, have found exponents of more than secondary importance in the ecclesiastical hierarchy. There was a resumption of contacts, a drawing closer which marks a change of course as regards the past, even though it is restricted to a few, significant, cases. In fact, the base communities which have maintained their commitment over time have less resonance in the means of information, but they have not stopped acting on the basis of their guidelines or their commitment, which is tendentially popular with a strong presence in the social and the political.

In practice, the situation of popular religiosity in Italy has its own complexity, not at once reducible within convenient frames of references, *parti pris*, or unidirectional interpretations. If assisted by historical, or diachronic analysis, sociological understanding moderates views which are too improvized to acquire a scientific gloss. It is not by chance that only at a distance of some years and after an inquiry, long enough to permit more value-free statements, is it possible to have an overall picture capable of extrapolating the essential developments, reducing exaggeration, and grasping the most characteristic and far-reaching effects. An approach which sustained only de Martino's view would have annulled attention directed to certain emerging phenomena of an innovative kind. On the other hand, too Gramscian a conception of religion would have starved the analysis, confining it within overly restrictive boundaries specific to one exclusive viewpoint.

I do not intend thereby to deny the weight of Gramsci's observations—at least at their outset—on certain famous scholars with Marxist backgrounds. One should not, indeed, pass over what he glimpsed at and alluded to in his work. De Rosa (1978, p. 190) hits the mark when he stresses the "disconcerting" use of fideistic language: "incarnation, the new Father, those struggling for God." This is not merely the residue of a popular religiosity acquired through family education. But in reality

> what interests Gramsci is the study of the structure of ecclesiastical power, its powerful, broad international ramifications, its political influence. It is clear from the context of the article, that he calls the attention of the proletariat to the organization of ecclesiastical power. . . . (De Rosa 1978, p. 197).

And yet Gramsci only looks at one part of the clergy, leaving aside other characteristics, including those related to the greater poverty of the Southern churches. Moreover, he stays faithful to his reading of religion as common sense ideology; and so he is sensitive to the popular experience of the Christian religion.

He identifies the peasant and bourgeois, rural and urban stratifications, but first divides the "religion of the people" from that of the religious intellectuals, the religion of the "simple souls" from that of the ecclesiastical hierarchy (Gramsci 1975, p. 2312). This does not, however, mean his judgment of popular religion is a tender one, as he considers it "trivial and base, superstitious and bewitched" (Gramsci 1975, p. 1855). At all events, "according to Gramsci, overcoming the objectivist, dualist vision of common sense, and thus of religion and folklore, is achieved in the perspective of historicism and the immanence peculiar to the philosophy of practice. This is a qualitative leap, which does not wish to underestimate what there is in the "experience" of the subaltern classes that is profound and basic. Philosophy is not the prosperity of a privileged few but is inherent in everyone even if unconsciously" (Vinco 1983, p. 109). Here, then, is a restoration of a positive value in the popular condition, one not incapable of grasping the deficiencies of society and religion.

In the situation where popular religiosity is expressed with values of a sociopolitical character, it is not rare to find the use of exceptional emblematic figures capable of addressing the interests of large popular strata. Among other typical examples in this context is the particular idea of "Christ the first socialist," quoted by De Rosa (1978, p. 205), but with no reference to a basic contribution on the subject, such as that edited by Nesti (1974). De Rosa speaks of this type of popular religiosity in dismissive terms as a more or less conscious operation to reduce Christ's message to purely human terms, something analogous to what some modern theology does by making Christ the historical exemplary expression of humanity, with no marks of transcendence, and making the ecclesiastical hierarchy with its doctrine a machine for repression and authoritative government (De Rosa 1978, p. 205).

Nesti on the contrary, argues that

the new political militancy, also bearing in mind the significant weight church religion exercises at the popular level, is accompanied by an autonomous "world-view" with explicit references to evangelical inspiration and the original witness of Christ. This does not mean that Italian socialism is characterized by pre-Marxist elements, and should thus long have remained an utopian socialism. Rather, one can state that the utopian dimension is an important part of the collective patrimony of popular socialism. . . . "Jesus the socialist" thus reveals the limits of schematic conceptualizations, the precariousness of widespread commonplaces, for which the Catholic world is the space of the religious, and the socialist world materialist-atheist, antireligious space. It brings back into discussion the meaning of the Catholic world as a religious, and as political, reality (Nesti 1974, pp. 82-83).

We have thus arrived at a point rather distant from the purely magical description of popular religiosity. The subject here is clearly political, and has produced a whole series of polemics between the various parties involved. Gramsci himself seemed to show no interest in this area of discussion, preferring rather to examine the role of the church as the organizer of communication between intellectuals and the "simple." Meanwhile, even now the sociological evidence does not refute the hypothesis of a widespread popular sentiment which reasserts the tradition centered on Christ as the ideal figure and model for the struggle against social injustice (Cipriani 1985; Cipriani, Rinaldi, and Sobrero 1979).

In this context religion is no longer the opium of the people. Change in conditions is not expected and called for as coming from outside. The solution has no magical character. If there has to be a miracle, it must arrive through decisive action by the people themselves, and not through sorcerers and other people's witchcraft. The traditional slowness of the church in following the development of events is certainly not a point in favor of utopian pressures. However, the simultaneous ideal and utopian character of religion does not exclude the possibility that believers and nonbelievers should find themselves side-by-side, united in claims for a different world. Along the road of political and labor union militancy, the obstacle of a magical culture may be a hindrance, as it is a constant, with roots going back to centuries past and which branch out into the contemporary world. This dialectic, now conflicting, now one of accommodation, is to be seen in numerous expressions of popular religioisty, with variations according to place and time which are not always predictable. Only a deeper study of individual cases can provide a more than superficial form of verification. Generalizations about popular religion run the risk of appearing mystifying and misleading.

Finally, one should make clear that any leveling out between religion and church religion, as opposed to magic, as proposed by de Martino and others, "shows traces of an ethnocentric perspective" (Nesti 1985, p. 93). The same should be said for Gramsci's argument, whose viewpoint is totally Italian, and indeed focusses mainly on Rome and its hierarchical ramifications.

THE DIFFUSION AND PERSISTENCE OF MAGICAL RELIGIOSITY

The legacy of a magical type of religiosity certainly does not date from recent times. Its roots are lost in past ages, and are interwoven with many vicissitudes which have often seen popular beliefs and those of the ecclesiastical summit counterposed. The case of witchcraft is emblematic in this regard, as it bears witness to a long resistance made possible through symbolic, allusive transformations, as in the case cited by Camporesi (1978, p. 227), on the

> relation between the invocation to the bread to rise, and the Madonna who makes those around her rise. The witch was possibly parodying the Holy Virgin, as happened in the carnival tradition and that of the Sabbatic spirit. Or should the Madonna here be identified with the mother of harvests, the spirit of fertility, the pagans' *Virgo coelestis,* bringer of the fertilizing rains?

The continuity between paganism, witchcraft and Christian-popular practices emerges in this illustration. There is a special stressing of the conflictual tension between the villain, the peasant, the pagan (that is, precisely through its derivation, the dweller in the *pagus,* the village), and the urban society of which the clergy is a basic part. Camporesi (1978, pp. 233-234) states this point clearly:

> Systematically attacked by the evangelizing missions of the Counter-Reformation; subjected to a methodical brainwashing and cleaning of memory by catechizings, sacramentalizings and mass confessions, two devotional and penitential acts knowingly orchestrated by the expert Catholic manipulators of consciences; fascinated by the radiant liturgy of the Church of Rome and its great mass spectacles—such as processions and "rogations"; watched over and spied on by the capillary web of the rural parish, the man of the fields had nonetheless continued to oppose the Church's cultural policy in the countryside. To its unending waves of forced evangelizing and religious messages devised by urban culture, with a strong class connotation (from the *potentes* of the cathedrals and the aristocratic hierarchy), he countered with his instinctive, archaic defense, which took the form of a kind of elementary "Nicodemitism," of a two-faced religious attitude oscillating between God and Satan, nature and relevation, materialism and spiritualism.

Aside from some over-emphasis, the passage just quoted brings out well the colonization—to use one of Habermas's (1981, pp. 563-567) expressions—of the "subaltern culture." The latter, in turn, defended itself by resorting to its own modalities, inherited from a past which once more became the present.

The former man of the fields is today represented not only by categories of peasants in general, but also by the economically more dependent social classes, those of the periphery, the marginal. The typical, but not exclusive, context of this situation is above all that of Southern Italy and the Islands. We find similar characteristics precisely in a figure who is now famous in the literature on Italian popular culture—Menochio, a sixteenth-century miller, admirably described by Carlo Ginzburg (1976). Ginzburg brings out heretical tendencies, his yearnings toward utopia, and his inventive spirit. The scene is set in Northern Italy, in Friuli, but the *religio rusticorum*, of which Menochio is an example, may be found with quite close resemblances elsewhere too, both in the North and the South. The accusations and suspicions raised against him were the same as those leveled against witches and warlocks (cf. Marwick 1982). All this formed part of a demonology which had already been expressed in fifteenth-century Europe (Mair 1969, p. 223).

In popular culture, the subject of demons as bitter adversaries of certain saints, especially St. Anthony, is a recurrent element which crosses over the bounds of the past and reaches even to us, as di Nola (1976, pp. 183-185) showed on several occasions. The relation with the supernatural is revealed in different fashions which change according to time and place, but with certain constants which remain unaltered through the centuries. This is proven by certain rites investigated by di Nola himself (1983). They involve magical treatments for hernias and impotence, as well as customs in the world of the countryside which combine religious and sexual motivations. The significance of all this is not a limited one, as there is mention explicitly of a "different historico-anthropological consciousness, of an European and Mediterranean diffusion of behavior, the formation of ideas and models, which frees research into tradition and religious matters from its exile in the Italian cultural provinces and can re-present it as a moment of universal history" (di Nola 1983, pp. 9-10). The conclusion the author was moving toward had moreover been already explicitly anticipated in another book: "every mythical representation and every ritual behavior are presented as based on reality (on that reality a culture takes to be reality). This allows one to qualify as true, culturally true, all religions, and leads one to avoid constructing mystificatory scales of value of greater or lesser truth within them" (di Nola 1974, p. 14). Hereby it is intended to safeguard properly the special value, among other things, of popular religiosity itself—something often considered inferior, without dignity, false, and simply needing to be purified of its excesses. In fact, apart from any consideration of value, its sociological importance remains unquestionable, along with its historico-cultural stratification, its appearance as experience shared by significant groups of the population. The attitude of rejection in its regard does not assist the scientific understanding of its dynamics, and moreover aids the development of groundless prejudices and unwarranted generalizations. Accusing certain popular behavior of superstition without even knowing its historical forms is an error into which certain intellectual circles linked to the church establishment have also often fallen.

The social change under way does not eliminate the magical, even if it differentiates it. There is a new urban way of living, with recourse to magicians and soothsayers even "among the skyscrapers" (Flamini 1968). De Spirito duly recalls this (1976, p. 139):

> one might speak of two magical worlds: one characterized by a more scientific-industrial culture, the other. . .more mythico-ritual. The first, though borrowing heavily from the second, adopting and adapting often and willingly its beliefs, formulae and magic techniques, grows and advances; whereas the second shrinks and lives on in the cracks. . . , in a part of the people and in the peasant classes.

On the spread of the former phenomenon there are few doubts, even if one can have some reservation regarding the relative reduction of the old-style magic, which others, on the other hand, map out in broad, well-documented forms by following four threads: "one involves the world of agricultural labor, another relates to religiosity, and finally, one concerns spells and the magic practices for curing illnesses. A fourth possible thread is that which emerges from local tales and traditions, and appears as the fantastic rethinking of traditions experienced as true and unquestionble" (Boggi 1977, p. 11).

This encourages one to speak of a real "magic industry" (Boggi 1977, pp. 12, 19), but also stresses that magic and religion are capable of coexisting. In fact, "in the fundamental moments of existence, magic and religion are found face to face: in danger of death, the healer, like the doctor, acts to give life, the priest to ensure a good death in the prospect of an ultramundane life" (Boggi 1977, p. 35).

However, there are other, nonconvergent aspects which separate the popular and the ecclesiastical traditions. Aside from the well-known dimension of the "socialist Christ," one should mention the anticlerical attitude of many areas of the country, where there have been quite lively political happenings (cf. Cipriani 1985), with confrontations causing considerable problems for the representatives of the clergy, in difficulties because of popular protest, often borne forward by means of religious manifestations of great significance for the public. For instance, a political dissent can begin from and during a religious feast.

Sometimes the conflict appears on the same ground as actions intended to resolve some situation of difficulty or sickness. In such cases, the peasant-healer (Cipriani 1979, pp. 303-320) and the priest-exorcist (Guggino 1978, pp. 167-184) have the same phenomena confronting them. The former uses magical formulas and invocations, the latter uses prayers and blessings. Their mistrust is mutual. The lay holy man may appear hostile to a representative of a clergy who maintains his privileged role in the social environment.

The magic "lives at the level of the everyday, the magician is behind our front door, the evil eye, the spell are closely intertwined with the network of social relations, the air is thronged with *beings*. These beings, or, if you prefer, spirits, enter the human body, appear in the shape of animals, and give life to plants" (Guggino 1978, p. 21). Recourse to magic occurs whenever science is unable to provide clear, satisfactory responses which do not permit reality to be managed without being managed by it, without escaping being acted upon as de Martino would say. If some utility is found at the level of magic, this is due to the convincing force of cultural facts, which orient people to read the events of existence in a particular way. It is a logic which appears irrational to external observers, but which corresponds perfectly to the criteria of a rationality internal to the processes of interpretation and cultural transmission in a popular context.

PLACES AND FORMS OF POPULAR RELIGIOSITY

Rossi (1971) was one of the first researchers of Italian popular religiosity. She provided a catalog of ritual ceremonies more or less recognized by the official Catholic church but particularly practiced by the "multitudes of faithful." The disctinction made by this scholar between liturgical and extraliturgical rites has a purely descriptive, expository function; in practice, the followers do not make much distinction between the two forms of religious experience. Her conclusions stress the condition of poverty which brings people and clergy together, or at least one type of clergy whose economic conditions do not appear rosy. Rossi wrote (1971, p. 186):

> Poverty, need, and the absence of structures push the poor person to make offerings, pay, deprive himself of things useful and often indispensable, to place them at the feet of the Madonna, or attach them to a saint's mantle. In this way the agricultural laborer, the artisan, the emigrant, for one day of the year, feels himself less poor; the act of offering makes him feel important, similar to the rich people of the village. . . and the mediators between the poor and the church, the representatives of the local clergy are equal with the faithful who abandon themselves to scenes of desperation, despised by the "high" clergy because they are poor and ignorant, because they accept being the unconscious mediators of the mechanism of exploitation.

As can be seen, the emphasis on the "culture of poverty" takes up some echoes of Gramsci, and more particularly the sentiment of Lewis (1959). At times, thereafter, her analysis is more direct, more strongly critical and polemical, with some loss of scientific credibility because of the pamphleteering tone of the approach, later confirmed in a slender booklet which appeared, with others, on the occasion of a TV series on magic in the Italian South (Barbati, Mingozzi, and Rossi 1978).

Gallini's study (1971) on the Sardinian novenas—a kind of pilgrimage involving long stays in the temporary villages springing up around sanctuaries, according to an archaic custom dating back to the aboriginal (Nuraghic) people—examines a smaller universe and has a more rigorous approach. The study concerns five festivities and the same number of communities. It was found that

> the making of the novena does not seem to be wholly absorbed into the field of Catholicism, and not only as regards those aspects of an extra-ecclesiastical society which might appear "lay" and "pagan," but which the whole village, on the contrary, rightly considers as a necessary part of the performance of any festivity. Profound conflicts regarding competence may break out between the ecclesiastical authorities and the organizing committee, with the latter tending to assert its own jurisdictional autonomy. At the outside, there is present at the novena a good number of people who reject Catholic religious practice (Gallini 1971, pp. 166-167).

From these simple observations one can infer an essential insight: the management of the mechanism of the festivity is taken over by the people of the village themselves. The organizational models themselves, as Gallini shows, are profoundly different: families and committee on one side, and the hierarchical structure of the church on the other. However, compromises and deals resolve the divergences and everything is arranged within the bounds of the common culture of the base. From this perspective one can explain the "paradox of the anticlericalism of a good part of the male population of the village, which deserts the church, thunders against the priests and then parades around a saint to make a novena" (Gallini 1971, p. 168).

In the city two special spaces are provided which do not come under the management of the church: chapels and votive shrines (cf. Provitera, Ranisio, and Giliberti 1978) which individuals or families build or look after to honor some saint. These "place themselves outside the official forms of religion and express a need and possibility for self-management of their own religious expressions on the part of the subaltern classes" (Provitera, Ranisio, and Giliberti 1978, p. 89).

This notion is taken up later by Prandi (1985, p. 11), who says:

> To reflect on a group of religious images of various periods and different technical manufacture, scattered over an area belonging to a historico-geographical context whose Catholic character has been dominant for many centuries means above all to question oneself about the structure of the religious model which has determined Catholicism in the long term, and one of whose most typical aspects is represented by just that capillary spread of sacred images, even outside the places officially set aside for religion.

The evidence bears witness to a long acquaintance with altars and devotions of a domestic, almost private, kind, which are moved from the direct control of the religious structure.

Because of these reminders, attached to the exterior of the place assigned to the official religion, it has been possible to consolidate through time bonds of neighborhood and group solidarity, both inside and outside the family.

Indeed, "one of the most important forms through which the people relates its presence to the sacred is the *"relation of presence."* It is because of this that signs and places which bring the sacred close to the life of the people take on special importance (cf. Orlando 1984). In some way they constitute the connnecting tissue of the religion "of the people," as Orlando calls it (1980), and establish a relation with the sacred through channels which are no longer subject to liturgical rules, but more fitting for the expectations of individuals.

RE-EVALUATION AND DISSENT IN POPULAR RELIGIOSITY

In the past few years, popular religioisity has re-acquired the consideration it was in the past denied at the level of the official church. In particular it has been explored as a dimension characteristic of the peasant and working classes (Giannotti 1977), but also as a special phenomenon related to the cult of the saints, among whom the figure of St. Anthony of Padua has an important place (cf. Giuriati 1979, 1983). The interconnection of this widespread type of religious behavior is such as to produce a whole series of resultant morphologies, such as, for example, the numerous publications of a devotional nature which in the *Messaggero di S. Antonio* find their best known and definitive expression (cf. Nesti 1980).

There are currently in Italy the bases for a diffuse presence of dynamic forces linked to "popular piety," the study of which is found in De Luca (1962), the friend of the communist leader Palmiro Togliatti, a penetrating forerunner. However, only recently has there been discussion of "popular faith" within a specifically churchly viewpoint, with contributions involving essentially one year—1979 (Bo 1979; Pizzuti and Giannoni 1979; Colombo et al. 1979; Brovelli et al. 1979).

On the other hand, political militancy itself is not wholly alien to convergence with the phenomenon of popular religion, even where the contrast of ideologies could lead one to think the reverse. Italy demonstrates many cases of compromise between politics and religion, of mixtures not free from clashes, even though social change has altered the connotations of the previous trend (Faenza 1979). The category of Italian Protestantism is also not extraneous to this picture, having always been linked to the experience of the popular "base" (Mottu and Castiglione 1977).

The oppositional character of popular culture, and thus of religiosity, has often been analyzed and sustained by Satriani (1968), but it has also essentially been expressed through numerous experiences of Catholic dissent, through the base communities which proliferated in the 1960s, linked to the movement of *Christians for Socialism* (*Cristiani per il Socialismo*). Unfortunately there are no in-depth studies of this historic event from a sociological standpoint. There is some movement in this direction along journalistic and theological lines

(Sciubba and Sciubba-Pace 1976; Barbaglio et al. 1980). Berzano's study (1977) on the base communities in the capital of world Catholicism itself—Rome— is all the more valuable. There, experience is said to show that "once the separation of power between priests and laymen, between summit and base, has collapsed, the Christian communities are responsible for creating their history and making their choices without having to await orders passively from a series of "delegates" placed on a hierarchical scale" (Berzano 1977, p. 169).

Ultimately, the religiosity of the base is not just bogged down in the magical incantations and mass demonstrations in the various Italian sanctuaries, but has potentialities of an innovatory nature. These, however, do not always have the strength to emerge and become fresh utopian pressures, in a greater awareness of the mechanisms of the functioning of contemporary society.

REFERENCES

Barbaglio, G., F. Barbero, G. Bof, M. Cuminetti, G. Franzoni, G. Girardet, A. Giudici, T. Motta, N. Negretti, G. Piana, G. Picinali, D. Pizzuti, R. J. Regidor, G. Riva, A. Rizzi, and M. Vigli. 1980. *Massa e Meriba. Itinerari di fede nella storia delle comunità di base.* Torino: Claudiana.

Barbati, C., G. Mingozzi, and A. Rossi. 1978. *Profondo Sud.* Milano: Feltrinelli.

Berzano, L. 1977. *Partecipazione sociale e nuove forme religiose.* Torino: Tempi di Fraternità.

Bo, V. 1979. *La religiosità popolare. Studi, ricognizione storica, orientamenti pastorali, documenti.* Assisi: Cittadella.

Boggi, R. 1977. *Magia, religione e classi subalterne in Lunigiana.* Firenze: Guaraldi.

Bronzini, G. B. 1980. *Cultura popolare. Dialettica e contestualità.* Bari: Dedalo.

Brovelli, F., D. Sartore, A. Gangemi, E. Cattaneo, L. Pinkus, F. Demarchi, M. Squillacciotti, P. Visentin, A. N. Terrin, A. Pistoia, S. Maggiani, D. Sartor, and S. Sirboni. 1979. *Liturgia e religiosità popolare. Proposte di analisi e orientamenti.* Bologna: Dehoniane.

Burgalassi, S. 1970. *Le cristianità nascoste.* Bologna: Dehoniane.

Burke, P. 1978. *Popular Culture in Early Modern Europe.* London: Temple Smith.

Camporesi, P. 1978. *Il paese della fame.* Bologna: il Mulino.

Cipriani, R., ed. 1979. *Sociologia della cultura popolare in Italia.* Napoli: Liguori.

Cipriani, R., G. Rinaldi, and P. Sobrero. 1979. *Il simbolo conteso. Simbolismo politico e religioso nelle culture di base meridionali.* Roma: Ianua.

Cipriani, R. 1985. *Il Cristo rosso. Riti e simboli, religione e politica nella cultura popolare.* Roma: Ianua.

Cires, A. M. 1976. *Intellettuali, folklore, istinto di classe.* Torino: Einaudi.

Colombo, G., L. Dani, R. De Zan, R. Fabris, G. Leonardi, A. Marangon, J. Pinell, L. Sartori, G. Sovernigo, A. N. Terrin, F. Trolese, and C. Valenziano. 1979. *Ricerche sulla religiosità popolare nella bibbia, nella liturgia, nella pastorale.* Bologna: Dehoniane.

De Luca, G. 1962. *Introduzione alla storia della pietà.* Roma: Edizioni di storia e letteratura.

De Lutiis, G. 1973. *L'industria del santino.* Firenze: Guaraldi.

de Martino, E. 1958. *Morte e pianto rituale nel mondo antico: Dal lamento pagano al pianto di Maria.* Torino: Boringhieri.

———. 1959. *Sud e magia.* Milano: Feltrinelli.

———. 1961. *La terra del rimorso: Contributo a una storia religiosa del Sud.* Milano: il Saggiatore.

————. 1975. *Mondo popolare magia in Lucania.* Roma-Matera: Basilicata (a cura e con prefazione di R. Brienza).

De Rosa, G. 1971. *Vescovi, popolo e magia nel sud. Ricerche di storia socio-religiosa dal XVII al XIX secolo.* Napoli: Guida.

————. 1978. *Chiesa e religione popolare nel Mezzogiorno.* Bari: Laterza.

De Spirito, A. 1975. "Magia, scienza e religione in alcune interpretazioni contemporanee." *Sociologia* 2:75-110.

————. 1976. *Il paese delle streghe: Una ricerca sulla magia nel Sannio campano.* Roma: Bulzoni.

di Nola, A. M. 1974. *Antropologia religiosa: Introduzione al problema e campioni di ricerca.* Firenze: Vallecchi.

————. 1976. *Gli aspetti magico-religiosi di una cultura subalterna italiana.* Torino: Boringhieri.

————. 1983. *L'arco di rovo. Impotenza e aggressività in due rituali del sud.* Torino: Boringhieri.

Faenza, L. 1979. *Comunismo e cattolicesimo in una parrocchia di campagna. Vent'anni dopo (1959-1979).* Bologna: Cappelli.

Ferrarotti, F. 1964. *La sociologia. Storia, concetti, metodi.* Torino: ERI.

Flamini, G. 1968. *I maghi tra i grattacieli.* Bologna: Dehoniane.

Gallini, C. 1971. *Il consumo del sacro: Feste lunghe di Sardegna.* Bari: Laterza.

Giannotti, S. 1977. *Giovani operai e religiosità popolare.* Roma: LAS.

Ginzburg, C., ed. 1979. "Religioni delle classi popolari." *Quaderni storici* 41:393-697.

Ginzburg, C. 1976. *Il formaggio e i vermi: Il cosmo di un mugnaio del '500.* Torino: Einaudi.

Giuriati, P. 1979. "The Devotion to St. Anthony in the Sanctuary of Padua (Pilot Research)." Pp. 191-203 in *Spiritual Well-Being: Sociological Perspectives,* edited by D. O. Moberg. Washington, DC: University Press of America.

————. 1983. *Devozione a S. Antonio. Ricognizione socio-culturale.* Padova: Messagero.

Giusti, S. 1975. *La prospettiva storicistica di Ernesto de Martino.* Roma: Bulzoni.

Gottschalk, L., C. Kluckhohn, and R. C. Angell. 1945. *The Use of Personal Documents in History, Anthropology and Sociology.* New York: Social Science Research Council.

Gramsci, A. 1966. *La questione meridionale.* Roma: Editori Riuniti.

————. 1975. *Quaderni del carcere.* Torino: Einaudi.

Greinacher, N. and N. Mette, eds. 1986. *Popular Religion.* Edinburgh: T and T Clark.

Guggino, E. 1978. *La magia in Sicilia.* Palermo: Sellerio.

Guizzardi, G., C. Prandi, M. Castiglione, E. Pace, and A. Morossi. 1981. *Chiesa e religione del popolo. Analisi di un'egemonia.* Torino: Claudiana.

Habermas, J. 1981. *Theorie des kommunikativen Handelns.* Frankfurt: Suhrkamp.

Kokosalakis, N. 1982. *Ethnic Identity and Religion. Tradition and Change in Liverpool Jewry.* Washington, DC: University Press of America.

Lambert, Y. 1985. *Dieu change en Bretagne. La religion à Limerzel de 1900 à nos jours.* Paris: Cerf.

Lanternari, V. 1962. *Movimenti religiosi di libertà e di salvezza.* Milano: Feltrinelli.

————. 1969. "Religione popolare e contestazione." *Testimonianze* 118.

————. 1975. *Religioni primitive e religione popolare.* Roma: Bulzoni.

————. 1977. *Crisi e ricerca d'identità.* Napoli: Liguori.

————. 1983. *Festa, carisma, apocalisse.* Palermo: Sellerio

Lazarsfeld, P. F. 1948. "The Use of Panels in Social Research." *Proceedings of the American Philosophical Society.*

Leslie, C., ed. 1960. *Anthropology of Folk Religion.* New York: Vintage.

Levi, C. 1964. *Cristo si è fermato a Eboli.* Torino: Einaudi.

Lewis, O. 1959. *Five Families: Mexican Case Studies in the Culture of Poverty.* New York: Basic Books.

Lombardi Satriani, L. M. 1968. *Contenuti ambivalenti del folklore calabrese: ribellione e accettazione nella realtà subalterna.* Messina: Peloritana.

————. 1973. *Folklore e Profitto: Tecniche di distruzione di una cultura.* Rimini-Firenze: Guaraldi.

————. 1974a. *Antropologia culturale e analisi della cultura subalterna.* Rimini-Firenze: Guaraldi.

————. 1974b. *Menzogna e verità nella cultura contadina del Sud.* Napoli: Guida.

————. 1979. *Il silenzio, la memoria e lo sguardo.* Palermo: Sellerio.

Mair, L. 1969. *Witchcraft.* London: Weidenfeld and Nicolson.

Makky, G. A. W. 1978. *Mecca: The Pilgrimage City. A Study of Pilgrim Accomodation.* London: Croom Helm.

Marwick, M., ed. 1982. *Witchcraft and Sorcery.* Harmondsworth: Penguin Books.

Mottu, H. and M. Castiglione. 1977. *Religione popolare in un'ottica protestante: Gramsci, cultura subalterna e lotte contadine.* Torino: Claudiana.

Nesti, A. 1970. *L'altra chiesa in Italia.* Milano: Mondadori.

————. 1974. *"Gesù socialista".* Una tradizione popolare italiana *(1880-1920).* Torino: Claudiana.

————. 1980. *Una cultura del privato: Morfologia e significato della stampa devozionale italiana.* Torino: Claudiana.

————. 1983. *Religioni e società nel Centro America.* Roma: Ianua (1984, S. José de Costa Rica: Flacso).

————. 1985. *Il religioso implicito.* Roma: Ianua.

Orlando, V. 1980. *La religione "del popolo".* Bari: Ecumenica.

————. 1984. *La religiosità popolare in Basilicata.* Potenza: Istituto Pastorale Lucano.

Oursel, R. 1978. *Pèlerins du Moyen Age.* Paris: Arthème Fayard (1978, Milano: Jaca Book).

Pettazzoni, R. 1958. *La Chiesa e la vita religiosa in Italia.* Bari: Laterza.

Pizzuti, D. and P. Giannoni. 1979. *Fede popolare.* Torino: Marietti.

Pizzuti, D., ed. 1985. *Sociologia della religione.* Roma: Borla.

Prandi, C. 1977. *Religione e classi subalterne.* Roma: Coines.

————. 1983. *La religione popolare fra potere e tradizione: Per una sociologia della tradizione religiosa.* Milano: Angeli.

————. 1984. *Le società nei simboli religiosi: Il contributo di "Social Compass".* Milano: Angeli.

————. 1985. *"Immagini popolari e memoria del sacro."* In *Luoghi e Immagini della Devozione Popolare nel Vicariato di Suzzara.* Suzzara: Banca di Credito.

Provitera, G., G. Ranisio, and E. Giliberti. 1978. *Lo spazio sacro: Per un'analisi della religione popolare napoletana.* Napoli: Guida.

Rami, L. 1972. *"Religiosità e magia nel sud."* Sociologia 3.

Rossi, A. 1971. *Le feste dei poveri.* Bari: Laterza.

Sanga, G. 1979. *Il peso della carne: Il culto millenaristico del profeta Domenico Masselli di Stornarella.* Brescia: Grafo.

Sartori, L., ed. 1983. *Pellegrinaggio e religiosità popolare.* Padova: Messagero.

Sciubba, R. and R. Sciubba-Pace. 1976. *Le comunità di base in Italia: Storia e cronaca.* Roma: Coines.

Secondin, B., J. L. González Novalin, E. Pacho, R. Moretti, J. López Gay, J. Castellano, R. Valabek, J. Rovira, A. Pigna, and V. Macca. 1978. *La religiosità popolare: Valore sprirituale permanente.* Roma: Teresianum.

Sturzo, L. 1956. *Il Partito Popolare Italiano.* Bologna: Zanichelli.

Thomas, K. 1971. *Religion and the Decline of Magic. Studies in Popular Beliefs in Sixteenth- and Seventeenth-Century England.* London: Weidenfeld and Nicolson.

Trede, T. 1889-1891. *Das Heidentum in der römischen Kirche: Bilder aus dem religiösen und sittlichen Leben Süditaliens.* Gotha: F.A. Perthel.

Vinco, R. 1983. *Una fede senza futuro? Religione e mondo cattolico in Gramsci.* Verona: Mazziana.

Vrijhof, P. H. and J. Waardenburg, eds. 1979. *Official and Popular Religion: Analysis of a Theme for Religious Studies.* The Hague: Mouton.

Wach, J. 1931. *Einführung in die Religionssoziologie.* Tübingen: J.C.B. Mohr (1986. Bologna: Dehoniane).

Weber, M. 1922. "Religionssoziologie." In *Wirtschaft und Gesellschaft.* Tübingen: J.C.B. Mohr (1961. Milano: Comunità).

THE CONTRIBUTORS

Peter L. Benson is President of Search Institute, Minneapolis, Minnesota. He received his Ph.D. in experimental social psychology from the University of Denver. Well known for his nationwide research on the governance and effectiveness of Catholic high schools, his most recent books are *Religion on Capital Hill* (with Dorothy L. Williams) and *The Quicksilver Years: The Hopes and Fears of Early Adolescence* (with Williams and Arthur L. Johnson), both published by Harper and Row.

Roberto Cipriani is Professor of Sociology of Knowledge at the University of Rome. He received two doctorates—one in literature and one in philosophy—from the University of Rome and has done post-graduate work in sociology and the social sciences. Dr. Cipriani was a Visiting Scholar at the University of California, Berkeley in 1982 and serves on the Executive Committee of the International Conference on the Sociology of Religion (CISR) and as Secretary for the Sociology of Religion Research Committee of the International Sociological Association. Professor Cipriani has done field research in Italy, Greece, and Mexico on diffused religion, popular religion, legitimation of religion and politics, symbols, and youth. His most recent publication is *Sociology of Legitimization* published by Sage in 1987.

Michael J. Donahue is a Research Scientist in Search Institute, Minneapolis, Minnesota. He was awarded the Ph.D. in personality-social psychology from Purdue University, and has been a postdoctoral fellow in the psychology of religion at Brigham Young University. Dr. Donahue published a meta-analysis of the research on intrinsic and extrinsic religousness, and is co-author (with Francis Kelly and Peter Benson) of *Toward Effective Parish Religious Education for Children and Young People: A National Study* published by the National Catholic Educational Association.

Barry van Driel is a doctoral candidate in social psychology at Stevenson College of the University of California, Santa Cruz. Formerly, he was a Research Assistant in the Department of Sociology at the University of Nijmegen, The Netherlands. He is conducting dissertation research on media responses to new religous movements in the United States, West Germany, and The Netherlands.

239

NeMar Eastman completed her baccalaureate degree in Sociology at the University of Tulsa, Tulsa, Oklahoma, and now is a law student at the same institution.

Joseph A. Erickson is a Research Consultant with Search Institute, Minneapolis, Minnesota, as well as a doctoral student in educational psychology at the University of Minnesota. He holds master's degrees in counseling psychology from the College of St. Thomas (St. Paul, Minnesota) and in youth ministry and religion from Luther Northwestern Theological Seminary (St. Paul, Minnesota). He is the co-author of two chapters in *Accusations of Child Sexual Abuse* edited by Hollida Wakefield and Ralph Underwager and published by Charles C. Thomas. Mr. Erickson is currently investigating perception of religious stimuli via multidimensional scaling techniques.

Richard L. Gorsuch is Director of Research and Professor in Fuller Theological Seminary's Graduate School of Psychology. He holds master's degrees from the University of Illinois and Vanderbilt University and earned the Ph.D. in personality, social psychology, and sociology from the University of Illinois. Dr. Gorsuch has published a textbook on factor analysis, other books, and approximately twenty-five articles in the psychology of religion, social psychology, personality, and other areas.

Lyman A. Kellstedt is Professor of Political Science at Wheaton College, Wheaton, Illinois. He received the Ph.D. degree from the University of Illinois. His current research involves the study of evangelicals and the political process. He is a member of the American Political Science Association and the Society for the Scientific Study of Religion.

James R. Kelly is Professor of Sociology and Director of the Graduate Program in Pastoral Planning and Research at Fordham University. He received his Ph.D. from Harvard University. He has published articles in *Sociological Analysis, Journal for the Scientific Study of Religion, Review of Religious Research, Journal of Ecumenical Studies,* and other periodicals. Dr. Kelly has served as vice-president of the Association for the Sociology of Religion and book review editor of the *Review for Religious Research*. He currently is researching, among other things, a social history of the abortion controvesy.

Brock K. Kilbourne is with the Department of Health Psychology at the Naval Research Center in San Deigo, California. He has been a Psychology Instructor with the University of Maryland, European Division and a NATO postdoctoral fellow at the Psychology Institute, University of Heidelberg, West Germany. He currently is a consultant on cults and religion to the Board of Trustees of the American Psychiatric Association and is author of numerous articles and has edited several books. Dr. Kilbourne received his Ph.D. in social psychology from the University of Nevada, Reno.

Lee A. Kirkpatrick received his Ph.D. in Psychology at the University of Denver. He is currently completing postdoctoral studies in Psychology at the University of South Carolina. His previous degrees were taken at Lynchburg College (Virginia) and the University of Texas at El Paso. He is a member of the American Psychological

Association, Society for the Scientific Study of Religion, and the Religious Research Association. His research interests include social psychology, the psychology of religion, and methods of research design and analysis.

Monty L. Lynn is Assistant Professor of Management Sciences at Abilene Christian University. He completed master's degrees at Cornell University and Brigham Young University and was awarded the Ph.D. in social-organizational psychology from Brigham Young. Dr. Lynn's research interests are in normative organizations, especially religious and health care institutions. He has about a dozen journal and proceedings publications and is a member of the Academy of Management, American Psychological Association, and Religious Research Association.

David O. Moberg is Professor of Sociology at Marquette University. Following a master's degree at the University of Washington, he earned the Ph.D. in sociology from the University of Minnesota. He has held two Fulbright professorships (The Netherlands and West Germany) and has taught and lectured on numerous college, university, and theological seminary campuses besides his long-term appointments at Bethel College of Minnesota and Marquette. He is the author of several books and numerous articles and is a former president of the Religious Research Association, Association for the Sociology of Religion, and Wisconsin Sociological Association. He also has held various leadership positions in the Society for the Scientific Study of Religion, International Conference on the Sociology of Religion (CISR), Sociology of Religion Research Committee of the International Sociological Association, and other professional organizations.

Johannis (Hans) J. Mol is Professor of Religious Studies at McMaster University, Canada. Professor Mol received his Ph.D. in sociology from Columbia University. Born in The Netherlands, he has held academic positions in Canada, New Zealand, and Australia. He is author or editor of fifteen books and monographs in the sociology of religion and has published some fifty papers as chapters in books or articles in refereed journals. He has served as secretary-treasurer for the Sociological Association of Australia and New Zealand and as president of the Sociology of Religion Research Committee of the International Sociological Association.

Judith A. Press is Educational Consultant for the Hartford Jewish Federation, a Lecturer at the Hebrew College, and Principal of Congregation B'nai Israel in Vernon, Connecticut. Dr. Press earned degrees at Yeshiva University, Hebrew College, and the University of of Connecticut before completing her Ph.D. at the University of Connecticut. She is presently researching intermarriage and conversion to Judaism.

Sheryl A. Purvis completed a bachelor's degree at the University of Tulsa and received her J.D. at Yale Law School. She is currently practicing law in Houston, Texas.

James T. Richardson is a Professor of Sociology at the University of Nevada Reno. He earned his Ph.D. from Washington State University and a J.D. from Nevada School of Law. Dr. Richardson has written and edited several books and numerous articles on various aspects of new religions. He was President of the Association for the Sociology of Religion in 1985-86.

E. Burke Rochford, Jr. is Assistant Professor of Sociology at Middlebury College in Vermont. He is presently studying the social, psychological, and political consequences of flooding in Tulsa, Oklahoma while continuing to research new religions and social movements. His *Hare Krishna in America* was published in 1986 by Rutgers University Press. He has recently published an article in the *American Sociological Review* and a chapter in *The Future of New Religious Movements* edited by David Bromley and Phillip Hammond and published by Mercer University Press.

Craig S. Smith, formerly a clinical psychologist at the Veterans Administration Medical Center, Martinez, California, is now providing career counseling at the Center for Ministry in Oakland. He earned degrees from the University of California, Berkeley, and American Baptist Seminary of the West before being awarded the Ph.D. by Fuller Theological Seminary's Graduate School of Psychology. Dr. Smith is a member of the American Psychological Association and the Society for the Scientific Study of Religion.

AUTHOR INDEX

Abramson, P.R., 124, 127, 131
Acock, A.C., 165, 176, 177
Ackerman, W., 195
Adamakos, H., 30
Adamek, R., 96, 106
Adorno, T.W., 3, 29
Aldrich, J.H., 131
Allport, G.W., 1-9, 13-15, 17-28, 29, 175, 176
Amon, J., 4, 5, 10, 13, 24, 25, 29
Andersen, S.M., 41, 53
Angell, R.C., 235
Anthony, D., 41, 42, 56, 58, 68, 71, 75, 78, 80, 81
Argyle, M., 159, 164, 165, 176
Aronson, E., 55
Asch, S.E., 34, 53
Ash, S., 59, 61, 78
Asher, H., 124, 131
Asher, W., 175, 181
Atkinson, M., 195
Atwood, M., 205, 214

Bachman, J.G., 155, 160, 172, 176, 179
Back, K.W., ix, 83, 84, 103, 106
Bahr, H.M., 155, 173, 176, 177
Bainbridge, W., 75, 78

Balch, R.W., 48, 53
Barbaglio, G., 234
Barbati, C., 231, 234
Barbero, F., 234
Barker, E., 46, 53, 76, 78, 80, 154, 176
Batson, C.D., 6, 8, 9, 23, 28, 29, 162, 163, 173, 174, 175, 177
Baum, G., 210, 214
Bealer, R., 154, 177
Beatty, K., 118, 131
Beck, J., 104, 106
Becker, H., 50, 53
Beckford, J.A., 33, 36, 39, 53, 59, 68, 73, 76, 78
Beit-Hallahmi, B., 159, 164, 165, 176
Bellah, R.N., 34, 35, 53
Benesh-Weiner, 137
Bengtson, V.L., 165, 176, 177
Benson, Peter L., ix, 153-181, 239
Berkowitz, L., 56, 151
Berton, P., 203, 209, 214
Berzano, L., 234
Bibby, R.W., 204, 206, 208, 210, 214
Bird, F., 73, 78
Blake, J., 105, 106
Blau, P.M., 47, 53
Blum, A., 69, 78

Bo, V., 233, 234
Bock, G.D., 166, 177, 184, 195
Bof, G., 234
Boggi, R., 230, 234
Bowlby, J., 28, 29
Brannie, M.T., 30
Braungart, R.G., 35, 54
Bridges, R., 29
Bromley, D., 36, 37, 39, 45, 46, 53,
          54, 55, 56, 59, 68, 73, 78, 81,
          82, 110, 131, 132, 162, 177
Bronzini, G.B., 219, 234
Brovelli, F., 233, 234
Brown, H.O.J., 95
Brown, J., 92, 93, 104
Brown, L.B., 24, 29, 55, 80, 178
Brown, P., 93, 104
Brown, S., 214
Brudney, J.L., 110, 124, 127, 131
Buber, M., 185, 195
Buckley, P., 62, 67, 68, 70, 79
Budner, S., 8, 29
Buehler, C.J., 173, 177
Burgalassi, S., 234
Burke, J., 80
Burke, P., 218, 234
Burns, J.E., 30
Burtchaell, J.T., 86, 106
Butcher, J.N., 44, 54
Butler, M., 171, 178
Byrn, R.M., 87

Callahan, D., 105, 106, 107
Callahan, S., 105, 106, 107
Calley, Lt., 135, 136
Camporesi, P., 228, 234
Caplow, T., 155, 177
Carey, R.G., 4, 29, 168, 177
Carson, R.C., 44, 54
Carter, J., 127
Carter, J.D., 30
Cartwright, D., 54
Castellano, J., 221, 236

Castiglione, M., 219, 233, 235, 236
Castillo, N.L., 24, 25, 30
Cattell, R.B., 9, 29
Cattaneo, E., 234
Chadwick, O., 81
Chalfant, H.P., 172, 180
Chilman, C.S., 170, 177
Cipriani, Roberto, x, 217-237, 239
Cires, A.M., 234
Clark, C.A., 165, 177
Clark, J., 41, 48, 52, 54, 55, 59, 61,
          67, 69, 78
Clarke, H., 214
Cohen, J., 195
Cohen, M., 107
Cohen, S., 195
Cohon, G.A., 205
Coleman, J.C., 44, 54
Coleman, J.S., 165, 177
Coleman, L., 58, 59, 75, 79
Colombo, G., 233, 234
Comrey, 66
Conrad, P., 44, 54, 75, 79
Converse, P., 214
Conway, F., 54, 57, 61, 62, 68, 69,
          70, 71, 73, 77, 79
Conway, M., 124, 126, 131
Cook, P., 30
Copeland, M., 110, 124, 127, 131
Cornwall, M., 165, 177
Cox, H., 209
Cox, H.E., 214
Crick, F., 101
Cromer, G., 40, 54
Crysdale, S., 203-204, 208, 214
Cuminetti, M., 234
Curry, E.W., 172, 180
Curtis, J., 214
Cutler, S.J., 110, 121, 123, 132

Daly, R., 59, 78
Daner, F., 67, 79
Dani, L., 234

Darley, J.M., 174, 177
Dashefsky, A., 184, 192, 195, 196
Dauser, D.B., 165, 177
Davis, K., 35, 50, 54, 55
Dawson, D.A., 170, 177
Dean, D., 8, 29
deBord, L.W., 169, 178
Delahoyde, 106
Delgado, R., 58, 61, 79
De Luca, G., 233, 234
De Lutiis, G., 234
Demarchi, F., 234
de Martino, E., 222, 223, 224, 225, 228, 234-235
De Rosa, G., 224, 226, 227, 235
De Spirito, A., 230, 235
De Zan, R., 234
Derks, F., 50, 55
Deutsch, A., 67, 68, 70, 79
deVaus, D.A., 168, 178
Dickinson, G.E., 154, 159, 160, 178
di Nola, A.M., 229, 235
Dittes, J.E., 2, 28, 29
Dobson, E., 131
Donahue, Michael J., ix, 2, 3, 4, 6, 7, 17, 25, 26, 28, 29, 153-181, 239
Douglas, W.G.T., 162, 180
Downton, J., 71, 79
Doyle, D.P., 171, 181
Driel, Barry van, ix, 35-56, 239
Dudley, M.G., 165, 166, 178
Dudley, R.L., 165, 166, 178
Duncan, O.D., 47, 53
Dunphy, Wm., 214

Eastman, NeMar, ix, 57-82, 240
Echemendia, R.J., 25, 26, 27, 30
Edwards, H., 204, 214
Eister, A., 35, 54
Eklin, C., 159, 177
Elifson, K.W., 5, 30, 171, 172, 178
Elkind, D., 154, 161, 178

Ensing, D.S., 30
Erdahl, L.O., 98, 106
Erickson, D., 167, 178
Erickson, Joseph A., ix, 153-181, 240
Erickson, M.L., 171, 179

Fabris, R., 234
Faenza, L., 233, 235
Fairfax, O., 95
Falgout, K., 30
Falwell, J., 109-132
Feagin, J.R., 1, 2, 3, 4, 5, 6, 7, 9, 13, 14, 15, 20, 23, 26, 30
Fein, L., 195
Ferm, R.C., 163, 178
Ferrarotti, F., 235
Festinger, L., 114, 131
Feuer, L., 35, 54
Fincham, F.D., 135, 136, 137, 151
Finney, J.R., 6, 9, 30
Flamini, G., 230, 235
Fleck, J.R., 24, 25, 27, 30
Folcik, J., 179
Ford, K., 170, 181
Forrest, J.D., 179
Foster, J.E., 28, 31
Fowler, J., 161, 178
Fox, S., 195
Francis, L.J., 170, 173, 178
Francome, C., 88, 97, 101, 103, 106
Frank, J., 42, 54
Franzoni, G., 234
Freedman, A.M., 56, 82
Freeman, J., 87, 106
French, J.R.R., Jr., 54
Frenkel-Brunswick, E., 3, 29
Freud, S., 76, 198, 214

Gabain, M., 180
Gaddy, G.D., 121, 131
Galanter, M., 58, 59, 62, 63, 67, 68, 70, 71, 73, 76, 77, 79

Gallini, C., 231, 232, 235
Gallup, G., 72, 79, 81, 106, 154, 155,
        157, 159, 163, 178, 199, 200
Gangemi, A., 234
Garfield, S.L., 50, 54
Garfinkel, H., 40, 54
Gary, L.E., 170, 179
Gerth, H., 215
Giannoni, P., 233, 236
Giannotti, S., 235
Giliberti, E., 232, 236
Ginzburg, C., 219, 229, 235
Girardet, G., 234
Gitlin, T., 54
Giudici, A., 234
Giuriati, P., 233, 235
Giusti, S., 235
Glasow, R.D., 105, 106
Glass, L., 66, 79
Glazer, N., 184, 195
Glock, C.Y., 53, 134, 151
Gockel, G.L., 167, 178
Goldman, N., 179
Goldman, R., 161, 178
Gonzalez Novalin, J.L., 221, 236
Gordon, D., 93
Gorsuch, Richard L., ix, 2, 133-152,
        163, 170, 171, 178, 180, 181,
        240
Goswami, Satsvrupa dasa, 76, 79
Gottschalk, L., 235
Graham, Billy, 95, 121
Graham, P., 81
Gramsci, A., 226, 231, 235
Granberg, B.W., 86, 106
Granberg, D., 86, 106
Gray, N., 93
Gray, R.A., 6, 29
Greeley, A.M., 159, 166, 167, 178,
        195
Greinacher, N., 218, 235
Gren, E., 95
Gruenberg, E., 80

Guerra, M.J., 157, 177
Guggino, E., 230, 231, 235
Guizzardi, G., 219, 235
Guth, J.L., 118, 131

Habermas, J., 228, 235
Hadaway, C.K., 171, 172, 178
Hahn, J., 134, 151
Hall, E.J., 85, 106
Hall, R., 89
Hamilton, V.L., 134, 135, 136, 148,
        149, 151
Hamm, P., 209, 214
Hammond, P.E., 215
Hargrove, B., 61, 79
Harris Poll, 96
Havighurst, R., 154, 178
Hayes, C.D., 170, 178
Heider, F., 114, 131
Heilman, S., 184, 195
Heirich, M., 163, 179
Helzer, J., 80
Hendrick, C., 5, 31
Hendricks, L.E., 170, 179
Hendry, B., 130
Henshaw, S.K., 179
Henty, M., 207, 215
Herberg, W., 34, 54
Hetherton, J.M., 207, 215
Hewitt, J.P., 49, 54
Hilty, D.M., 5, 30
Himmelfarb, H., 184, 195
Hindson, E., 131
Hirschi, T., 171, 179
Hoge, D.R., 3, 4, 5, 10, 13, 24, 25,
        26, 27, 28, 30, 154, 161, 164,
        165, 166, 168, 179, 180
Holzner, B., 72, 80
Hood, R.W., Jr., 2, 28, 30, 31, 110,
        116, 122, 127, 131, 134, 152,
        163, 181
Hopkins, R.P., 52, 54
Horan, D.J., 106, 107

Horner, A.J., 24, 25, 30
Howe, I., 195
Hughes, M., 86, 107
Hunt, R.A., 2, 4, 5, 28, 30
Hunter, J.D., 112, 113, 131

Inciardi, J., 77, 79
Izzo, A., 170, 179

Jacobs, J., 73, 79
James, W., 162, 179
Jaspars, J.M., 124, 136, 137, 151
Jelen, T.G., 85, 107
Jensen, G.F., 171, 179
Jenson, J., 214
Jessor, R., 174, 179
Jessor, S.L., 174, 179
Johnson, A.L., 177
Johnson, M.A., 166, 179
Johnson, S.D., 110, 121, 123, 127,
    131, 132
Johnston, L.D., 155, 159, 160, 172,
    176, 179
Johnstone, R., 167, 179
Jones, E.E., 54
Jones, E.F., 171, 179
Judah, S., 67, 76, 79

Kahoe, R.D., 24, 30, 162, 163, 179
Kandermans, B., 86, 107
Kantner, J., 170, 181
Kaplan, H.Y., 56, 82
Kaslow, F., 154, 179
Kay, B., 214
Keating, B., 154, 178
Kecmanovic, D., 41, 54
Keeter, L., 165, 179
Kelemen, M.L., 30
Kelleher, M., 77, 79
Kellstedt, Lyman A., ix, 109-132,
    240
Kelly, F.D., 165, 166, 167, 175, 179
Kelly, James R., ix, 83-107, 240

Kelman, 135
Kennedy, D., 101, 107
Kenniston, K., 79
Kent, L., 171, 181
Kilbourn, W., 204, 214
Kilbourne, Brock K., ix, 33-56, 71,
    77, 79, 240
Killian, L.M., 86, 107
Kim, B., 73, 79
King, M.B., 2, 4, 5, 28, 30
Kirkpatrick, Lee A., ix, 1-31, 134,
    152, 240
Kirsch, M., 66, 79
Klapper, J.T., 37, 55
Kluckhohn, C., 235
Kohlberg, L., 175, 179
Kojetin, B., 6, 28, 29, 30
Kokosalakis, N., 218, 235
Koop, C.E., 95
Kopplin, D., 8, 30
Kraus, S., 37, 55
Kriesberg, L., 54
Kun, 137
Kuner, W., 63, 68, 80

Laabs, C., 161, 180
Lader, L., 88, 90, 104, 107
Lamanna, M.A., 107
Lambert, R., 214
Lambert, Y., 221, 235
Lang, G., 55, 184, 195
Lang, K., 55
Langner, T., 81
Langone, M.D., 48, 54, 55, 59, 71,
    77, 78, 80
Lans, J. van der, 50, 55
Lanternari, V., 221, 235
Lasch, C., 35, 55
Lawrence, 135
Lazarsfeld, P.F., 235
Leahy, P.J., 85, 86, 88, 91, 102, 107
LeDuc, L., 214
Lee, A., 206

LeMoult, J., 58, 80
Leonardi, G., 234
Leone, M., 54, 78
Leslie, C., 219, 235
Levenson, H., 8, 30
Levebre, Archbishop, 202
Levi, C., 235
Levine, S., 59, 63, 67, 68, 70, 71, 73, 80
Levinson, D.J., 3, 29
Lewis, O., 231, 235
Liebman, R.C., 110, 132
Lincoln, R., 179
Lindsell, H., 95
Lindt, G., 38, 48, 55
Lindzey, G., 55
Lipset, S.M., 110, 127, 132
Lofland, J., 72, 80, 185, 195
Lombardi Satriani, L.M., 235-236
Lopez Gay, J., 221, 236
Lucksted, O., 57, 80
Luft, G.A., 166, 179
Luker, K., 85, 86, 87, 88, 97, 104, 107
Lyman, S., 69, 81
Lynn, Monty L., x, 241

Macca, V., 221, 236
Machalek, R., 72, 81
MacMurray, B., 79
MacPhillamy, D., 63, 68, 78, 80
Maggiani, S., 234
Maher, B., 54, 71, 77, 80
Maier, L., 90
Mair, L., 229, 236
Makky, G.A.W., 219, 236
Mall, D., 106, 107
Malony, H.N., 6, 9, 29, 30, 134, 152
Malthus, T., 97
Manno, B.V., 157, 177
Marangon, A., 234
Marsden, G., 121, 132
Martell, D., 57, 80

Martin, T.K., 173, 176
Marwick, M., 229, 236
Marx, G., 80
Marx, J., 72, 80
Marx, K., 198, 214
Marx, P., 93
Marzen, T.W., 107
Masterson, J., 72, 80
McCormick, E., 102
McCormick, N., 170, 179
McCourt, K., 159, 178
McCready, W.C., 159, 166, 178, 179
McFadden, J., 93
McGee, M.G., 170, 180
McHugh, J., 91
McHugh, P., 69, 78
McIntosh, D., 6,8, 28, 29, 30
Meadow, M.J., 24, 30, 162, 163, 180
Meisel, J., 214
Melton, J., 57, 80
Menochio, 229
Mette, N., 218, 235
Michael, S., 81
Mikolaski, S.J., 208, 214
Miller, A.H., 110, 124, 127, 132
Miller, D.E., 48, 55
Mills, C., 69, 80
Mills, C.W., 215
Mills, J., 159, 177
Mingozzi, G., 231, 234
Moberg, David O., x, 140, 151, 235, 241
Mobley, G.M., 121, 132
Mohr, J.C., 104, 107
Mol, Johannis (Hans) J., x, 197-215, 241
Moon, Sun Myung, 39, 56
Moore, B., 205, 215
Moore, K., 173, 180
Morehead, L., 130
Moretti, R., 221, 236
Morgan, R.L., 5, 30
Morossi, A., 219, 235

Morris, R.J., 28, 31, 110, 116, 122, 127, 131
Moscovici, S., 34, 55
Motta, T., 234
Mottu, H., 233, 236
Mueller, C., 95
Mullin, M., 173, 181
Murray, E.J., 5, 31
Myers, J., 30

Nagel, T., 107
Nathanson, B.N., 84, 107
Neeman, J., 29
Negretti, N., 234
Neilson, W.A., 162, 180
Nelsen, H.M., 154, 159, 160, 161, 165, 169, 180
Nelson, R.J., 95, 107
Nesti, A., 220, 226, 227, 228, 233, 236
Newman, P.C., 215
Newport, F., 111, 112, 130, 132
Nie, N., 126, 132
Nisbet, R., 40, 54
Nordquist, T., 64, 81
Normandin, Y., 202

Oliver, D., 46, 56
Olsen, J., 165, 177
O'Malley, P.M., 155, 172, 176, 179
Opler, M., 81
Orlando, V., 233, 236
Orvaschel, H., 80
Oursel, R., 219, 236

Pace, E., 219, 235
Pacho, E., 221, 236
Padover, S.K., 214
Paloutzian, R.F., 163, 180
Pammett, J., 214
Pargament, K.I., 5, 25, 26, 27, 30, 134, 136, 151, 152
Parris, F., 79

Patrick, J.W., 4, 30
Patterson, T.E., 37, 55
Pattison, E., 71, 72, 80
Peatling, J., 161, 180
Peek, C.W., 172, 180
Personnaz, B., 34, 55
Peter, 137
Petersen, D.M., 171, 172, 178
Petrillo, G.H., 161, 164, 165, 166, 167, 168, 179
Pettazzoni, R., 236
Piaget, J., 161, 180
Piana, G., 234
Piazza, T., 134, 151
Picinali, G., 234
Pierard, R.V., 110, 123, 132
Pigna, A., 221, 236
Pinal, J.H. del, 105, 106
Pinard, M., 214
Pinell, J., 234
Pinkus, L., 234
Pistoia, A., 234
Pizzuti, D., 218, 233, 234, 236
Pollak, G., 184, 195
Poloma, M., 119, 132
Pool, I.D., 56
Pope Paul VI, 202
Posterski, 210
Potvin, R.H., 154, 157, 159, 160, 161, 164, 167, 168, 169, 180, 181
Prabhupada, A.C.B. Swami, 60, 73, 74, 76
Prandi, C., 218, 219, 220, 232, 235, 236
Press, Judith A., ix, 183-196, 241
Proudfoot, W., 134, 152
Provitera, G., 232, 236
Purvis, Sheryl A., ix, 57-82, 241

Quay, E.A., 106, 107

Raab, E., 110, 127, 132
Rabkin, J., 79

Rabkin, R., 79
Radler, D., 155, 180
Rajneesh, B.S., 39, 62
Rambo, L.R., 72, 80, 162, 180
Rami, L., 236
Ranisio, G., 232, 236
Raven, B.H., 37, 54
Reagan, R., 109, 127
Regenstreiff, P., 214
Regidor, R.J., 234
Regier, D., 80
Reichardt, C.S., 29
Reimer, B., 73, 78
Remmers, H., 155, 180
Rennie, T., 81
Richardson, H., 58, 80
Richardson, James T., ix, 33-56, 57,
        59, 80, 81, 82, 162, 177, 241
Reiff, P., 76, 80
Riesman, D., 34, 55
Rinaldi, G., 227, 234
Rist, R., 185, 195
Ritzema, R.J., 134, 147, 152
Riva, G., 234
Rizzi, A., 234
Robbins, T., 41, 42, 56, 58, 61, 68,
        71, 72, 75, 78, 80, 81
Robinson, J.P., 30
Robinson-Brown, D.P., 170, 179
Roche, A., 202, 215
Rochford, E. Burke, Jr., ix, 57-82,
        242
Rockefeller, N., 97
Roebuck, J., 170, 180
Rohde, D.W., 131
Rokeach, M., 34, 56
Rosen, A., 81
Rosenberg, A.H., 52, 56
Rosenberg, M., 173, 180
Rosik, C.H., 164, 180
Rosoff, J.I., 179
Ross, J.M., 1-9, 13-15, 17-25, 29,
        175, 176

Ross, L., 40, 56
Ross, M., 64, 66, 68, 75, 81
Rossi, A., 231, 234, 236
Rossi, P.H., 167, 178
Roszak, T., 67, 81
Rothenberg, S., 111, 112, 130, 132
Rovira, J., 221, 236
Rutter, M., 72, 81

Sadock, B.J., 56, 82
Saint Anthony, 229, 233
Salter, N., 63, 67, 68, 70, 80
Sanford, R.N., 3, 29
Sanga, G., 236
Sanua, V.D., 195
Sartor, D., 234
Sartore, D., 234
Sartori, L., 219, 234, 236
Satriani, 233
Scanlan, T., 107
Schaeffer, E., 95
Schecter, R., 78
Scheidler, J., 93
Schmidt, G., 8, 30, 134, 136, 152
Schneider, J., 44, 54
Schoem, D., 184, 196
Schwartz, L., 69, 81
Schwartz, M., 314
Sciubba, R., 234, 236
Sciubba-Pace, R., 234, 236
Scott, M., 69, 81
Scroggs, J.R., 162, 180
Sears, D.D., 37, 56
Secondin, B., 221, 236
Shapiro, E., 81
Shapiro, H., 184, 192, 195, 196
Shapiro, T., 59, 79
Sharpsteen, D., 29
Shaver, P., 28, 30, 134, 152
Shaw, A., 101, 106, 107
Sherif, C.W., 46, 56, 138, 140, 149, 152
Sherif, M., 34, 46, 56, 138, 140, 149,
        152

Shields, J., 154, 180
Shupe, A., 37, 39, 45, 46, 48, 54, 56,
    59, 68, 78, 81, 110, 114, 120,
    121, 131, 132
Sidorsky, D., 195
Siegelman, J., 54, 57, 61, 62, 68, 69,
    70, 71, 73, 77, 79
Silberman, C., 184, 196
Simmonds, R.B., 55, 64, 66, 68, 70,
    71, 78, 81
Simpson, J.H., 86, 107, 110, 113, 132
Singer, M., 41, 52, 56, 59, 61, 65, 69,
    70, 81, 82
Singer, P., 101, 107
Singh, S., 170, 180
Sirboni, S., 234
Sklare, M., 196
Skonovd, N., 72, 73, 80, 81
Sloane, D.M., 175, 164, 168, 180
Smidt, C., 119, 132
Smith, C.B., 164, 180
Smith, Craig S., ix, 133-152, 242
Smith, E.I., 173, 179
Snow, D., 72, 81
Sobrero, P., 227, 234
Solomon, T., 59, 68, 73, 81
Somerhill, L., 90
Sorell, G.T., 166, 179
Sovernigo, G., 234
Spero, M., 65, 69, 70, 81
Spilka, Bernard, 4, 6, 8, 24, 28, 29,
    30, 134, 136, 152, 163, 166,
    168, 169, 170, 173, 177, 181
Spardlin, W., 134, 152
Squillacciotti, M., 234
Srole, L., 72, 81
Stacey, W., 114, 120, 121, 132
Stanley, S., 29
Stanton, J., 106, 107
Starbuck, E.D., 162, 181
Stark, R., 171, 179, 181
Stephenson, M., 206, 215
Stewart, M.W., 55, 57, 80

Stockton, R.R., 110, 132
Stone, F., 196
Stoner, S., 173, 180
Strommen, M.P., 178
Sturzo, L., 236
Sullivan, M., 134, 136, 152
Sussman, M.B., 154, 179
Suziedelis, A., 159, 160, 181
Szasz, T., 75, 81

Tamney, J.B., 110, 114, 121, 123,
    127, 131, 132
Tarrance and Associates, 111, 130
Terrin, A.N., 234
Thomas, D.L., 165, 173, 177, 180, 181
Thomas, K., 218, 236
Thompson, A.D., 175, 181
Togliatti, P., 233
Tooley, M., 101, 107
Trede, T., 223, 236
Trolese, F., 234
Turnbull, H.R., 100, 101, 107
Tweed, D., 29

Ungerleider, J., 65, 66, 68, 70, 77, 81

Valabek, R., 221, 236
Valenziano, C., 234
Van Driel (see Driel)
Venable, G.D., 170, 178
Ventimiglia, J.S., 37, 39, 54
Ventis, W.L., 28, 29, 162, 173, 177
Verba, S., 126, 132
Vigli, M., 234
Vincenzo, J., 5, 31
Vinco, R., 226, 236
Visentin, P., 234
Vrijhof, P.H., 218, 237

Waardenburg, J., 218, 237
Wach, J., 237
Walter, O., 118, 131
Warren, R.K., 30

Watson, J., 101
Watson, P.J., 28, 31
Wattenberg, M., 110, 124, 127, 132
Wax, R.H., 185, 196
Weber, M., 98, 211, 215, 237
Weed, S., 165, 177
Weigert, A.J., 165, 177, 180, 181
Weiner, 137
Weiss, A., 66, 68, 82
Weissman, M., 80
Wellisch, C., 65, 66, 68, 70, 77, 81
West, L.J., 41, 56, 61, 69, 82
Westoff, C.F., 179
Weyreich, P., 92
Whitney, R.E., 37, 56
Wilcox, C., 110, 124, 127, 132
Will, J., 121, 132
Willets, F., 177
Williams, D.L., 159, 177
Williams, R., 121, 132
Willke, J., 105, 107
Wilson, 163
Wilson, B., 36, 56, 78, 198, 211, 215
Wilson, J., 214

Wilson, W.W., 3, 31
Wood, J., 80
Wood, M., 86, 107
Wood, P.K., 157, 159, 177
Woodrow, R., 93
Worthington, E.L., 165, 177
Wright, S., 59, 73, 82
Wulf, D., 179
Wuthnow, R., 110, 132, 179

Yankelovich, D., 34, 56
Yankelovich, Skelly and White Poll,
    96
Yeager, R.J., 157, 177
Yeats, J.R., 175, 181
Yela, M., 4, 5, 10, 13, 24, 25, 29
Yinger, J.M., 110, 121, 123, 132
Young, C., 134, 152
Yule, W., 81

Zaretsky, I., 54, 78
Zelnick, M., 170, 181
Zemel, J., 69, 81
Zimbardo, P.G., 41, 53

SUBJECT INDEX

Abortifacients, 105
Abortion, 110, 113, 115-117, 129,
    130, 171
  controversy, 83-108
Ad Hoc Committee in Defense of
    Life, 93
Adolescence and religion, ix, 153,
    181
Advertising, 206
Africa, viii
Age
  and adolescent religion, 157-159
  and church attendance, 200-201
  and conversion, 162-163
  and voting, 124, 125
AIDS, 114, 115, 117, 129
Alcohol abuse, 67, 77, 171, 209
Alcoholics Anonymous (AA), 205,
    211
Alienation, 8, 35, 210, 213
Alternative religions, 33-56
  (see Cults; New Religions)
Alternatives to Abortion Interna-
    tional, 90
Altruism, 173-174, 175
American Citizens Concerned for
    Life, 102, 103
American Law Institute, 87, 89, 96

American Life League, 92-93, 94, 103
American Life Lobby, 93
American society, 34-36, 46, 110, 111
Americans United for Life, 93
Amish, 38
Ananda Marga, 63, 64
Anglicans, 199, 200-201, 203, 207,
    211-212
Anomie, 87, 213
Anticlericalism, 230, 232
Anti-cult movement, 33, 36, 39, 41,
    43-49, 69, 74
Anti-Semitism, 187
Apostasy, 72, 153
  (see Defection)
Association for the Study of Abor-
    tion, 89
Atrocity tales, 37-38, 39
Attachment theory, 28
Attributions, 8, 28
  error, 40
  to God, ix, 133-152
  theory, 28, 134-136
Australia, 206, 208

Baba Family, 62
Baptists, 105, 157, 169, 206
  Baptist Federation, 208

Fellowship of Evangelical Baptists, 208
Southern Baptist Convention, 95, 131
Bar/Bat Mitzvah, 183, 188, 193
Base communities, 217, 225, 233-234
Bible, 155, 159, 161, 204
Birth control, 85-86, 88, 97, 202
  information, 113, 115, 116-117, 129
Birthright, 90
Bishops' Pro-Life Action Committee, 94
Blacks
  and adolescent sex, 170-171
  attitudes of, 115-116
  religion, 160
Book of Common Prayer, 211-212
Born-again Christians, 111, 112, 210
Brainwashing, 43, 51, 53, 57, 58, 68, 75, 162
Bread for the World, 95
Brethren, 206
Bureaucracy, 101, 211

Canada, x, 197-215
Capitalism, 52, 100
Catholic Church, x, 91, 198
  attendance, 200-201, 208
  attitudes toward, 119, 121
  criticisms of, 48
  dissent in, 217, 225, 233
Catholicism, 199, 202-203, 219
  and abortion, 84, 85, 87-89, 91-95, 102, 103, 104n
  and magic, 222-225
  and popular religion, 217-237
Catholics, 113, 114-116, 164, 173, 207
  high school students, 157, 159, 165, 167, 174
Catholic Worker, 93
Causal inference, 133-152

Charismatic Christians, 128, 208
Children of God, 59, 62, 63, 65
China, 99
Christ, the socialist, 226-227, 230
Christian Action Council, 90, 95
Christianity, 212
Christian Right, ix, 109-132
Christian Science, 38
Christians for Socialism, 217, 233
Christology, 112, 113
Church attendance, 23, 155-156, 159, 160, 207, 208
  in Canada, 199-201, 202-203
Church membership, 154, 199, 207-208
Church of England, 198-199
  (see Anglicans)
Church-state issues, 75, 207
  (see Abortion; Falwell platform)
Clergy, 212, 217, 228, 230, 231
Cognition, 160-162
Communism, 53, 111
  and religion, viii, 198
Confessional, 202
Connecticut Mutual Life Report on American Values, 96, 106
Conversion, 42, 72, 73, 162-163
  An Age of, 57
Counterculture, 34-35
Cults, 33-56, 76n
  leaders, 40
  therapeutic effects, 42, 48, 52, 71-72
  (see Anti-cult movement; New religious movements)
Cult syndrome, 43

Day care, 194
Defection, 57, 59-61, 72-74, 76n, 77-78
  (see Apostasy)
Defense spending, 115, 117, 129
Delinquency, 171-172

Democrats (Party), 124, 126-127
Democrats for Life, 93
Demonology, 229
Denomination, and adolescents, 168, 169
Deprivation, cultural, 184
Deprogramming, 45, 52, 58, 68, 71, 73, 75, 77
Development, religious, 154, 160-169, 176
Deviance, religious control of, 153
    social construction of, 49-50, 53
Deviance amplification, 172
Differentiation, 207, 213-214, 225
Dissonance, cognitive, 49
    cultural, 184
Divine Light Mission, 59, 62, 63, 65, 67, 71
Doe v. *Bolton,* 90
Down's syndrome, 100
Drugs, 34, 67, 70, 77, 171, 172, 174

Eastern religions, viii
Economic individualism, 33-56
Ecumenism, 95
Education, and adolescent religion, 166-167
    and church attendance, 200
    Jewish, 183-196
    parochial, 167
    (*see* Catholics, high school students)
Egalitarianism, 83, 99-104
Ego-involvement, 138, 141, 142, 143, 146, 149
Eidetic reduction, 186
Emancipation, 207
Empathy, 175
England, 207
Episcopalians, 94, 118, 161
Episcopalians for Life, 95
Epoche', 186
Equal opportunity, 100

Equal Rights Amendment (ERA), 86, 110, 113, 114, 115, 117, 129
Erhard Seminars Training (est), 61, 62, 66n
Esalen Institute, 61
Ethics, religion and, 98, 173
Ethnicity, 160
Ethnographic research needs, 48
Eugenics, 101
Europe, viii
Euthanasia, 92, 100, 101, 104, 106
Evangelical Christians, 96, 109-132, 197, 209, 210, 214
    defined, 112-113, 131
Evangelicals for Social Action, 93, 103
Evangelism, 112
Ex-cultists, 68
    (*see* Defection)
Exorcism, 223, 230
Experiential religion, 157, 159
Extraversion, 173
Extrinsic religiousity, 1-32, 157, 159, 164, 175
    Extrinsic residual, 14-23, 25-26
    Personal-extrinsic, 10-23, 25-28
    Social-extrinsic, 10-23, 25-28
Extrinsic Religious Values Scale, 3

Faith, 2
    stages, 161-162
Falwell platform, ix, 109-132
Families for Life, 93
Family, 46-48, 110, 211
    tension, 166
    (*see* Parents)
Feminism, 86, 88, 97, 110, 118
Feminists for Life, 86, 93, 96, 102, 103
Folk religion, 219
France, 207
Freedom
    of churches, 207
    personal, 59, 75

Friends, 172
Friends for Life (UCC), 95
Fundamentalists, 64, 84, 85, 92, 95,
        105, 109, 113, 114, 118, 120,
        124, 128, 155, 169, 197
    definition, 130-131

Gallup Poll, 154, 199, 200
Gender, and adolescent religion,
        159-160
Generation Gap, 35, 165
German society, 198
God, ix, 112, 205, 212
    attributions to, 133-152
    belief in, 154, 155
    closeness to, 157
Golden Rule, 173

Habitat for Humanity, 95
Hanukkah, 193
Hare Krishna, 58, 59-68, 69, 72-78
    defection from, 60-61, 72-74, 77
Hatch Amendment, 92, 94
Healers, 223, 230
Hebrew school, ix, 183-196
    curriculum, 193-194
    purposes, 187-189
Hindu group, 62
Hispanics, religion of, 160
Hockey Night cult, 204
Homosexuality, 110, 113, 114-115,
        117, 129-130
Horoscopes, 206, 211
Humanae Vitae, 202
Human Life International, 93
Hyde amendments, 97

Ideology, secular, 202-205, 209-211
    totalitarian, 36, 51
Idolatry, 205
Individualism, 33-56, 103, 202
Infanticide, 92, 98, 101, 106
Information disease, 61, 71

Information power, 37
Inheritance, 47
Integration, 211, 213-214
Intent, 137-138, 141, 146-147
International Society for Krishna
        Consciousness (ISKCON),
        59-78
Intolerance of Ambiguity Scale, 8
Intrinsic-extrinsic religiousity, ix, 1-
        32, 175
    factor analyses of, 3, 4-5, 9-14, 24,
        25
Intrinsic religion, 1-32, 157, 159, 160,
        164, 174, 175
Ireland, viii, 207
Islam, viii
Israel, 111, 113, 114-115, 117, 130
Italy, x, 217-237

Jehovah's Witnesses, viii, 38, 208
Jesuits, 198
Jesus Christ, 111, 112, 120, 130-131
Jesus People, 63, 64, 78
Jewish(ness), 183, 186-187, 194-195
Jews, and abortion, 88, 93
    education of, 183-196
    and retention of children, 164
Jonestown, 38
Just Life, 93, 96, 102

Latin America, viii
Latter Day Saints, 208
Legitimation, reciprocal, 220
Liberalism, 97, 99, 100, 106
Libertarians for Life, 93
Liberty Foundation, 129
Life Amendment Political Action
        Committee, 93
Lifestyle, and religion, 169-175
Lobbying, 45, 94
Locus of Control scales, 8
Lord's Day Alliance, 205
Luck, 133, 138, 147, 148

Lutherans, 118
  Lutheran Church in America, 95
  Missouri-Synod Lutheran, 95, 161
Lutherans for Life, 95

Magic, 217, 221-231
Mai Lai massacre, 135, 136
Marxism, 198, 226
Mass media, 36-40, 52, 222
McDonald's as religion, 205
Meaning, 185, 220
Medicalization, 45, 75
Me generation, 35, 210
Mennonites, 38, 157, 209
Mental health, 41-45, 173, 175
  and new religions, 57-82
Meritocracy, 100
Methodists, 94, 118, 207, 208
Methodists for Life, 95
Middle East, viii
Middletown, 155
Mind control, 61, 69, 76n
  (see Brainwashing)
Miracles, 137
Moonies, 76, 77-78
  (see Unification Church)
Moral development, 175
Morality, 85, 204
Moral Majority, viii, 84, 113-114,
    116, 121, 123, 127, 129
Mormons, viii, 208, 213
  youth, 164-165
Motivation, 28, 77, 86, 135, 140, 141,
    142-144, 146
Motives, 69, 134
Movies, 40

Narcissism, 210
Nascent permanence, ix, 83, 103-104
National Assn. for the Repeal of
    Abortion Laws, 84, 89-90
National Committee for a Human
    Life Amendment, 94

National defense, 111, 113, 114-117, 129
National March for Life, 93
National Organization for Women
    (NOW), 86, 113, 114, 115,
    116, 117, 129
National Pro-Life Action League, 93
National Right to Life Committee,
    86, 91-93, 102
Neuroticism, 173
New Christian Right, 84
New religious movements, 35-56, 57-
    82, 154
  defectors from, 57, 59-61, 62, 65,
    68-69, 71, 72-74
New Right, 102
News magazines, 37, 38
Newspapers, 38, 40
Noetic correlate, 186
Novenas, Sardinian, 231-232
Nuclear freeze, 115, 117, 129

Operation Rescue, 93
Opportunity structure, 49, 52
Orthodoxy, 23, 157, 159

Paganism, 223, 228
Palmreaders, 206
Parents, 153, 163-165, 167, 168, 170,
    172
  discord, 160, 166
Pearson Foundation, 90
Peer influence, 164, 168
Pentecostals, 109, 118-120, 123, 124,
    126, 128, 131, 206, 208, 213
Personality, adolescent, 169, 172-
    173, 175
Phenomenology, 184-185, 218
Planned Parenthood Assn., 104
Pluralism, 84-85, 95, 104
Poland, 207
Politics, religion and, 109-132, 233
Popular religion, 217-237
  definition, 218-220

Pornography, 110
Poverty, 97, 219, 231
Prayer, 23, 150, 154, 155, 157, 159,
    209
Prayers, 183, 188, 190, 212
Pregnancy, adolescent, 170-171
Prejudice, 174, 175
Presbyterians, 94, 118, 199, 207
Presbyterians for Life, 95
Priests, 225, 230
    (see clergy)
Prolifers for Survival, 93, 96, 102,
    103
Proreligiousness, indiscriminate, 26
Protestants, 199, 206
    and abortion, 85, 88-89, 92, 93,
        94-95
    evangelical, 84, 109-132
        (see Evangelical Christians)
    Italian, 233
    liberal, 164
    mainline, 157, 169
Psychiatry, 43-45, 58, 75-76
Psychologizing, 40
Psychology, 43-45
    of religion, 5, 169-170
Psychometrics, 1-32
Psychotherapy, 42, 50
Public opinion, 37

Quakers, 93
Quality of life, 100-102, 104, 106

Race, religion and, 160
Racial injustice, 111
Rajneesh movement, 39, 62
Rationalization, 197-198, 204, 208,
    211, 222
Religion, definition, 2, 219
    and social science, vii-viii
Religion, types of
    comforting, 157, 173
    horizontal, 157, 159, 174

liberating, 157, 159
prophetic, 207
restricting, 157
vertical, 157, 159, 174
    (see Extrinsic; Intrinsic)
Religious beliefs, 154, 155, 161, 204
Religious Coalition of Abortion
        Rights, 104n
Religious education, 166-167
    Jewish, 183-196
Religious practices, 155, 157, 158-
        159, 199-201, 208-209
Republicans (Party), 121, 123, 124,
        125, 126, 127, 128
Resesarch, social, viii
    limitations, 174-176
Resource mobilization, 87
Responsibility vs. causation, 136-137
Revival, mid-century, viii
Right-to-life movement, ix, 83-108
Rituals, 223, 231
Roe v. Wade, 89, 90, 91, 95, 96, 98,
        104n, 105

Sacralization, 214, 217
Salience of religion, 119, 120, 123,
        125, 140
Salvation Army, 38, 206, 207
Sanctioning, 133-152
Sanctity of life ethic, 101, 102, 103,
        104
San Gennaor's blood cult, 222
Schooling, 153, 166-167
    Hebrew, 183-196
School prayer, 110, 111, 113, 114,
        115-116, 117, 129
Schools, private and public, 111
School textbooks, 111
Scientology, 58, 59, 62-65, 78
Scotland, 207
Secular humanism, 92
Secularization, viii, x
    of Canada, 197-215

Self conceptions, 52, 72, 76, 168
Self-esteem, 165, 172-173
Self growth/help groups, 51, 61
Sexual intercourse, adolescent, 170-171, 172, 174
Siblings, 169
Sins, deadly, 206
Social class, 168-169
  (*see* Socioeconomic status)
Social control, 49, 57-82, 174
Socialism, 226-227, 230
Socialization, 128, 164, 184, 194, 204
Social movements, 83-89, 95-96, 103-104
Socioeconomic status, 119, 121-122, 124-126, 168-169
Sociology of religion, 84, 95-96, 218
South Africa, viii
Spirits, 231
Spiritual guidance, 76
Spiritual maturity, 162
Spiritual surrogates, 34
Sports, 205
Status degradation, 40
Stereotyping, 38, 39-40, 43, 84, 104
Sunday, 205
Sunday school, 167, 184
Symbolic interation, 49-50
Synagogue attendance, 200
Syncretism, 224

Teachers, 191
Television, 37, 40, 122-123
  religious, 121, 125, 128
Theological self-classification, 140-150
Theology, and church attendance, 208
  liberal, 203-204
Thinking, religious, 160-162
Thornburg v. *American College of Obstetricians and Gynecologists,* 90

3 HO, 63
Tnevnoc cult, 48
Totalitarianism, 36, 51
Traditions, transmitting, 189
Triangulation, viii
Tuition tax credits, 115, 117, 129

Unification Church, 37, 38, 58, 62, 63, 65, 67, 68, 71, 76n, 77
  ex-members, 77-78
  members, 42
  and mental health, 59
United Church of Canada, 199, 200-201, 203-204, 206
United Church of Christ, 94, 95
United Church Renewal Fellowship, 208
U.S. Catholic Conference, 91
U.S. Coalition for Life, 93
U.S. Constitution, 58-59
  First Amendment, 58, 75
  Fourteenth Amendment, 103
Urbanism, 203

Values, 210-211
  secular, 205-206, 211-212
  terminal, 34
  traditional, 35
  transmission of, 165-166
Vatican II, 88, 202, 220
Violence, 37
Volunteerism, 175, 194
Voting, 124

Welfare, 97, 102, 103, 111
Well-being, 212
  psychological, 59, 77, 90
Wholeness, 211
Witchcraft, 206, 227, 228
Women Exploited by Abortion, 96
Women's Liberation Movement, 206
Women's rights, 86, 110, 113
  (*see* Feminism)

Youth, 34, 40, 153-181, 210
    rebellion, 40
Youth culture, 165

Zen Buddhism, 59, 63, 78